D0500234

Eyewitness

to

Wall Street

400 Years of Dreamers, Schemers, Busts, and Booms

David Colbert

BROADWAY BOOKS

New York

Broadway Books titles may be purchased for business or promotional use or for special sales. For information, please write to: Special Markets Department, Random House, Inc., 1540 Broadway, New York, NY 10036.

Permissions begin on page 371.

BROADWAY BOOKS and its logo, a letter B bisected on the diagonal, are trademarks of Broadway Books, a division of Random House, Inc.

Visit our website at www.broadwaybooks.com and the author's website at www.eyewitnesshistory.com

Library of Congress Cataloging-in-Publication Data

Colbert, David.
Eyewitness to Wall Street: 400 years of dreamers, schemers, busts, and booms / David Colbert.
p. cm.
Includes bibliographical references and index.
1. Wall Street. 2. Capitalists and financiers—United States—History.
3. Securities—United States—History. 4. Finance—United States—History. I. Title.

HG4572 .C67 200
332'.0973—dc21
2001025169

FIRST EDITION

Designed by Fearn Cutler

ISBN 0-7679-0660-8
1 3 5 7 9 10 8 6 4 2

To my mother,
dedicated student and brilliant teacher of the financial markets.

Contents

Contents • xi

Contents • xiii

Contents • xv

xvi • Contents

Eyewitness to Wall Street

Introduction

Nothing changes: New York was founded by a publicly traded company that encouraged colonists to buy stock with debt.

Everything changes: In 1999, Merrill Lynch, by most accounts the most powerful firm on Wall Street a couple of years earlier, was shaken by upstart Internet brokerages.

Most of this book covers recent history: the easy money of the "Go-Go" 1960s; the treacherous 1970s, which sank dozens of brokerages; the 1980s, when greed was good (how quaint those mere multimillion-dollar fortunes seem today); the Internet boom of the 1990s; and the shape of things to come.

Yet the early years are just as revealing and relevant. Eyewitnesses to the first stock exchanges, centuries ago, noted the distinct mind-sets of bulls and bears. In the 1600s, a savvy trader achieved the first "corner" of a financial market in America by hiding barrels of wampum beads—the general currency even among European colonists—making the beads so scarce their value quadrupled.

Throughout, one discovers the story of the country is linked closely to the financial markets. For instance, the nation's capital is Washington, D.C., because New York City and Philadelphia traded away the honor in return for Congress's agreement to borrow money—at a stiff interest rate—from local financiers.

It's also apparent that the getting and spending of the Street typifies national character in a way the financial centers of other countries—such as London's "City"—do not.

The casual explanation is that Americans worship wealth. But few cultures can claim otherwise. The particular American emphasis requires a more thoughtful explanation. Touring America at the beginning of the twentieth century, English author H. G. Wells wrote, *"America is still, by virtue of its great Puritan tradition and in the older sense of the word, an intensely moral land. Most lusts here are strongly curbed, by public opinion, by training and tradition. But the lust of acquisition has not been curbed but glorified."* Another English-man, James Bryce, who visited a couple of decades earlier, told his countrymen, *"The share market of New York is the most remarkable sight in the country after Niagara and the Yellowstone Geysers."* Bryce's explanation is more subtle than Wells's: *"It can hardly be doubted that the pre-existing tendency to encounter risks and 'back one's opinion,' in-born in the Americans, and fostered by the circumstances of their country, is further stimulated by the existence of so vast a number of joint-stock en-terprises, and by the facilities they offer to the smallest capitalists. . . . The habit of speculation is now a part of their character."*

I learned as a child that my mother has "the habit of specula-tion." Her car radio seemed constantly tuned to market updates. (This was during the bear market of the 1970s, so the reports seemed dismal to me; only later did I learn that Mom, a natural skeptic, correctly saw the slump as more than a quick correction and was shorting the blue chips brilliantly.) I can still hear the radio an-nouncer's emphatic sign-off: "The name of the game is *In*-forma-tion." That announcer identified a pattern in the story of Wall Street. Two hundred years before my mother listened to stock prices broadcast over radio, speculators established an ingenious system to speed information from New York to Philadelphia, the other great trading center of the country. They built a series of towers between the two cities, manning them with signalmen who relayed price in-formation. (The process took about half an hour.) During the Civil War, Jay Cooke used the telegraph to organize a nationwide sales force for Treasury bonds. The new technology allowed him to raise money faster than the government needed it. Today few people trade without real-time quotes, an advantage that only a few years ago was reserved for professionals and subscribers to expensive services.

Other patterns also appear:

—Emotion and intellect are in constant conflict. *"Opinions change from moment to moment,"* observed one of the eyewitnesses. *"Hope and fear are equally vehement and equally irrational; men are constant only in inconstancy, superstitious because they are skeptical, dis-trustful of patent probabilities, and therefore ready to trust their own fan-cies or some unfathered tale."* He was writing in 1688. More than three hundred years later, eyewitness Matthew Klam, watching a day trader in action, was confused when the trader suddenly canceled an order placed just a moment earlier. *"Why did you cancel?"* Klam asked. *"It was spooky,"* the day trader said. *"I don't get this stock."*

—Readers will notice a familiar phrase, "New Era," appears a few times, only to be discredited. There certainly have been truly new eras on Wall Street, important changes in commerce and the economy. But when the phrase is heard often, one can bet that people are projecting unrealistic dreams onto the market. Investor Bernard Baruch, lucky enough to sit out the 1901 panic, observed coldly, *"As with most financial panics the stage had been set in advance by extravagant hopes and talk of a 'New Era.' Varied factors contributed to this surge of optimism. Our victory over Spain had stirred fantastic dreams of imperialism and dazzling predictions of new foreign markets. The public was in the stock market as never before."* In 1928, Frederick Lewis Allen recalled, *"The new era had arrived, and the abolition of poverty was just around the corner."* Are we in a "new era" of commerce now, at the dawn of the Internet age? Certainly. Have all natural laws been repealed? Not yet.

—Professionals play follow the leader. In bull markets, professionals pile on to the best-performing stocks, until a select few companies are carrying the burden of market performance. Edward Johnson III of Fidelity Investments, recalling the quick decline of the "Nifty Fifty" stocks that defied gravity in the mid-1970s, said the mob mentality was unavoidable. *"It was a performance game,"* he said, *"and if you didn't own the Nifty Fifty, you were behind."* By the late 1980s, Johnson said, the stocks had changed but the principle had stayed the same: *"Instead of its being the Nifty Fifty, it's the Nifty 500, whatever is in the S&P. All of the geniuses have figured out that the best way to have a glorious party is to all join the index. And the only problem is that all of the money is flowing into a limited number of securities and the index is no longer an index. It's making its own market."*

—Just as they pile on, professionals panic. As the eyewitnesses here reveal, professionals and institutions are usually the first and the biggest sellers during any sharp market drop. That makes sense, of course. They sell because they can. They're closer to the information, and to the trading floor. And as Johnson pointed out, they're being publicly judged against the performance of others. They can't lie to their neighbors about selling a stock at its peak.

The focus here is on people, not numbers. The eyewitnesses share a knack for revealing the human side of business: the brilliant successes, the con men, the tycoons and robber barons, the rivalries, the mob mentality of the Street and investors, the corporate battles. As Commodore Vanderbilt once telegraphed to some double-crossing partners: *"Gentlemen: You have undertaken to cheat me. I will not sue you, for the law takes too long. I will ruin you."* He did.

Following the pattern of *Eyewitness to America* and *Eyewitness to the American West*, I've drawn material from diaries, private letters, memoirs, and reportage, to bring the story of the Street to life as only firsthand reports can.

One difference in this book is what constitutes an eyewitness. Many of the accounts come from business reporters who pieced together the whole story from several firsthand sources. This points to a difficulty all business historians face. Business, by its competitive nature, is generally conducted in private by people who don't want the public to know precisely what is happening. For instance, one must assume, simply because the law of averages applies to all of us at times, that convicted felon Ivan Boesky has once or twice lapsed into truthfulness. But for the full story of the 1980s insider trading scandals we need to read reporters such as James Stewart, author of *Den of Thieves*.

That human focus is not celebrity journalism. What it reveals is often essential. Veteran business writer and author Stanley H. Brown tells the story of an assignment he gave a class of journalism students in 1981. He wanted, as concisely as possible, the crux of the story about the newly merged Shearson and American Express. The one student who passed the assignment wrote just a single sentence: *"A man named Sandy Weill will not stay in business long with a man named James Robinson III."* Three years later, Robinson, the classic "Southern gentleman," had pushed out the Brooklyn-born Weill. No one questioned that it was a clash of ego and personality. Of course, everything changes: In 1998, Weill transformed the financial services industry with the Travelers-Citibank merger. And just as certainly, nothing changes: As part of that bargain, Weill agreed to be cochairman with Citibank chief John Reed, a buttoned-down technologist; but less than two years later Reed was out.

A final thought: Without denying that "the lust for acquisition" and "the habit of speculation" are central to the Wall Street story, or that greed and selfishness are evident throughout this book, one should appreciate that Wall Street has been a hub of constructive enterprise for centuries. For example, no stocks were ever manipulated more than the railroad stocks of the nineteenth century; yet the companies they supported were often more than mere corporate shells. Wall Street is intimately connected with building the nation, helping allies win two world wars, and funding municipalities across the country. Consider this story from Travers Bell, a founder of the first black-owned investment bank to be a member of the New York Stock Exchange: *"We thought our best hope [for becoming an underwriter of municipal bond issues] would be to try to find some black mayors. The only place we could find them was down in rural towns in the South. Mound Bayou, Mississippi, was a classic because it was the oldest black municipality in the U.S. It had never had a financing, and here we came, knocking on doors and saying, 'We want to do a bond issue.' And this guy says, 'What's a bond issue?' So we did a housing issue there. As a result, Mound Bayou is a very progressive town today. Maynard Jackson [later mayor of Atlanta] was a lawyer in his own Atlanta law firm at that time, just a lawyer. We made him co-bond counsel in the Mound Bayou deal. It was the first time a black firm had ever been a bond counsel in a bond issue."*

That's yet another pattern you'll discover. Wall Streeters, while enriching themselves, have also improved and enriched the nation.

PART ONE

Financing the New World

"The prodigious increase of the Netherlanders in their domestic and foreign trade, riches, and multitude of shipping is the envy of the present, and may be the wonder of all future generations."

Josiah Child, 1688

Timeline

1519 — Spain conquers Mexico, rich in gold and silver—Spanish *reals* will be most trusted currency in early U.S.

1519 — Bohemia mints thaler (origin of "dollar")

1531 — First European stock exchange opens in Belgium

1602 — Hot IPO is Dutch East India Co., first modern public company. Double-digit yields until dissolution in 1799

1606 — Virginia Company of London granted charter

1611 — Dutch develop stock exchanges

1625 — New Amsterdam settled

1637 — Height of Tulipmania in Holland; single flower bulbs trade for large fortunes

1653 — 12-foot-high wall built across lower Manhattan

1666 — Trader corners wampum by burying it, price quadruples

1675 — Fishing company becomes first corporation in America

1685 — Path behind city wall becomes Wall Street

1690 — Massachusetts issues first paper money in colonies

1694 — Bank of England established

1698 — Trinity Church opens March 13

1720 — Mississippi and South Sea bubbles pop—crises in French and British economies

1721 — First American insurance company is established in Philadelphia

1729 — Ben Franklin prints money for Pennsylvania

THE SCENE IN THE 1600s

New Amsterdam

Arnoldus Montanus
Montanus, a Dutch trader, saw the town in 1670.

On the Manhattans island stands New Amsterdam, five miles from the Ocean. Ships run up to the harbor there from the sea with one tide. The city hath an earthen fort. Within the fort, and on the outermost bastion towards the river, stand a windmill, and a very high staff, on which a flag is hoisted whenever any vessels are seen in Godyn's bay. The church rises with a double roof between which a square tower looms aloft. On one side is the prison, on the other side of the church the governor's house. Without the walls are the houses mostly by Amsterdamers. On the river side stand the gallows and whipping post. A handsome, public tavern adorns the farthest point. Between this fort and this tavern is a row of suitable dwelling houses: among which stand out the warehouses of the West India Company.

From the First IPO to the South Sea Bubble, 1621–1720

Josef de la Vega & Daniel Defoe

From the start, European settlement of New York was a publicly traded commercial venture. The colony of New Netherlands and its capital of New Amsterdam were established by the Dutch West India Company in 1621. "West," as the company was known, was one of the blue-chip stocks of the Amsterdam Exchange, the most sophisticated in Europe. ("East," the Dutch East India Company, was formed to trade in Asia.) In contrast, Massachusetts and Pennsylvania were religious sanctuaries; Virginia was owned by a private consortium that soon failed and became sponsored by the Crown.

The Dutch colonists were granted more freedom than their British neighbors, many of whom lived as little better than employees. The Dutch colonists were also given an opportunity that has become deeply imbedded in American culture: indebting themselves to buy stock.

New Amsterdam was the perfect spot for traders and merchants. The huge harbor, though well protected, is just a quick sail from the open sea — closer than Philadelphia to the ocean, safer than Boston. Just as important, the Dutch emphasis on fair trade allowed commerce from various European colonies and Caribbean islands to pass through New Amsterdam.

Although the town was practical and unpretentious — it would trail Philadelphia and Boston in sophistication for a couple of centuries — other nations took notice of the Dutch success. When war between Britain and the Netherlands broke out in 1652, Peter Stuyvesant, the governor of New Netherlands, ordered the capital's men to build a half-mile-long wall of sharpened logs, reaching twelve feet high, across what was then the northern edge of the city.

Stuyvesant was right to guess the British were coming; but in 1664 they came by sea, not land. After British frigates were spotted off Long Island, the governor rushed a letter to the nearby towns. "This capital is the object aimed at," he wrote, "which if lost, all is lost, there being no other place ca-

pable of offering any resistance." He "earnestly required and requested" the towns to send him every third man to defend New Amsterdam. But colonists did not comply. "We ourselves are living here on the Flatland without any protection," wrote one town council, "and must leave wives and children seated here in fear and trembling, which our hearts would fail to do."

The outcome, though inevitable, held a few surprises. First, it was peaceful. Second, and perhaps more important, it was indulgent. The British intelligently agreed to mild surrender terms that allowed the colony to continue doing business. In the "Articles of Capitulation" the British agreed that "Any people may freely come from the Netherlands and plant in this country, and that Dutch vessels may freely come hither, and any of the Dutch may freely return home, or send any sort of merchandise home in vessels of their own country." As well, "All differences of contracts and bargains made before this day by any in this country, shall be determined according to the manner of the Dutch." Even the elected officials were allowed to remain in office. In short: business as usual.

The British did demand one immediate change. The city, like the colony, was renamed New York, in honor of the duke who had financed the successful invasion.

The log wall became an anachronism as the city grew beyond its old northern border. It was torn down in 1698. By then, however, it had given a name to the street that ran along it.

By bringing Dutch commerce into their fold, British business culture leaped forward. British economists had long envied the strong currency, secure banks, reasonable interest rates, and fluid markets of the Netherlands, one·of the most advanced economies in the world. Now their American colonies would benefit from Dutch business acumen.

A cornerstone of the Dutch economy was the Amsterdam Stock Exchange. "Confusion of confusions" was the phrase used in 1688 by eyewitness Josef de la Vega, a Portuguese Jew who had moved to the Netherlands to escape the Inquisition. "This enigmatic business is at once the fairest and most deceitful in Europe, the noblest and the most infamous in the world, the finest and the most vulgar on earth. It is a quintessence of academic learning and a paragon of fraudulence; it is a touchstone for the intelligent and a tombstone for the audacious, a treasury of usefulness and a source of disaster. It has necessarily been converted into a game, and merchants in it have become speculators."

Although to the uninitiated like de la Vega it was an awesome spectacle, to the modern eye it seems remarkably familiar:

The Exchange is an enclosed building surrounded by columns. (Some people lean against these columns of the Exchange, others hide behind them.) The way in which the transactions are concluded is as ridiculous as the game itself. Handshakes or hand-slaps are the signs of agreement. But how painful! A member of the Exchange opens his hand and another takes it, and thus sells a number of shares at a fixed price, which is confirmed by a second handshake. With a new handshake a further item is offered, and then there follows a bid. The hands redden from the blows (I believe from the shame that even the most respected people do business in such an indecent manner as with blows.) The handshakes are followed by shouting, the shouting by insults, the insults by impudence and more insults, shouting, pushes, and handshakes until the business is finished.

Reading de la Vega, one also notices the psychology of speculation has changed very little:

The speculator fights his own good sense, struggles against his own will, counteracts his own hope, acts against his own comfort, and is at odds with his own decisions. There are many occasions in which every speculator seems to have two bodies so that astonished observers see a human being fighting himself. If, for example, there arrives a piece of news which would induce the speculator to buy, while the atmosphere prevailing at the stock exchange forces him to sell, his reasoning fights his own good reasons. At one moment his reasoning drives him to buy, because of the information that has just arrived. At the other it induces him to sell because of the trend at the Exchange. People who get involved in this swindle resemble the English Quakers who believe to contain in their bodies an inner light that advises them.

In his description of the seventeenth-century Amsterdam Exchange, de la Vega included some advice that rings true for those investing today:

Never give anyone the advice to buy or sell shares, because, where perspicacity is weakened, the most benevolent piece of advice can turn out badly. Take every gain without showing remorse about missed profits, because an eel may escape sooner than you think. Whoever wishes to win in this game must have patience and money, since the values are so little constant and the rumors so little founded on truth. A twenty per cent drop in the stock prices is not large enough to be considered a serious blow; as the price may drop twenty per cent overnight, it may also rise fifty per cent in the same period. . . . It is foolish to think you can withdraw from the Exchange after you have tasted success.

Britain's early steps toward market scholarship began about 1705, when a Scotsman named John Law put forth "several Proposals to Remedy the Difficulties the Nation is under from the great Scarcity of Money." His prescription was simplistic: "The use of banks has been the best method yet practis'd for the increase of money. So far as they lend they add to the money, which brings a profit to the country, by imploying more people, and extending trade." But Britain wasn't ready for easy credit, so Law moved to France, where his views were accepted. He was granted a charter for the private Banque Générale in 1716, and allowed to print money. In 1717 he formed the Compagnie d'Occident ("Company of the West"—best known as the Mississippi Company), which enjoyed a monopoly on trade in Louisiana and Canada. Law hoped it would mimic the success of the Dutch West India Company.

The company grew through mergers and acquisitions—including a merger with Law's bank, which had since been made the national bank. But the company produced too little profit. The speculative bubble that had followed its creation burst in 1720. Law wisely left France.

By then the stock fever had spread to England. The highest flier was the South Sea Company, which owned the rights to British trade with South America and the South Sea Islands. Founded in 1711, it had followed Law's lead in 1720 by assuming responsibility for the national debt, swapping its stock for government bonds. In January of that year the price of a share was £128½; in August it was £1,000.

A staggering variety of new companies hoping to ride the wave of speculation offered stock to the inexperienced British public. Their businesses ranged from "improving the art of making soap" and "trading in hair" to "a grand American fishery" and even "a company for carrying on an undertaking of great advantage, but nobody to know what it is."

You know how the story ends. An anonymous Massachusetts pamphleteer was unsympathetic:

When I heard the first news of the South-Sea stock rising to such a considerable height, that a person who had one hundred pounds in that stock could sell it at a thousand or eleven hundred, I could only think the people concerned in this new contrivance were a company of mad-men. At least they look'd like a company of gamesters, eagerly gaming daily, lest their chance should be at an end. And when I heard of men of low degree being advanced to their coaches, what could I think but the world is turning upside down. But all on a sudden the scale is turned; the next news is that abundance are broke by the fall of stocks. It's fallen from eleven hundred to under three hundred, and none cares to buy. Families have been ruined, brought to poverty, and turned beggars. The trade of the city of London, one of the finest in the world, hath been very much shortened. Few ships have been built, or fitted to sea, during the reign of the South-Sea Company.

But why do I talk of South-Sea stock only? Is not Mississippi stock as bad, or worse? Are not Holland, and Spain, and others, contriving to be at the same sport? Truly, as far as I can learn, the greatest part of Europe is infatuated with the same spirit!

One Londoner of the time, Daniel Defoe, author of Robinson Crusoe, *suffered from a gambling bug. Despite knowing the odds were against making a profit in the stock market, he couldn't resist trying. Occasionally he vented his frustration in verse:*

Some in clandestine companies combine
Erect new stocks to trade beyond the line
With air and empty names beguile the town
And raise new credits first, then cry 'em down
Divide the nothing into shares
And set the crowd together by the ears.

At other times he stuck to prose, such as this general attack on the game as it was played during the South Sea era:

If you talk to [brokers] of their occupation, there is not a man but will own 'tis a compleat system of knavery; that 'tis a trade founded in fraud, born of deceit, and nourished by trick, cheat, wheedle, forgeries, falsehoods, and all sorts of delusions; coining false news, this way good, that way bad; whispering imaginary terrors, frights, hopes, expectations, and then preying upon the weakness of those whose imaginations they have wrought upon, whom they have either elevated or depressed.

The [stock] jobbers, hardened in crime, are at last come to exceed all bounds, and will some time or other, make it absolutely necessary to the Government to demolish them. I know they laugh at the suggestion, and have the pride to think it impracticable to restrain them. " 'Tis impossible," said one. "There is no way in the world to suppress us unless the Government should first pay all the public debts. [If they do,] they will be apt to hang themselves."

Though John Law's schemes ended in scandal and financial disaster, they were the foundation of the plan adopted by the U.S. Congress after the Revolution.

PART TWO

The Revolution and "The Monied Men"

"It is my fixed opinion that America has much more to fear from the effects of the large quantities of paper money than from the operations of Howe and all the British generals."

Joseph Eggleston, Jr., *1777*

Timeline

1764 — Britain's Currency Act bans paper money in colonies

1775 — American Manufactory of Woolens, Linens, and Cottons is first public U.S. industrial

1776–1781 — Revolutionary War

1781 — Congress charters private Bank of North America

1784 — Bank of New York, oldest continuing bank, established

1789 — Washington inaugurated at Federal Hall on Wall Street

1790 — Federal government assumes war debts, issues bonds that become basis of U.S. securities markets

1791 — Congress charters semi-private First Bank of the United States; will close in 1811

1792 — Congress opts for "dollars" (set at 371.25 grains of silver) and "cents," rather than "pounds"

1792 — Former Treasury official William Duer tries to manipulate markets, causes run-up then crash

THE SCENE IN THE 1700S

"Frugal and Industrious"

Andrew Burnaby

The British succeeded in preserving Dutch commercial culture. In the 1750s a visitor noted, "Many are the instances of persons who came here distressed by their poverty, who now enjoy easy and plentiful fortunes. The people, both in town and country, are sober, industrious, and hospitable, though intent upon gain."

Andrew Burnaby, a clergyman, visited about the same time:

The city contains between two and three thousand houses, and 16 or 17,000 inhabitants, is tolerably well built, and has several good houses. The streets are paved, and very clean, but in general they are narrow; there are two or three, indeed, which are spacious and airy, particularly the Broad-Way. The houses in this street have most of them a row of trees before them; which form an agreeable shade, and produce a pretty effect.

The college [now Columbia University] when finished, will be exceedingly handsome: it is to be built on three sides of a quadrangle, fronting Hudson's or North River, and will be the most beautifully situated of any college, I believe, in the world.

The inhabitants of New-York, in their character, very much resemble the Pennsylvanians: more than half of them are Dutch, and almost all traders: they are, therefore, habitually frugal, industrious, and parsimonious. Being, however, of different nations, different languages, and different religions, it is almost impossible to give them any precise or determinate character.

There are several houses pleasantly situated upon East River, near New-York, where it is common to have turtle-feasts; these happen once or twice in a week. Thirty or forty gentlemen and ladies meet and dine together, drink tea in the afternoon, fish and amuse themselves till evening, and then return home in Italian chaises, a gentleman and lady in each chaise. In the way there is a bridge, about three miles distant from New-York, which you always pass over as you return, called the Kissing Bridge; where it is part of the etiquette to salute the lady who has put herself under your protection.

"Not Worth a Continental," 1776–1781

The Rivington Royal Gazette, *Alexander Hamilton, and the Buttonwood Brokers*

War is expensive as hell. And when the Revolution began, there was no Wall Street to which the Continental Congress could turn for ready cash. Among other things, the war assembled pools of capital that became the germ of American banking and the basis for the first traded securities. But because capitalism runs counter to another American dream, the agrarian utopia, those early banking schemes met stiff resistance. In simplest terms, farmers such as Virginia's Thomas Jefferson did not want to be indebted to financiers. The specifics of the disputes, and how they were settled, still affect us today.

"The enormous pay of our Army," wrote Philadelphia businessman Robert Morris in 1776, "the immense expenses at which they are supplied with provisions, clothing, and other necessaries, and, in short, the extravagance that has prevailed in most departments of the public service, have called forth prodigious emissions of paper money, both Continental and Colonial." A few years after the war began, one American officer wrote home, "By the arts of monopolizers and extortioners, and the little, the very little, attention by authority to counteract them, our currency is reduced to a mere name." Occasionally one still hears "not worth a Continental," referring to the dollars issued by the Continental Congress.

Certain Loyalists were delighted by the financial crisis. Rivington's Royal Gazette *printed this notice on May 7, 1781:*

The Congress is finally bankrupt! Last Saturday a large body of the inhabitants with paper dollars in their hats by way of cockades paraded the streets of Philadelphia, carrying colors flying, with a dog tarred, and instead of the usual appendage and ornament of feathers, his back was covered with the Congress' paper dollars. This example of disaffection, immediately under the eyes of the rulers of the revolted provinces, in solemn session at the State House assembled, was directly followed by the jailer, who refused accepting the bills in purchase of a glass of rum, and afterwards by

21

the traders of the city, who shut up their shops, declining to sell any more goods but for gold or silver. It was declared also by the popular voice that if the opposition to Great Britain was not in future carried on by solid money instead of paper bills, all further assistance to the mother country were vain and must be given up.

"We seem to have pursued our paper projects as far as prudence will warrant," said Virginia's James Madison, later President, with some understatement. The paper money was redeemed for specie—coined money—at the rate of forty paper dollars to one dollar of hard cash.

The man who would lead (and sometimes prod) the colonies through the crisis was Alexander Hamilton. Surprisingly, he studied an unlikely source, the discredited economist John Law, for a solution to the economic problems facing the young nation. "This country is in the same predicament in which France was previous to the famous Mississippi scheme projected by Mr. Law," he wrote. "Its paper money like ours had dwindled to nothing, and no efforts of the government could revive it, because the people had lost all confidence in its ability."

Hamilton looked past Law's scandalous reputation to coldly examine his theories, and decided Law was right to "unite the interest and credit of rich individuals with those of the state." The problem wasn't in the theory, he believed, but rather in its application. "The foundation was good but the superstructure too vast. The proprietors aimed at unlimited wealth and the government itself expected too much; which was the cause of the ultimate miscarriage of the scheme and of all the mischiefs that befell the Kingdom [of France] in consequence."

He asked Congress "to select what is good in this plan and in any others that have gone before us, avoiding their defects and excesses." In the following letter, he outlined specifics.

The only plan that can preserve the currency is one that will make it the *immediate* interest of the monied men to cooperate with government in its support.

The plan I would propose is that of an American bank, instituted by authority of Congress for ten years. . . . The Bank to furnish Congress with an annual loan of two millions sterling if they have occasion for it at 4 per cent interest. The government to share one half of the whole stock and profits of the Bank. . . .

This scheme stands on the firm footing of public and private faith. It links the interests of the state in an intimate connection with those of the rich individuals belonging to it. It turns the wealth and influence of both into a commercial channel for mutual benefit.

The essence of the plan was entirely practical. The country could only raise money from people who had it. Those people would want something in return. Congress had no way to guarantee repayment without promising to levy taxes.

Congress chartered the Bank of North America in 1781. It was established in Philadelphia by Robert Morris, who was given charge of rescuing the country's finances. "I have great expectations from the appointment of Mr. Morris," George Washington remarked to a friend, "but they are not unreasonable ones; for I do not suppose that by Art magick, he can do more than recover us, by degrees, from the labyrinth into which our finance is plunged." Morris was a controversial choice. He had already been investigated for allegedly taking advantage of earlier government positions, and was involved in various schemes to profit from the war. But Congress had been swayed by Hamilton's arguments to let financiers profit from supporting the new nation. Morris demanded, and was given, sweeping powers. One eyewitness called him "a pecuniary dictator." Prickly and autocratic, he remained controversial throughout his tenure. And he certainly exploited the distress of the colonists for personal profit. But his efforts, backed by his credit and reputation, helped the colonies borrow enough money to successfully conclude the war. After the war he served as one of Pennsylvania's first senators. Ironically, after a failed speculation in western land he went bankrupt and was sent to debtor's prison.

After the Revolutionary War, New York became the capital of the United States. How the capital was moved, first to Philadelphia and then to Washington, D.C., is a story closely connected to Wall Street history. In return for votes in favor of the national debt, Hamilton had arranged for congressmen from the northern states—which, not coincidentally, had the most to gain from a large financing scheme—to vote that the new federal government would be located in the south. Hamilton genuinely believed a national debt would bind the union, quite tentative at the time. He had written a few years earlier, "A national debt, if it is not excessive will be to us a national blessing; it will be powerful cement of our union. It will create a necessity for keeping up taxation to a degree which without being oppressive, [and] will be a spur to industry."

Thomas Jefferson, disliking finance and financiers, distrustful of any policy that might subordinate state government to Congress, would later recall the Compromise of 1790 as one of his greatest errors. By every democratic philosophy upon which the country was based, Jefferson was right. But one has to wonder if there would have been a country without Hamilton's willingness to be pragmatic.

Shortly afterward, an immense scandal hit Wall Street. The consequences of that incident continue to shape our markets.

The villain in the story was William Duer, a former member of the Continental Congress and a successful war profiteer. Duer lived lavishly with his heiress wife, Kitty Alexander, hosting dinner parties at which more than a dozen different wines might be served.

As Assistant Secretary of the Treasury, under Alexander Hamilton, Duer used insider knowledge to speculate in government securities. Hamilton was not amused. Duer resigned his post and continued to speculate, sometimes with insider knowledge, sometimes bluffing.

In 1791, Duer concocted a scheme to manipulate the stock price of the Bank of New York, one of the most widely traded and trusted securities of the time. In partnership with Alexander Macomb—which, for Duer, meant he was using Macomb's money rather than his own—Duer began buying Bank of New York stock, and simultaneously floating the rumor that the institution would be bought by the federally chartered Bank of the United States in Philadelphia.

To that simple plan, Duer added a twist. He simultaneously bet that the price of Bank of New York would drop. He advised one of the country's richest families, the Livingstons, to do the same. He had let the Street think he was using Macomb as a front for investing; in fact, he was using Macomb's money to set up the market for a fall.

Duer had outsmarted himself. The markets rose and rose and rose, forcing him to scramble to cover his positions. Eventually people realized he couldn't make good on his deals or his debts. A letter captures the chaos that followed:

I wrote you in my last [March 21] that Duer was to come forward yesterday — but on Friday he was arrested & sent to prison — the inclosed address was printed yesterday, & has had some effect in softening the minds of the people — I confess I have but little hopes that he will ever be able to do anything — What he has done with near half a million of cash is astonishing—

Among the many who have lent him are A Robertson it [is] said 80,000 — Mr Leake 30,000 — H Cruger 8 or 9,000 — N Cruger as much — Miss Beekmans 15,000 — old Simmons 7,000 — Clason 5,000. Dr Bard 2,000 — besides shopkeepers, Widows, orphans — Butchers, Carmen, Gardeners, market women, & even the noted Bawd M—— Macarty — many of them if they are unpaid are ruined

Duer's going to prison may be his protection — much has been said of mobbing him by the lower classes to whom he owes money. Platt I imagine must among many others be a considerable sufferer by Duer

— In short everything is afloat & confidence destroyed —

This Town has recd a shock which it will not get over in many years — happy is the man who is far removed from the confusion & distress that prevails —

"The confusion still increases in New York," another eyewitness wrote a friend, "and I expect to hear daily that they have broke open the jail and taken out Duer and Walter Livingston, and hanged them; the most prudent of those who have failed have run off, and I think we shall have much such riots as there was in London in 1780."

Even before the crash, Hamilton had been appalled by his associate's machinations. " 'Tis time," he said, "there must be a line of separation between honest men and knaves, between respectable stockholders and dealers in the funds, and mere unprincipled gamblers."

Shortly after the Duer scandal, and in direct response to it, the predecessor to the New York Stock Exchange was formed. On May 17, 1792, two dozen brokers who regularly met under a buttonwood (sycamore) tree in downtown Manhattan signed a pact — the Buttonwood Agreement:

We, the subscribers, brokers for the purchase and sale of public stocks, do hereby solemnly promise and pledge ourselves to each other that we will not buy or sell from this date, for any person whatsoever, any kind of public stocks at a rate less than one quarter of one percent commission on the specie value, and that we will give preference to each other in our negotiations.

The Buttonwood brokers presented themselves as the most honorable of the lot. However, in return for dealing with them, customers paid a premium. That's still the essence of the New York Stock Exchange. The

harshest criticisms of the NYSE over the next two centuries—that it was a private club and enjoyed price-fixing—were expressed in that early covenant. But the club was not the powerhouse it is today. Though it was important in New York, Philadelphia was still the nation's financial center.

The Buttonwood traders, however, did a brisk business in their first hot IPO, the Bank of New York. Other banks and then canal companies were among its strong issues in the following years.

Soon after joining forces, the traders began to meet indoors, at a coffeehouse, distinguishing themselves from the "curb traders" who worked outside—yes, even in winter—until the 1920s. (The Curb Exchange was renamed the American Stock Exchange in the 1950s.) By 1817, the association had grown large enough to require a code of conduct. A formal constitution was adopted, and the name of the organization became the New York Stock & Exchange Board. It met in a rented room at 40 Wall Street.

PART THREE

From the Buttonwood Tree
to the Civil War

"All the banks have stopped payment . . . I walked down Wall Street, and had a convincing proof of the great demand for money, for somebody picked my pocket."

Frederick Marryat, *1837*

Timeline

1792 — On May 17, in wake of Duer scandal, 24 brokers sign Buttonwood Agreement, forerunner of NYSE

1803 — Louisiana Purchase, financed by U.K.'s Barings

1812 — War; Stephen Girard and John Astor buy U.S. bonds

1815 — First stock table appears in N.Y. *Commercial Advertiser* on March 10

1816 — Second Bank of the United States chartered

1817 — Buttonwood brokers est. New York Stock & Exchange Board; rent space at 40 Wall Street; adopt code of conduct

1824 — N.Y. Gas Light Co. (now Con Edison) established

1826 — Prime, Ward & King est., first U.S. investment bank

1827 — Baltimore & Ohio RR est. on February 28; RR stocks lead for next century

1830 — March 16 is the lowest NYSE volume day ever: 31 shares

1832 — President Andrew Jackson refuses to renew charter of Second Bank of the United States; orders its funds given to state banks the next year. Bank will close in 1841

1835 — Great Fire levels lower Manhattan

1836 — Pres. Jackson requires hard cash for land purchases

1837 — Panic. Hundreds of banks fail. European capital flees. Harsh seven-year depression begins

1840 — U.S. establishes independent Treasury

1844 — Samuel Morse invents telegraph

1846–48 — Mexican War: U.S. gains land; speculation will follow

1848 — "Eureka!"—Gold found in CA; rush begins in 1849

1848 — "City of the Big Shoulders"—Chicago Board of Trade est.

1853 — NYSE's first disclosure requirements

1854 — Penn. Rock Oil Co. est., first U.S. petroleum company

1857 — Panic and depression follow runaway gains in land and RRs

1861–1865 — Civil War

1861 — Sec. of Treasury Chase calls on Jay Cooke to sell bonds

1861 — First federal income tax

1862 — "Greenbacks" created—not redeemable for gold

1863 — National currency replaces innumerable local banknotes

1863 — New exchanges arise as war effort drives financial markets

THE SCENE IN THE EARLY 1800S

The Great Fire and the New Exchange

Philip Hone

The opening of the Erie Canal in 1825 firmly established New York as the country's most important port. Shortly afterward, President Andrew Jackson closed Philadelphia's Second Bank of the United States, ending that city's dominance of finance. Wall Street and New York City were about to grow, together, into the country's financial and merchant center.

That growth was briefly interrupted in December 1835, when most of colonial New York south of Wall Street was destroyed in a fire that raged for two days. Philip Hone, businessman, former mayor, and, most important, diarist, recorded the scene.

Nearly one half of the first ward is in ashes; 500 to 700 stores, which with their contents are valued at $20,000,000 to $40,000,000 are now lying in an indistinguishable mass of ruins.

The night was intensely cold, which was one cause of the unprecedented progress of the flames, for the water froze in the hydrants, and the engines and their hose could not be worked without great difficulty. The firemen, too, had been on duty all last night, and were almost incapable of performing their usual services.

The fire originated in the store of Comstock & Adams in Merchant Street, a narrow crooked street, filled with high stores lately erected and occupied by dry goods and hardware merchants, which led from Hanover to Pearl Street.

When I arrived at the spot the scene exceeded all description; the progress of the flames, like flashes of lightning, communicated in every direction, and a few minutes sufficed to level the lofty edifices on every side. It had crossed the block to Pearl Street.

Girard's Bank, Philadelphia, 1814

James Parton

John Jacob Astor is often mistakenly named as the premier financier of the early republic. He actually ran second to a man barely remembered today. In the mid-1800s, when a magazine began a series titled "American Mercantile Biography," the editor declared, "At the head of this department conspicuously is the name of Stephen Girard. It has inscribed itself upon the pages of our country's history, and is identified with our earliest commercial progress. Where better could we begin in presenting the memoirs and the portraits of Eminent Merchants? Mr. Girard's history will require but little comment, being familiar to most of his countrymen."

Nowadays, a little comment is due the quirky man who bought the assets of the First Bank of the United States when its charter expired in 1811, and propped up the country during the War of 1812.

Within the memory of many persons still alive, "old Girard," as the famous banker was usually styled, a short, stout, brisk old gentleman, used to walk, in his swift, awkward way, the streets of the lower part of Philadelphia. Though everything about him indicated that he had very little in common with his fellow-citizens, he was the marked man of the city for more than a generation.

His aspect was rather insignificant and quite unprepossessing. His dress was old-fashioned and shabby; and he wore the pig-tail, the white neck-cloth, the wide-brimmed hat, and the large-skirted coat of the last century. He was blind of one eye; and though his bushy eyebrows gave some character to his countenance, it was curiously devoid of expression. He had also the absent look of a man who either had no thoughts or was absorbed in thought; and he shuffled along on his enormous feet, looking neither to the right nor to the left. There was always a certain look of the old mariner about him, though he had been fifty years an inhabitant of the town. When he rode it was in the plainest, least comfortable gig in Philadelphia, drawn by an ancient and ill-formed horse, driven always by the master's own hand at a good pace.

I perceived that the store of my son John (Brown &
was in danger, and made the best of my way by Front
around the Old Slip to the spot. We succeeded in getti
the stock of valuable dry goods, but they were put
square, and in the course of the night our labors were re
unavailing, for the fire reached and destroyed them. . . .

At this period the flames were unmanageable, a
crowd, including the firemen, appeared to look on with tl
thy of despair, and the destruction continued until it r
Coenties Slip, in that direction, and Wall Street down to th
including all South Street and Water Street; while to th
Exchange Street, including all Post's stores, Lord's beauti
William Street, Beaver and Stone Streets, were destroyed

The splendid edifice erected a few years since by th
ality of the merchants, known as the Merchants' Ex
and one of the ornaments of the city, took fire in the re
is now a heap of ruins. The facade and magnificent
columns fronting on Wall Street are all that remain of t
ble building, and resemble the ruins of an ancient
rather than the new and beautiful resort of the mercha

I have been alarmed by some of the signs of th
which this calamity has brought forth: the miserable w
who prowled about the ruins, and became beastly drun
champagne and other wines and liquors with which the
and wharves were lined, seemed to exult in the misfortu
such expressions were heard as "Ah! They'll make no m
per cent dividends!"

The stock exchange built a new home. Six years after th
November 17, 1841, Hone made note of the opening:

The rotunda of the Merchants' Exchange in Wal
the magnificent room in which the merchants of Ne
are to "congregate," was opened this day for their use.
perb edifice will be an ornament to the city, but a very l
cern for the stockholders, of which number I am one.

Many feared, many served, but none loved this singular and lonely old man. Never was there a person more destitute than Girard of the qualities that win the affection of others. His temper was violent, his presence forbidding, his usual manner ungracious, his will inflexible, his heart untender, his imagination dead. He was odious to many of his fellow-citizens, who considered him the hardest and meanest of men.

The war of 1812, which suspended commerce, made this merchant so enormously rich. In 1811, the charter of the old United States Bank expired; and the casting-vote of Vice-President George Clinton negatived [vetoed] the bill for rechartering it. When war was imminent, Girard had a million dollars in the bank of Baring Brothers in London. This large sum, useless then for purposes of commerce—in peril, too, from the disturbed condition of English finance—he invested in United States stock and in stock of the United States Bank, both being depreciated in England. Being thus a large holder of the stock of the bank, the charter having expired, and its affairs being in liquidation, he bought out the entire concern; and, merely changing the name to Girard's Bank, continued it in being as a private institution, in the same building, with the same coin in its vaults, the same bank-notes, the same cashier and clerks.

Girard was the very sheet-anchor of the government credit during the whole of that disastrous war. If advances were required at a critical moment, it was Girard who was promptest to make them. When all other banks and houses were contracting, it was Girard who stayed the panic by a timely and liberal expansion. When all other paper was depreciated, Girard's notes, and his alone, were as good as gold. In 1814, when the credit of the government was at its lowest ebb, when a loan of five millions, at seven per cent interest and twenty dollars bonus, was up for weeks, and only procured twenty thousand dollars, it was "old Girard" who boldly subscribed for the whole amount; which at once gave it market value, and infused life into the paralyzed credit of the nation.

Jackson Closes the Bank of the United States
Washington, July 10, 1832

Andrew Jackson

The financial community's relations with Washington have never been worse than during President Andrew Jackson's battle with the Second Bank of the United States. A semi-private institution, the Bank— named not for its size but because it was established after the charter of the first such bank expired—enjoyed a monopoly on federal government banking. It was headed by one of the country's brightest men, Nicholas Biddle, as accomplished in the arts as in finance. (Thomas Jefferson had selected him to edit the journals of Lewis and Clark.) Among the untitled aristocracy of the new republic, Biddle stood first, and knew it.

"Nicholas Biddle is the Napoleon of finance," wrote James Gordon Bennett, editor of the New York Herald. *"He is twice as great as Henry Clay—twice and a half as great as Daniel Webster—and eight or ten times as great as Martin Van Buren. 'I would sooner be Nicholas Biddle in Wall Street,' said our ex-Mayor [Philip Hone], 'than any potentate in the world.' Nicholas Biddle walks around the street like a spirit from heaven—saying to the hurricane of commerce, 'peace'—and telling the storm of speculation, 'be still.' He is the genius—the impersonation of the 'calm summer morning.' As he entered or emerged from this bank or that bank, people gazed, gazed and gazed."*

But Biddle wasn't President. That office was held by a backwoods populist who hated blue bloods. The two men tangled several times. Finally, when the charter of the Second Bank of the United States expired, Jackson refused to extend it. He sent his veto to the Senate with the following explanation.

This act seems to be predicated on the erroneous idea that the present stockholders have a prescriptive right not only to the favor but [also] to the bounty of Government. It appears that more than a fourth part of the stock is held by foreigners and the residue is held by a few hundred of our own citizens, chiefly of the richest class.

For their benefit does this act exclude the whole American people from competition in the purchase of this monopoly and dispose of it for many millions less than it is worth. This seems the less excusable because some of our citizens not now stockholders petitioned that the door of competition might be opened, and offered to take a charter on terms much more favorable to the Government and country.

But this proposition, although made by men whose aggregate wealth is believed to be equal to all the private stock in the existing bank, has been set aside. The bounty of our Government is proposed to be again bestowed on the few who have been fortunate enough to secure the stock and at this moment wield the power of the existing institution. I can not perceive the justice or policy of this course.

It has been urged as an argument in favor of rechartering the present bank that the calling in of its loans will produce great embarrassment and distress. The time allowed to close its concerns is ample, and if it has been well managed its pressure will be light, and heavy only in case its management has been bad. If, therefore, it shall produce distress, the fault will be its own, and it would furnish a reason against renewing a power which has been so obviously abused. But will there ever be a time when this reason will be less powerful? To acknowledge its force is to admit that the bank ought to be perpetual, and as a consequence the present stockholders and those inheriting their rights as successors be established a privileged order, clothed both with great political power and enjoying immense pecuniary advantages from their connection with the Government.

The Bank continued to operate under a state charter until 1841, when it declared bankruptcy. Biddle had resigned his post two years earlier.

With the closing of the bank, Philadelphia ceded preeminence in the nation's financial markets to Wall Street. Volume on the New York Stock Exchange already exceeded volume on the Philadelphia Exchange, thanks to trading in Erie Canal bonds. Now Wall Street would pull ahead in credit. Though Philadelphia's Jay Cooke & Co. would dominate government finance during the Civil War, even that honor would be short-lived.

Jackson can't be faulted for wanting the riches enjoyed by the Bank's owners to be shared by more people. He may even have made superior legal arguments. But his plan for the nation's finances did indeed "produce great embarrassment and distress." The flood of paper that poured from the state-chartered banks established during his administration led directly to one of the worst financial collapses in American history.

The Panic of 1837

Frederick Marryat

"Another failure," complained businessman and former New York City mayor Philip Hone in his diary entry for January 31, 1834. "Wall Street was thrown into consternation this morning by the failure of John G. Warren & Son, a house in good credit and one of the most extensive in their line as brokers. If Gen. Jackson had visited Wall Street this morning, he might have been regaled with a sight similar to that of the field of battle at New Orleans. His killed and wounded were to be seen in every direction, and men enquiring with anxious solicitude, 'Who is to fall next?' "

Hone blamed President Andrew Jackson for the calamity because Jackson had promoted the establishment of state banks, each of which was allowed to issue banknotes. The inflation of the economy with paper currency backed by questionable assets was followed, of course, by a collapse. In May 1837, the panic became general.

Marryat was a British naval officer and novelist.

My appearance at New York was very much like bursting into a friend's house with a merry face when there is a death in it.

Two hundred and sixty [banking] houses have already failed, and no one knows where it is to end. Suspicion, fear, and misfortune have taken possession of the city. Had I not been aware of the cause, I should have imagined that the plague was raging. All the banks have stopped payment in specie [coin money], and there is not a dollar to be had. I walked down Wall Street, and had a convincing proof of the great demand for money, for somebody picked my pocket. The militia are under arms, as riots are expected. Affairs are now at their worst, and now that such is the case, the New Yorkers appear to recover their spirits.

The distress for change has produced a curious remedy. Every man is now his own banker. Go to the theatres and places of public amusement, and, instead of change, you receive an I.O.U. from the treasury. At the hotels and oyster-cellars it is the same thing. Call for a glass of brandy and water and the change is fifteen tickets, each "good for one glass of brandy and water." At an oyster-shop, eat a plate of oysters, and you have in return seven tickets, good for one plate of oysters each. It is the same everywhere. The barbers give you tickets, good for so many shaves; and were there beggars in the streets, I presume they would give you tickets in change, good for so much philanthropy.

Hence arises another variety of exchange in Wall Street.

"Tom, do you want any oysters for lunch today?"

"Yes!"

"Then here's a ticket, and give me two shaves in return."

A few statistics underlie Marryat's colorful observations. From 1829 to 1837 the number of banks in the country more than doubled; the value of the banknotes they issued tripled; their loans almost quadrupled.

President Jackson had watched in dismay at the uncontrolled growth, aware that many of the new banks flouted the few laws regulating them. Despite having opened the banking system to the states, he had been no supporter of a freewheeling economy. If anything, he was determined to slam on the brakes.

Much of the growth was due to the get-rich-quick scheme of that era: borrowing money, usually from an unsteady bank, to buy Western land from the government's General Land Office. Alarmed by the runaway speculation, Jackson proposed that the government refuse payments in banknotes and accept only gold or silver. Failing to win support from legislators, he waited until Congress's session ended and enacted his proposal as an executive order.

The Panic of 1837 began just a few months after Jackson's second term ended. More than 600 banks had failed by the time the economy turned around six years later.

The Great Bear:
Jacob Little, 1850

William Worthington Fowler

First canal companies then railroads were the darlings of Wall Street during the first half of the nineteenth century. Though old-fashioned to us, those industries were thoroughly modern in their appeal: They promised speed. Everything—people, merchandise, information—would move faster, faster, faster.

Though the fascination is familiar, a contemporary observer would be horrified by the way share prices were manipulated. Wall Street was laissez-faire in those days, a century or so before meaningful government regulation. Only the speed of printing presses limited how many shares were issued, and when. Was someone accumulating stock in your company? Print more certificates. Or perhaps you intended to declare a dividend? Might as well have some of your confederates secretly buy shares in the open market.

One of the sharpest traders of the time, Daniel Drew, eventually managed to get himself elected a director and treasurer of the Erie Railroad, making his control of the stock price complete. A rhyme went:

> When Unc'e Dan'l says "Up"
> Erie goes up.
> When Unc'e Dan'l says "Down"
> Erie goes down.
> When Unc'e Dan'l says "Wiggle waggle"
> Erie bobs both ways.

A skeptical trader named Jacob Little became the most famous speculator on Wall Street. Known as the Great Bear because of his predilection for selling short, Little had arrived on the Street in 1817, the same year the New York Stock & Exchange Board was established. By the time he was profiled by William Worthington Fowler, author of the classic Twenty Years on Wall Street, *Little had made and lost several fortunes.*

The sound of the half hour stroke after ten, from the belfry of Trinity, had hardly died away, when looking towards Wall Street, I saw approaching, a quaint figure, holding in its hand a roll of stock certificates. It disappeared down a basement office at the corner of William Street and Exchange Place, but was up again on the sidewalk in a twinkling. A tall, slight figure, with a stoop, a black alpaca coat hanging loosely about it, walking towards the crowd at a rapid pace.

What a strange face! The coloring a vivid darkness, a clear-obscure, like a tropical night. The eyes dark, with a dreamy, introverted look—the eyes of a philosopher or poet, the drooping, sagacious nose of a financier, and the flexible mouth of an orator. The expression mobile, changing not only emotionally, but in the shape of the features. As he paused on the fringes of the crowd, his lips were suddenly protruded, as if the market were something to be tested by the sense of taste, and then as suddenly withdrawn to their natural position. Again they were puckered up, and protruded as if he were preparing to kiss something, perhaps a plump profit. Every motion and look spoke the Wall Street man, and something more.

Jacob Little! A great name for twenty years in Wall Street! Banker, broker, operator in stocks, exchanges and cotton, he ran through the whole scale, sounding all the heavy notes, from high to low. He would reign the king of the market, fight a dozen pitched battles, suffer defeat, abdicate, and then once more ascend the throne, all in the space of six months. Master of every kind of game played in stocks, rings, corners, sleight-of-hand, beggar your neighbor, bluff, lock-up and bar-out, straddling two horses going different ways, he had the skill as well as the nerve to play them all, and for the most part came out the winner.

Circumstances decided his future career and policy, as they have that of so many other men of mark. If he had commenced his life as a stock operator in 1861 he might have been a great "Bull," and have shared with Cornelius Vanderbilt, the spoils and honors of his campaigns. But soon after he started in business, the financial omens all portended [a] great revulsion; this fact, and the failure of several banks, organized by Jacob Barker, his former employer, inspired him with distrust as to the future value of stock-securities, and so he became a "Bear."

Of course his numerous bear operations made him fair game for a corner, and sometimes he found himself surrounded by an army of bulls, whereupon he would retreat to his last fortress, and after making terms with his besiegers would surrender, and then proceed to re-organize his shattered forces. But he was generally a hard man to corner, and occasionally, when his antagonists thought they had accomplished their purpose, he would turn on them and rout them with great slaughter.

In the latter years of his life he failed for a large amount, and, as usual in such cases, gave his notes to settle the indebtedness. Certain friends of his held some of these notes, and not expecting ever to call on Mr. Little for payment, or that he would ever be able to pay them, had cancelled them, and wiped the indebtedness from their books. But the maker of the notes one day put in an appearance for the purpose of taking them up, having just made one of his great hits. He expressed the greatest indignation on finding the notes had been cancelled, and insisted on paying their amount, which he accordingly did.

The closing years of Jacob Little convey to all who would sell stocks short, a still more instructive lesson. Still clinging to the objects of a pursuit which was to him a passion, his face bearing the marks of the fierce struggles of his life, a broken weird-looking old man, he haunted the Board Room like a spectre where he had once reigned as a king, offering small lots of five shares of the same stock, the whole capital whereof he had once controlled. Where then were the piled millions which that cunning hand and scheming brain had rolled up? Where the prestige of his victories on 'Change? Gone, scattered, lost. Poor and unnoticed, he passed away from the scene, and left nothing behind him but the shadow of what was once a great Wall Street reputation.

The Panic of 1857

George Templeton Strong

The 1848 discovery of gold in California had several dramatic effects on the economy. It literally increased the money supply, as gold was mined and coined. The number of financial institutions, and the value of their banknotes and bonds, increased at an even greater rate. The value of Western land rose sharply. And the railroad and shipping companies enjoyed a boom that seemed to have no end.

In 1857 the end came, suddenly.

"Up to August 1857, our commercial affairs were generally prosperous," wrote J. S. Gibbons, an employee of the New York Clearing House, which settled transactions between banks. "The most sagacious of our city bank officers saw no indications of an unusual storm in the commercial skies." Those bank officers were delusional. There had been indications of a downturn, such as a sharp drop in stock prices on August 8 as banks began calling loans. But for every dip an apparently distinct explanation was offered.

Then, as Gibbons recalled: "On the twenty-fourth of August the suspension of the Ohio Life Insurance and Trust Company was announced. It struck on the public mind like a cannon shot. An intense excitement was manifested in all financial circles, in which bank officers participated with unusual sensitiveness and want of self possession. Flying rumors were exaggerated at every corner. The holders of stock and of commercial paper hurried to the broker, and were eager to make what a week before they would have shunned as a ruinous sacrifice. Several stock and money dealers failed, and the daily meetings of the Board of Brokers were characterized by intense excitement. Every individual misfortune was announced on the news bulletins in large letters, and attracted a curious crowd, which was constantly fed from the passing throng."

Eyewitness George Templeton Strong was a well-connected lawyer.

October 10. We seem foundering. Affairs are worse than ever today, and a period of general insolvency seems close upon us. People say "we must reach the bottom soon," but the bottom has certainly come out. Depression and depletion are going on without sign of any limit and promise to continue till we reach the zero point or universal suspension [of specie payments]. This attack is far more sudden, acute, and prostrating than that of 1837. Will the banks stand it? I think not, and predict their downfall within ten days.

People's faces in Wall Street look fearfully gaunt and desperate. There are two or three millionaire friends of mine whose expression is enough to knock off three per cent a month extra from the market value of their paper. I know of at least two "great houses" that are trembling to their foundations. No merchant or banker, no man who has an obligation outstanding, can feel safe unless he has the needful gold in his own custody. He may be worth any amount in stocks or bonds or land, and yet be unable to raise five thousand dollars a week hence.

The Bowery Bank stopped yesterday. So did the little "East River Bank," I believe. This afternoon as I came uptown there was a crowd besieging the Bowery Savings Bank. I don't know how strong it may be, but if it falls, there will be a run on the other savings banks.

October 13. Here is the "crisis" at last. The community is at length actually enjoying the long-anticipated pleasure, perhaps questionable, of annihilating its own property as fast as possible. The chemical reaction of debtor and creditor has brought the financial crucible to a red heat and the elements are now finally deflagrating. The decisive process of decomposition has set in.

Morning was cloudy. From Hanover Street to Nassau, both sidewalks were densely packed with business men, capitalists, and operators. It was a most "respectable" mob, good-natured and cheerful in its outward aspects but quivering and tingling with excitement. They laughed nervously, and I saw more than one *crying*.

October 14. We have *burst*. All the banks declined paying specie this morning, with the ridiculous exception of the Chemical, which is a little private shaving-shop of the Joneses with no depositors but its own stockholders.

October 22. Walking down Broadway you pass great $200,000 buildings begun last spring or summer that have gone up two stories, and stopped, and may stand unfinished and desolate for years, or on which six Celts are working instead of sixty. Almost every

shop has its placards (written, not printed) announcing a great sacrifice, vast reduction of prices, sales at less than cost. In Wall Street
every man carries Pressure, Anxiety, Loss, written on his forehead.
This is far the worst period of public calamity and distress I've ever
seen, and I fear it is but the beginning.

*Banks resumed specie payments on December 12. "The majority of the
human race," wrote Strong, was "in liquidation." After a similar crisis
a few years later, Bancroft Davies, reporter for* The Times *of London,
concluded that America needed to learn from British finance. "If New
York, instead of 29 or 30 petty banks managed by petty men, without a financial policy, each institution struggling to maintain itself in a rivalry
with all the others, unable to expand while any of its associates were contracting — if, instead of such a powerless confederation of capital as this,
New York had an institution like the Bank of England, or the Bank of
France, or the old Bank of the United States, I believe that the disasters
of the past week might have been prevented." Several decades and disasters later, the United States would agree, establishing the Federal Reserve
System.*

War Bonds and Greenbacks
Washington, 1861–63

Salmon P. Chase

Secretary of the Treasury Salmon P. Chase's schemes to raise funds for the Civil War have had a lasting effect on Wall Street and the nation. Invention, however, was the child of necessity. Just prior to Abraham Lincoln's election, the federal government spent less than $175,000 a day; a year later, with the Civil War underway, it was spending about $1.5 million. Meanwhile, the markets were jittery. "The Board of Brokers is in decided panic," wrote lawyer George Templeton Strong in his diary entry for October 24, 1860. "Stocks are going down. Cause, the anticipation of trouble growing out of Lincoln's election." The real selling began soon after the vote. "Stocks have fallen heavily today," Strong noted on November 13, "and I think they will fall much lower before this game is played out. One can buy in yet more profitably a fortnight hence. Southern securities are waste paper in Wall Street. Not a dollar can be raised on them. Who wants to buy paper that must be collected by suit in the courts of South Carolina and Georgia?"

"The Treasury is now rather hard run," Chase confessed to a friend a few days after the first battle of the war. "It would be a great comfort to me if you New York gentlemen could be patriotic enough to take some Five Millions of the Treasury Notes." Chase also outlined a plan that revealed an instinct for mass marketing: "I propose to issue Treasury Notes, in Denominations Of 50, 100, 500, 1000 and 5000$ bearing Interest Of 7 3/10 per cent per annum. I adopt this rate for the convenience of calculation, and because I think it, under the circumstances, about fair. At this rate, the Interest on $50 will be, say one Cent a day—on $100 Two Cents, and so on. An endorsement of Interest, calculated at this rate, on the back, will, I think, add somewhat to the attractiveness of the investment. For this Loan, I propose a Subscription, to be opened all over the country, Ten per cent to be paid at the time of subscribing, and the balance in Four Monthly Instalments thereafter."

Soon afterward Chase struck a deal with someone who shared his insight:

FROM JAY COOKE & CO., BANKERS, PHILADELPHIA
JULY 12TH 1861

Dear Sir,

After some days negotiation I have to submit the following for your consideration—

Messrs Drexel & Co of this city are willing to join our house in opening a first class Banking Establishment in Washn. at once—trusting to our energy capital & credit for success, as well as those natural advantages that would legitimately & honestly flow towards us from your personal friendship & the fact that our firm was ardently & fully with the Administration.

Drexel & Co & ourselves would represent at least 2½ to 3 millions of capital not all in cash, nor all immediately available but still good as a basis without referring to our own standing & credit, which we may say, is, after 22 years active business in this city, now on a firmer basis than ever—we would refer to Drexel & Co as the heaviest house in Philada. with correspondents all over this land & doing also a heavy business in Germany, Mr Reed their New York partner & active agent there has probably transacted more business in Gov loans & Treasy notes than any other N York firm & is the particular frd of Mr Cisco [a Treasury official] & stands very high as a business man.

We propose to give personal attention to the business at Washn. with a view of making our services valuable to yourself during the coming 3 or 4 years, Mr A. J. Drexel (the head of the house of Drexel & Co) & myself will reside in Washn. most of the time & in this arrangement we shall include my Bro H D who will have a share in the profits — We would wish to make our business mostly out of the Treasury operations, & we feel sure that we could by having a proper understanding with yourself greatly help you in the management of your vast negotiations—at the same time if we could not thus prove our value to you we should not expect your continued influence & favor—

If you feel disposed to say to us, if our plans commend themselves fully to your judgement that you will give us the management of the Loans to be issued by the Government

during the war allowing us a fair commission on them subject of course & entirely to your supervision & advice we are
ready to throw ourselves into the matter heartily & at once &
will go down & have an interview with you [to] explain our
plans & if encouraged by you go to work at once—

> *Very Respy*
> *Jay Cooke*

*Cooke was the right man for the job, having trained in a Philadel-
phia firm that used popular advertising to sell securities, including bonds
that financed the war with Mexico in 1846.*

*To sell Chase's bonds he organized a national system of salespeople
(eventually numbering 2,500), expediting transactions with the newly invented telegraph. Appealing to patriotism and compassion, he advertised
in newspapers and billboards.*

*The effort succeeded far beyond anyone's expectations. Cooke quickly
earned a unique reputation and role. During a later crisis, Chase
pleaded, "It will be necessary to raise the conversions to a million of dollars per day. Can this be done? Are you willing to undertake it?"*

*Could it be done? Cooke's selling outpaced Chase's spending. By the
end of the war he had sold almost a billion dollars' worth of bonds.*

*All Cooke's work was done despite minuscule commissions. He accepted
those commissions in part to distinguish himself from other bankers,
knowing he could profit by earning interest on the "float"—money his
bank had received on behalf of the government but had not yet transferred
to the Treasury. However, Chase did not allow much room for such manipulation. (Negotiating a later bond issue, Chase tried to limit that
practice with language so stiff that Cooke replied, "Some passages of this
letter are more fit for instructions to a fool or dishonest agent than one de-
serving confidence & tried and trusted heretofore to millions.") In any
event, the low pay wasn't reflected in his work, which was undoubtedly
motivated by his belief in the Union cause.*

*The most obvious legacy of Chase's Civil War financing schemes was
the establishment of a national currency. As hard as it may be to believe
today, given the worldwide importance of American dollars, prior to the
Civil War people used an ever-changing assortment of notes from individual banks, notes issued by individual states, specie (gold or silver), or
some combination of all three.*

Chase's currency, which came to be called greenbacks, was controver-

sial primarily because the bills were not redeemable for specie of equal value. But that wasn't the only innovation the country had to accept. To distribute the notes and maintain public confidence in them, Chase created a precursor to the Federal Reserve System, which he sketched in a letter to a friend: "Its main features are, the preparation and supply of a uniform Currency by the United States; the issue of it by organization under the law, throughout the country; and the security afforded to the holders, by the deposit of United States Bonds in the Treasury department. This arrangement will bring to the support of the public credit the whole banking interest of the country." (In contrast to the tight control with which Union finances were conducted, the Confederacy's efforts were chaotic. To be fair, the South might never have been able to overcome the handicap of a cash-poor agrarian economy. In any case, its efforts were unsophisticated: newly printed money accounted for more than half its costs in the war, compared to less than 15 percent for the North. Accordingly, inflation hit the South much harder.)

Chase was walking in the footsteps of Alexander Hamilton, who faced similar crises during the Revolutionary War. Ironically, when Chase became Chief Justice of the United States after the war, he tried to undo much of his work. "The National Bank Act," he later said, "was the greatest mistake in my life. It has built up a monopoly which affects every interest in the country. It should be repealed, but before that can be accomplished, the people should be arrayed on one side, and the banks on the other, in a contest such as we have never seen before in this country." He opposed his own Legal Tender Act just as strongly, ruling it unconstitutional in a decision that would have forced the retirement of all the greenbacks issued had not President Ulysses S. Grant appointed two Supreme Court justices whose votes overturned the decision. Despite himself, Chase fulfilled a goal he once stated during the war: "I hope, not without some reason, to be able to convert our financial troubles into permanent benefits to the country."

To Chase one must also give credit, reluctantly, for a final innovation with staying power. He introduced the income tax.

The Gold Exchange, 1866

Horace White

Within weeks of the U.S. government's decision to issue currency that was not redeemable in gold, speculators created a market where one could buy gold with greenbacks. When confidence in the Union fell, more greenbacks were needed to buy gold. When confidence rose, the value of the greenbacks rose also. The informal market eventually became the Gold Exchange, perhaps the rowdiest market in Wall Street history.

Horace White was editor of the Chicago Tribune *and later U.S. Treasurer.*

Imagine a rat-pit in full blast, with twenty or thirty men ranged around the rat tragedy, each with a canine under his arm, yelling and howling at once, and you have as good a comparison as can be found in the outside world of the aspect of the Gold Room as it strikes the beholder on his first entrance. The furniture of the room is extremely simple. It consists of two iron railings and an indicator. The first railing is a circle about four feet high and ten feet in diameter, placed exactly in the center of the room. In the interior, which represents the space devoted to rat killing in other establishments, is a marble cupid throwing up a jet of pure Croton water. The artistic conception is not appropriate. Instead of a cupid throwing a pearly fountain into the air, there should have been a hungry Midas turning everything to gold and starving from sheer inability to eat.

The other railing is a semicircle twenty or thirty feet from the central one. The outer rail fences off the "lame ducks and deadbeats," men who have once been famous at the rat-pit, but have since been cleaned out. Solvency is the first essential of the Gold Room. Nothing bogus is allowed to interfere with the serious nature of the business in hand. Nevertheless, these "lame ducks and deadbeats" cannot keep away from the place. Day after day they come and range themselves along this iron grating and look over at the rat-pit with the strongest expression of intelligent vacancy and longing despair that can be found out of purgatory. They seem to be a part of the furniture of the room. While I was there I did not see one of them move or speak, and when they winked it was with much the same spirit that an owl at mid-day lowers the film over his eye and lifts it again.

The indicator, which is the third piece of furniture in the room (or the fourth if we count the deadbeats), is a piece of mechanism to show the changes in the market. It is something like an old-fashioned Dutch clock, seven or eight feet high, with an open space at the top, disclosing three figures and a fraction, as in 141½ [meaning 141½ greenbacks to 100 gold dollars] where the market stood when I entered. The figures being movable, a slight manipulation will manifest any change in the market. Connected with the indicator is a plain desk with a book on it, in which are recorded all the movements of the indicator, with the hour and minute at which each takes place. The floor of the establishment is a pavement with circular steps or terraces rising from the center to the circumference. "Neat but not gaudy" is the general aspect of the premises. Of course such an institution could not exist without a telegraph office. Accordingly we find one communicating with the Gold Room by a row of windows through which dispatches are constantly passing.

Having given the appearance of the concern, we now come to business. Three things are in demand—lungs, note books, and pencils. Wow-wow-wow, yah-yah-yah, from twenty or thirty throats around the pit all at once, and kept going from morning till night, from Monday till Saturday, is what presents itself to the ears of the beholder. The voices of the gentry around the circle are for the most part tenori, with now and then a falsetto and a basso. I shall not soon forget a basso profundo in the ring, who drew his breath at regular intervals and announced his desires with a seriousness truly remarkable. He was a thick set man, with capacious chest, shaggy head, keen eyes, and rusty whiskers, which curved upward from his inferior maxillary line in the most determined manner. He cocked his head on one side, thrust his chin as far over the railing as possible, and made himself heard every time. He put in his B-flat in regular cadence, like the trombone performer in a mill pond, of a summer's evening, drowning for the moment all the fiddles of the frog community.

The government shut down the Gold Exchange briefly, but the speculation couldn't be stopped, so the Exchange was allowed to reopen. The free-floating currency sank to its low in 1863, at 287 greenbacks to 100 dollars of gold.

The Exchange operated until dollars were again backed by gold in 1875.

PART FOUR

Wall Street in the Gilded Age

"I have never walked down Fifth Avenue alone without thinking of money. I have never walked there with a companion without talking of it. I fancy that every man there, in order to maintain the spirit of the place, should bear on his forehead a label stating how many dollars he is worth, and that every label should be expected to assert a falsehood."

Anthony Trollope, 1860

Timeline

1867 — Stock ticker developed by Edward A. Calahan

1867 — Crédit Mobilier scandal—congressmen gain from railroad embezzlement

1868 — NYSE members allowed to own and sell "seats"

1868 — Jay Gould, Daniel Drew, and Jim Fisk battle Vanderbilt for Erie RR

1869 — September 24: "Black Friday"; prices collapse as gold corner fails

1871 — Continuous trading of all stocks on NYSE—"specialists" stick to "posts" on trading floor

1873 — Jay Cooke & Co., financier of Union, collapses on September 19; panic closes NYSE for ten days; Morgan will become leading bank

1874 — Chicago Produce Exchange est. (later becomes Chicago Mercantile Exchange)

1878 — Wall Street installs some of the first telephones in U.S.

1878 — To support Western mining states, Congress requires govt. purchases of silver and fixes its exchange rate with gold— inflation will undermine U.S. currency as silver is coined

1879 — U.S. agrees to redeem greenbacks; public prefers paper

1882 — Rockefeller organizes Standard Oil trust

1883 — Charles Dow and Edward Jones print *Customer's Afternoon Letter*, renamed *Wall Street Journal* in 1889

1883 — NYSE gets its first electric lights

1884 — Dow creates first "average" of stock prices

1884 — Dow adds first "industrial," American Sugar, to average

1893 — Silver mining has inflated U.S. currency; foreign capital flees; panic and depression follow; U.S. stops buying silver

1895 — J. P. Morgan teams with Rothschilds to sell gold to Treasury, becoming de facto central bank

1895 — NYSE tells companies to send annual reports of finances

1896 — The use of silver to back currency is hot issue in presidential election; gold standard wins

1896 — *Wall Street Journal* publishes average of industrial stocks

THE SCENE IN THE GILDED AGE

The Idle Rich

Ward McAllister

After the Civil War, the country quickly got back to business, more of which flowed through Wall Street and New York than ever before. The growth of the federal government and the national-ization of currency concentrated the economy to the benefit of Northern bankers. Building began on the transcontinental railroad and other industrial efforts, channeling hundreds of millions more through the stock and bond markets. Electricity and petroleum be-came the foundation of new industries.

Add to those efforts the magical effect of fraud—which may have been the rule rather than the exception, especially during the Grant administration—and you create more than a few grand for-tunes and grandiose displays.

One might guess from the tone of this eyewitness account that McAllister was amused by New York society. In fact, he was ob-sessed with it, and with his own role as its gatekeeper. It was the Georgia-born McAllister who contrived the idea of "the Four Hun-dred," the select few people in New York "who mattered." (One ver-sion of the story is that only 400 people could fit into the ballroom of McAllister's famous patron, Mrs. William B. Astor.)

Up to this time for one to be worth a million of dollars was to be rated as a man of fortune, but now bygones must be by-gones. New York's ideas as to values, when fortune was named, leaped boldly up to ten millions, fifty millions, one hundred millions; and the necessities and luxuries followed suit. One was no longer content with a dinner of a dozen or more, to be served by a couple of servants. Fashion demanded that you be received in the hall of the house in which you were to dine by from five to six servants, who, with the butler, were to serve the repast—the butler, on such occasions, to do alone the headwork, and under him he had these men in livery to serve the dinner, he to guide and direct them. Soft strains of music were introduced between the courses, and in some houses gold replaced silver in the way of plate; and everything that skill and art could suggest was added to make the dinners not a vulgar display but a gastronomic effort evidencing the possession by the host of both money and taste.

The great event in the fashionable world was a ball. At one, six quadrilles were danced. There was the hobbyhorse quadrille, the men who danced in it being dressed in "pink" and the ladies wearing red hunting coats and white satin skirts, all of the period of Louis XIV. In the Mother Goose quadrille were Jack and Jill, Little Red Riding Hood, Bo-Peep, Goody Two-Shoes, Mary, Mary, Quite Contrary, and My Pretty Maid. The opéra bouffe quadrille was most successful. But of all of them, the star quadrille, containing the youth and beauty of the city, was the most brilliant. The ladies in it were arrayed as twin stars in four different colors, yellow, blue, mauve, and white. Above the forehead of each lady, in her hair, was worn an electric light, giving a fairy and elflike appearance to each of them.

The Battle for Erie, 1868

William Worthington Fowler

No other takeover battle matches this one. It held as much public interest as another event underway at the same time, the impeachment of President Andrew Johnson.

The Erie Railroad was an odd line. In theory, it linked the port of New York City with the Midwest. In reality, because it had been designed by politicians careful to protect interests like the Erie Canal, it did not begin in the city or reach Buffalo, the canal's important Lake Erie terminus. Historian John Steele Gordon noted that when built it was "the longest railroad in the world, running, almost literally, between nowhere and nowhere." Financing for railroad was just as disordered. Eventually it was backed by so many different securities that people had difficulty keeping them straight. Crafty traders constantly exploited the confusion. The line would become known as "The Scarlet Woman of Wall Street."

Despite these problems, and the occasional bankruptcy, Wall Street's two toughest operators wanted it. Cornelius Vanderbilt already controlled some of the best lines in the country: the New York & Harlem, the New York Central, and the Hudson River Railroad. Tough, and not above sharp dealing, Vanderbilt was nonetheless a legitimate businessman by the standards of his day: he tried to operate his company at a profit. Daniel Drew, on the other hand, was a timeless crook. He gained control of the Erie line in 1857 after manipulating its stock for several years as a broker. Once in charge of the company's finances, he played with the stock price to earn profits from trading, while simultaneously skimming the railroad's revenue. He was aided in this fight by two men who almost made him look respectable. James Fisk and Jay Gould were shameless swindlers, celebrated for their audacity.

The Erie battle began when Vanderbilt, a minority investor in the line, grew tired of Drew's accounting antics and made a bid for control. Wall Street speculators tried to anticipate the outcome and arbitrage accordingly. Did Vanderbilt have enough money to buy all the Erie shares that might hit the market—including those dumped by Drew and his ac-

complices in an effort to soak Vanderbilt's capital? If so, the price would rise, meaning one should hold or buy. But if Vanderbilt's effort failed, the market might have an oversupply of shares, meaning prices could suddenly drop.

William Worthington Fowler was the author of Twenty Years on Wall Street.

The whole market hung on one word—*Erie*. The strident voice of George Henriques, the Vice President of the Open Board [a stock exchange that rivaled the NYSE and at one point had a larger volume], was heard calling off in quick succession, Government Bonds, State Bonds, Pacific Mail, New York Central, then a pause, a shadow rippled across his face and a shiver ran through the hall as he ejaculated in a tone still more strident—*Erie!* For ten minutes bedlam seemed to have broken loose. Every operator and broker was on his feet in an instant, screaming and gesticulating. The different Vanderbilt brokers stood each in the center of a circle, wheeling as on a pivot from right to left, brandishing their arms and snatching at all the stock offered them.

As the presiding officer's hammer fell and his hoarse voice thundered out, "That will do, gentlemen, I shall fine any other offer," Erie stood at 80. The crowd leaving the other stocks not yet called, poured into the street, where nothing was heard but Erie. Vanderbilt's brokers had orders to buy every share offered, and under their enormous purchases the price rose, by twelve o'clock, to 83.

Meanwhile, [Drew's broker] William Heath had not been idle. The fifty thousand shares of stock which had been given him to sell, had been distributed in lots of five and ten thousand shares to his sub-agents, and by half-past one, they had all been disposed of.

In the very height of this battle between giant avarice, fighting like a demon with his fellow over the grave of all the passions, a whisper was heard which sent an electric thrill through the whole market. This whisper, breathed thus, was "thousands of shares of fresh certificates, dated three days back, and in the name of James Fisk, Jr., are on the street." The price dropped like lead to 71. Vanderbilt had lost the day.

The news of this disaster was carried to him by a friend, who asked if he would now sell his Erie? He roared a thundering No! His situation was indeed critical, loaded as he was with ten millions of fresh Erie stock, which marked down the intrinsic value of the stock to 50, to say nothing of the huge blocks of Central, Hudson, and Harlem, which he was carrying on his aged shoulders. Any lack of nerve would have produced a financial collapse, which would have involved himself and thousands of others in frightful loss, and perhaps ruin. But he never flinched.

His first move was to punish his adversaries, by bringing them under the process of the court, whose injunction they had disregarded. The executive committee of the Erie Board were holding high festival over their triumph, at the offices of the company, at the foot of Duane Street, on the morning of the 11th of March. Uncle Daniel's corrugated visage was set into a chronic chuckle. Jay Gould's financial eye beamed and glittered, and the blonde bulk of James Fisk, Jr., was unctuous with jokes, when a messenger arrived, conveying to them the intelligence that process of the court had been issued, to punish them for contempt of its mandates, and would soon be placed for service in the hands of the high sheriff's spongy officers. Then there were hurryings to and fro in the Erie Railroad Office.

A few moments later, and the policeman on that beat observed a squad of respectably dressed, but terrified looking men, loaded down with packages of greenbacks, account books, bundles of papers tied up with red tape, emerge in haste and disorder from the Erie building. Thinking perhaps that something illicit had been taking place, and these individuals might be plunderers playing a bold game in open daylight, he approached them, but he soon found out his mistake, they were only the executive committee of the Erie Company, flying the wrath of the Commodore, and laden with the spoils of their recent campaign.

By three o'clock that afternoon the fugitives had established their headquarters at Taylor's Hotel, in Jersey City, and were sheltered from the process of the New York Courts under the broad aegis of the free and sovereign State of New Jersey. They were provided with ammunition in the shape of from six to ten millions of money, principally the proceeds from the sale of one hundred thousand shares of new Erie stock, which they had saddled upon Vanderbilt, and now were ready to open fire all around, though at long range.

The old proverb, that laws are cobwebs which catch only smal' flies, while the large flies break through and escape, was now fully illustrated. The litigation which followed was a carnival for the legal fraternity. The fees of one of the lawyers amounted to $150,000. This was only one item in a bill of costs payable to an army of attorneys and counselors. The files of the courts were stacked with affidavits and counter affidavits, complaints, answers, replies, demurrers and orders. The Supreme Court rang with the criminations and recriminations of the rival factions, while reluctant witnesses were stretched upon the rack and badgered and threatened in order to elicit from them the dark secrets of the stock-trade. The gravest insinuations were made against the purity of the judicial ermine.

Outside the courts of law, the battle was renewed in other fields. The press, siding with one party or the other, teemed with articles and affidavits affecting the combatants by forestalling public opinion. In the Legislature of New Jersey, an act was passed making the Erie Railway Company a corporation of that State. In the Legislature of New York, a bill was introduced for the purpose of legalizing the new issue of Erie stock, providing for a broad gauge connection between New York and Chicago, and forbidding the consolidation of Erie with Central. The securing of the passage of this bill was entrusted to Jay Gould, a master of diplomacy, who, braving the process for contempt which was out against him, succeeded in establishing himself in Albany, fortified with a trunk full of greenbacks, and proceeded to lobby for its passage. The Erie Company leveled another blow at Vanderbilt, by lowering the tariff of freights and passengers on their road to a ruinous rate.

Meanwhile the withdrawal of the vast sum carried away by the conspirators into New Jersey had created a stringency in the money market, and stocks declined in a semi-panic. New York Central fell from 132 to 108. The market was full of rumors affecting the solvency of Vanderbilt. He had declared his intention to hold up Erie, if he had to mortgage every dollar of property he possessed. But could he do it? He was exposed to fresh issues of Erie stock, which it was reported his opponents had threatened to make. Some of his associates, terrified at the prospect, threw their New York Central stock upon the market. Heavy bets were made, that the bill legalizing the new issue of Erie stock would pass the Legislature, and that New York Central would go down to par. The whole street seemed to be selling Central. When it reached 108¾, it wheeled and shot back to 111, amid the consternation of the bears, who still persisted in selling.

Monday, April 20th, was a dark, cloudy day. The effect of the weather upon stocks is very apparent. That strange, and many-chorded instrument, the human nerve, is nowhere more delicately strung, or more responsive to the subtlest influences, than in the orchestra of stock-speculation.

At twelve o'clock, meridian, the news reached the Long Room, that the Erie bill had passed by a large majority. The bears (who generally sympathized with the Erie faction) now sold Central short on every side. The skies grew black, and a pouring shower followed, amid which the strong hand of the Commodore, regardless of the elements which were against him, hoisted the enormous bulk of Central to 120. How did it happen, that he had thus resumed his grip on Central? Had a settlement been made by the litigants?

Vanderbilt understood the character of Drew. He knew, and said that he had "no backbone," and would be inclined to compromise. The event proved that he knew his man. Hardly had the Erie confederates been installed in Taylor's Hotel, when his younger, and more robust associates, noticed the workings of his timid, vacillating nature. He had been borne along by their stronger wills, and now felt painfully his trying position. He missed his pleasant fireside, where he had so often toasted his aged limbs, and dreamed of panics. One evening he was missed from the conclave; where could he be? His associates distrusted him, and put detectives on his track. He was followed to Weehawken ferry, and it was ascertained, that he was making secret visits to New York. From that time, he was never free from the surveillance of detectives. He drew out the money, which had been brought over at the time of his flight, and carried it to New York. James Fisk, Jr., attached his securities in Jersey City, and compelled him to restore it.

Under the process of the court, Daniel Drew was liable to be immured in Ludlow Street jail. But Sunday brings, besides its other blessings, immunity from arrest. One Sunday in April saw the "old man" at the house of the Commodore. Once more he shed salt tears and supplicated for mercy. "The gentle dew of mercy" was dropped upon him, and a few days after that he was seen in Broad Street, on a week day. Rumors began to spread, but nothing definite was known for some weeks. The rise in Central, however, told the story to those who chose to put two and two together. The terms of this settlement have lately been made public in the most thorough manner, in the great suit of the Erie Railway Company vs. Cornelius Vanderbilt. He was relieved of fifty thousand shares of Erie stock, and received therefor, $2,500,000 in cash, and $1,250,000 in bonds of the Boston, Hartford and Erie Company, at 80. He also received the further sum of $1,000,000 for the privilege given the Erie Company thus purchased, of calling upon him for his remaining fifty thousand shares at 70, any time within four months. This settlement was effected late in April.

The Erie Company was now under the control of Jay Gould, who had been chosen president, and James Fisk, Jr., who had been chosen comptroller of the company. The leaders of the Tammany [political] ring, Peter B. Sweeney, and William M. Tweed, were added to the Board of Directors. During the four months prior to the 24th of October, 1868, fresh issues of Erie stock had been forced upon the market. The capital stock had been increased by two hundred and thirty-five thousand shares, and now stood at $57,766,300. The stock-price ran down to 44.

The upstarts Fisk and Gould had amazed the Street by beating both Vanderbilt and Drew. They continued Drew's tradition of draining profit from the line and using it as a tool for speculation. It was the Erie treasury that supported their plan to corner the country's gold supply—the scheme that ended in Black Friday.

Black Friday, 1869

The New York Times *and George S. Boutwell*

What would lead two speculators, even two as bold as Jay Gould and James Fisk, to attempt a corner of the United States gold supply? Could it even be done?

Gould believed he had figured a way. In the notorious Gold Room, about $100,000 would buy contracts for more than the $20 million in gold and gold certificates Gould guessed to be owned privately in New York and available for quick delivery.

There was a possible complication: about $100 million of U.S. government gold was held in New York. As the price rose, the government would have incentive to sell. That incentive would become stronger if a panic began. Gold would be needed to calm the markets. So Gould and Fisk had to prevent the U.S. government from selling. Fortunately for them, the administration of President Ulysses S. Grant was notoriously corrupt. Gould and Fisk knew they could win friends in high places. The only question was, How high?

The New York Times *reported the action:*

WEDNESDAY, SEPTEMBER 22

The excitement in Wall-street on Wednesday was at white heat late in the day on Gold. [The] sensation related to the speculation and practical *corner* in gold. And here about 3 o'clock Wednesday afternoon appeared on the scene the inevitable and irrepressible Fisk, Jr. His presence in the Gold Room was signalized by the rapid rise in gold from 137½ to 141½ [greenback dollars for $100 in gold], and by the offers of wagers for any part of $50,000 that its price would reach 145.

At the time, the price in London for the same amount of gold was about $105.

The other engineers of the movement were not idle, nor had they been through the earlier part of the day. They not only *bulled* gold with a will, but talked freely of the warrant which they had from Washington that the Government would not interfere with them. The highest official in the land was quoted *as being with them*, and he, of course, controls the action of the Secretary of the Treasury and the New-York Assistant Treasurer.

THURSDAY, SEPTEMBER 23

By 9 o'clock the belligerent parties in the gold speculation had begun to take shots at each other. Transactions were at once made at 142½, or more than one point above the highest futures of the day before. In a short time, amid intense excitement, the price began to rise, and it sold rapidly up to 144 and 144¼.

As the roar of battle and the screams of the victims resounded through New Street, it seemed as though human nature was undergoing torments worse than any that Dante ever witnessed in hell. Throughout the afternoon, the Long Room [the stock exchange] was constantly crowded by a "mob of gentlemen" who maintained themselves in a state of enthusiasm far surpassing anything we ever witnessed, either at a Southern camp-meeting or a Havana cock-fight. In fact, the condition both of the Long Room and the Gold Room was vividly and accurately described by an ingenuous rustic on the steps of the Gold Room, who, when asked by an excited operator what were the features of the market, replied, "Simply howling."

We were told by brokers that not since the war times of 1864–5 had they seen the street in such a state of perturbation as during the last two days; and it is more than likely that to-day will see a continuation of the "heated term."

Crowds were inside the rooms and outside—crowds were standing here and there—crowds were constantly hurrying to and fro in all parts of New, Broad, Wall, Nassau and William streets.

Old operators in the street say that the bull clique which now controls the gold market is the most powerful clique we have had in gold since the war—if not the greatest that has appeared since gold went above par [when $100 of greenbacks were worth $100 of gold] eight years ago.

The names of the parties who are supposed, if not positively known, to compose this clique are freely mentioned; but we do not propose to injure any man's reputation here by accusing him of being a member of the *Ring*.

Of course it is to the advantage of this clique that the largest stories of their power should be circulated, and that the wildest schemes in regard to gold should be attributed to them. They are thus enabled the more effectually to carry out their purposes, and to strike their adversaries with dismay.

Did they really have the President in their pocket, or were they bluffing? As Secretary of the Treasury George S. Boutwell explained afterward, the answer wasn't clear, especially to Gould and Fisk.

Their confidence was in Mr. A. R. Corbin, a brother-in-law of the President, who under the influence of various considerations, which appear to have been personal and pecuniary to a very large extent, lent himself to the task of influencing the President. As a matter of fact, his attempts were very feeble and misdirected and of no consequence whatever. Indeed, such is my opinion of the President, and such my belief as to his opinion concerning Mr. Corbin, that nothing which Mr. Corbin did say, or could have said, did have or could have had the least influence upon the President's opinion or conduct. It is, however, also true that Fisk and Gould employed Corbin and gave him consideration in their undertakings out of which he realized some money. I received information also, which may not have been true, that they suggested to him that he might become president of the Tenth National Bank, which had a very conspicuous part in the events which culminated in Black Friday. . . .

I called upon the President after business on the 23rd of September, and made a statement of the condition of the gold market in the city of New York, as far as it had been communicated to me during the day. I then said that a sale of gold should be made for the purposes of breaking the market and ending the excitement. He asked me what sum I proposed to sell. I said: "Three million dollars will be sufficient to break the combination."

He said in reply: "I think you had better make it $5,000,000."

Without assenting to his proposition or dissenting from it, I returned to the department, and sent an order for the sale of $4,000,000 of gold the next day.

The order was to the assistant treasurer in these words: "Sell $4,000,000 gold tomorrow, and buy $4,000,000 bonds." The message was not in cipher, and there was no attempt to keep it secret. It was duplicated, and sent by each of the rival telegraph lines to New York.

Within the space of fifteen minutes after the receipt of the despatch, the price of gold fell from 160 to 133 [dollars per ounce], and in the language of one of the witnesses, "half of Wall Street was involved in ruin."

At the congressional hearings into the incident, it was revealed that Gould had proven himself even more slippery than Fisk. After receiving early news of Grant's actual position, he kept that news from Fisk and switched from buyer to seller.

Some of Fisk's comments before Congress are still quoted. "Nothing is lost save honor," he said. And when asked where all the money went, he replied lyrically that it had "gone where the woodbine twineth." To a congressman who didn't know that woodbine—honeysuckle—was often planted around outhouses to cover their smell, Fisk offered a prosaic explanation: "Up the spout."

Carnegie's Career Begins, 1869

Andrew Carnegie

The Gilded Age was not just one scandal after another. Real businesses were built, including some that endure.

Andrew Carnegie, one of the most impressive entrepreneurs of that time or any other, took his first job shortly after emigrating to the United States from Scotland as a child. He combined precocious individual skills with organizational ability, perfectly fitting him for the new Industrial Age. He understood his businesses well enough to operate them, yet also knew the value of delegating control to talented managers. Among his notable protégés were Henry Clay Frick and Charles M. Schwab (grandfather of the discount brokerage founder known from television ads).

Mark Twain, who knew him well, called him the Human Being Unconcealed. "He is just like the rest of the human race," explained Twain, "but with this difference, that the rest of the race try to conceal what they are and succeed, whereas Andrew tries to conceal what he is but doesn't succeed. He never has any but one theme, himself. Not that he deals in autobiography; not that he tells you about his brave struggles for a livelihood as a friendless poor boy in a strange land; not that he tells you how he advanced his fortunes steadily and successfully against obstructions that would have defeated almost any other human being similarly placed; not that he tells you how he finally reached the summit of his ambition and became lord over 22,000 men and possessor of one of the three giant fortunes of his day; no, as regards these achievements he is as modest a man as you could meet anywhere, and seldom makes even a fleeting reference to them; yet it is as I say, he is himself his one darling subject, the only subject he for the moment—the social moment—seems stupendously interested in."

Though best known for his steel fortune, Carnegie's early career included railroads and, as he describes in this social moment, bridgebuilding.

One day in 1869 the gentleman in charge of the [St. Louis Bridge Company] enterprise, Mr. Macpherson (he was very Scotch), called at my New York office and said they were trying to raise capital to build the bridge. He wished to know if I could not enlist some of the Eastern railroad companies in the scheme. After careful examination of the project I made the contract for the construction of the bridge on behalf of the Keystone Bridge Works. I also obtained an option upon four million dollars of first mortgage bonds of the bridge company and set out for London in March, 1869, to negotiate their sale.

During the voyage I prepared a prospectus which I had printed upon my arrival in London, and having upon my previous visit made the acquaintance of Junius S. Morgan, the great banker [and father of John Pierpont Morgan], I called upon him one morning and opened negotiations. I left with him a copy of the prospectus, and upon calling next day was delighted to find that Mr. Morgan viewed the matter favorably. I sold him part of the bonds with the option to take the remainder; but when his lawyers were called in for advice a score of changes were required in the wording of the bonds. Mr. Morgan said to me that as I was going to Scotland I had better go now; I could write the parties in St. Louis and ascertain whether they would agree to the changes proposed. It would be time enough, he said, to close the matter upon my return three weeks hence.

But I had no idea of allowing the fish to play so long, and I informed him that I would have a telegram in the morning agreeing to all the changes. The Atlantic cable had been open for some time, but it is doubtful if it had yet carried so long a private cable as I sent that day. It was not an easy matter to number the lines of the bond and then going carefully over them to state what changes, omissions, or additions were required in each line. I showed Mr. Morgan the message before sending it and he said, "Well, young man, if you succeed in that you deserve a red mark."

When I entered the office the next morning, I found on the desk that had been appropriated to my use in Mr. Morgan's private office the colored envelope which contained the answer. There it was: "Board meeting last night; changes all approved." "Now, Mr. Morgan," I said, "we can proceed, assuming that the bond is as your lawyers desire." The papers were soon closed.

While I was in the office Mr. Sampson, the financial editor of *The Times*, came in. I had an interview with him, well knowing that a few words from him would go far in lifting the price of the bonds on the Exchange. American securities had recently been fiercely attacked, owing to the proceedings of Fisk and Gould in connection with the Erie Railway Company, and their control of the judges in New York, who seemed to do their bidding. I knew this would be handed out as an objection, and therefore I met it at once.

I called Mr. Sampson's attention to the fact that the charter of the St. Louis Bridge Company was from the National Government. In case of necessity appeal lay directly to the Supreme Court of the United States, a body vying with their own high tribunals. He said he would be delighted to give prominence to this commendable feature. I described the bridge as a toll-gate on the continental highway and this appeared to please him. It was all plain and easy sailing, and when he left the office, Mr. Morgan clapped me on the shoulder and said, "Thank you, young man; you have raised the price of those bonds five percent this morning."

"All right, Mr. Morgan," I replied, "now show me how I can raise them five percent more for you." The issue was a great success, and the money for the St. Louis Bridge Company was obtained. I had a considerable margin of profit upon the negotiation. This was my first financial negotiation with the bankers of Europe. Mr. Pullman told me a few days later that Mr. Morgan at a dinner party had told the telegraphic incident and predicted, "That young man will be heard from."

In 1901 Carnegie sold his extensive steel holdings to the U.S. Steel Corporation, established by Junius Morgan's son, J.P. He then retired to devote himself fully to philanthropy. By the time of his death in 1919, Carnegie had endowed various charities and foundations with $350 million.

A footnote to history: While America was still officially a neutral observer of World War I, Charles M. Schwab, who had negotiated the U.S. Steel deal and become the president of the combined operation, received an offer of $100 million—much more than market value—for his controlling interest. The offer came from the German government, which hoped to choke Britain's steel supply. Schwab refused.

The First Women Brokers
February 5, 1870

New York Sun

When sisters Victoria Woodhull and Tennie C. Claflin opened a broker-age in the Hoffman House hotel, it was a front-page story in every New York paper.

Woodhull & Claflin opened their office at 10 a.m. Mr. Edward Van Schalck was the first gentleman who called upon them. The ladies received him very cordially. They told him that as soon as they were firmly established they should be happy to receive his orders for the purchase of stock. While Mr. Van Schalck was conversing with the members of the firm Mr. George B. Alley and Mr. Abram B. Baylis entered, and wished the new firm much joy. Meanwhile, Mr. Van Schalck departed. A few minutes afterward Messrs. Wm. B. Beekman, George H. Bend and John Bloodgood paid the ladies a visit and left apparently satisfied that the firm was well established and meant to have their fair share of business in Wall street. Mr. S. J. Blood and the handsome George T. Bonner were the next calls.

At 10:45 a.m. Mr. Edward H. Van Schalck paid the firm a second visit. He had been to the barber's and his really handsome face glowed with enthusiasm. He was accompanied by the dignified H. A. Bostwick, the lithe James Boyde, the gentlemanly Edward Brandon and Hugh Hastings. The latter gentleman regarded the ladies with evident astonishment and bluntly told them that they could not succeed. At this Mr. Van Schalck became quite indignant and told Mr. Hastings that he ought to know that ladies made the most successful lobbyists and he saw no reason why they should not become successful bankers. After further conversation the party left. Daniel Drew and O. D. Ashley meanwhile paid their respects to the partners. Mr. Drew was evidently deeply impressed with the importance of the movement. As he went out the door he met Jay

Cooke and Mr. John Bonner, who acknowledged that they had called out of mere curiosity.

At half past 11 o'clock Mr. Edward H. Van Schalck and Hugh Hastings paid a third visit to the new banking house. Mr. Van Schalck had changed his cravat and now wore one of blue silk of huge dimensions and exquisitely tied. During their visit numerous capitalists entered the room. These gentlemen listened to the business plans of the new firm with skeptical faces, but heartily wished the ladies success in their undertaking.

At twenty minutes after twelve, Mr. Edward H. Van Schalck and Mr. Hugh Hastings again entered the room. Mr. Van Schalck wore a new hat, and Mr. Hastings had a gorgeous rose in the lapel of his coat. They wanted to know how Central stood. Miss Claflin sprang to the instrument and shouted "Before call 94½."

The next visitors were S. W. Harned and Rufus Hatch. These gentlemen looked at the principal of the house with grim silence, and departed without vouchsafing a word. On the threshold they were met by the Hon. Oliver Charlick, John R. Jacquelin, and Charles A. Lemont. The ladies listened to Mr. Charlick's advice with much interest. He gave them some points on Long Island stock, which they jotted down upon ivory memorandum books, after sweetly thanking him for his information.

At 2 p.m. the firm were surprised by a visit from the Hon. Edward H. Van Schalck and Hugh Hastings. Mr. Van Schalck wore an elegant diamond pin and his boots had received a bright polish. Mr. Hastings had had his hair parted in the middle, and wore a stand up collar, with the points turned down. Close upon the heels of this party we noticed George Henriques, W. R. Travers and Mr. H. R. Le Roy. Mr. Travers told the ladies that they would lose money in Wall street, Mrs. Woodhull replied that they did not come to Wall street to lose money, but to make money.

At 3 p.m. the partners were agreeably surprised by a visit from Mr. Edward H. Van Schalck and the Hon. Hugh Hastings. Both gentlemen wore brass dress coats with polished blue buttons, pearl colored pantaloons and green kid gloves. They were accompanied by Robert Walker, John K. Warren and M. A. Wheelock. The party departed after looking at the closing prices.

Just as the office was being closed the Hon. Edward H. Van Schalck and Hugh Hastings called upon the fair bankers. They were told that it was after business hours and if they had any orders to give they would be received after 9 o'clock on Monday morning. Messrs. Van Schalck and Hastings bowed and retired.

Helped in part by stock tips from their friend and mentor Cornelius Vanderbilt, the sisters were successful brokers. They even profited on Black Friday.

Eventually they closed shop to pursue more radical interests. Victoria's fearless nature made her famous far beyond Wall Street. She advocated and practiced free love, became the first woman to address the U.S. Senate, ran for President (abolitionist Frederick Douglass was her running mate), fought for women's suffrage, and was the first American publisher of Karl Marx's Das Kapital.

Philadelphia's Last Gasp
September 18, 1873

Alvred B. Nettleton

Philadelphia was blindsided by the final blow to its status as a financial center. Eyewitness Alvred Nettleton, a manager at the office of bond powerhouse Jay Cooke & Co. and later Assistant Secretary of the U.S. Treasury, described the mournful day in a letter to his wife.

Entering my side office and sitting down at my desk, the first person I saw was our janitor William, who took pains to hand me the latest edition of the previous evening's paper. My eye at once rested on the startling head-line: "Suspension of Jay Cooke and Company!"

If I had been struck on the head with a hammer, I could not have been more stunned and devoid of ideas! I rubbed my eyes to see if I was quite awake, and finally sat down and read through the despatches from New York and the statements of the Philadelphia reporters.

As the morning wore on, the crowd in the street in front of the office, and for several blocks either way in Third and Chestnut, increased, until passage was well-nigh impossible; very few depositors or creditors of Jay Cooke and Company were present, but nearly all expected a general smash among the banks, and the excitement was astounding. The members of the firm did not expect the suspension twelve hours before it occurred. The storm struck them so suddenly and the demands for money from depositors were so very large that not an hour was given in which to effect arrangements for tiding over the emergency.

Saturday morning I went to New York to attend to matters of the house. The scene at the corner of Wall and Nassau Streets I shall never forget. For squares in every direction the streets were a solid mass of black hats, and surging back and forth, while men gesticulated, shouted and rushed to and fro. The doors of Fisk and Hatch, E. D. Randolph and Company and Jay Cooke and Company, "all in a row" on Nassau Street, were closed, and curious crowds were coming and going and gazing at the doors and windows. A "run" was in progress on the Fourth National Bank, across the way from Fisk and Hatch, and this redoubled the excitement. Long rows of anxious men, with checks in their hands, waited impatiently for their turns to come, and scores of panicky depositors constantly swelled the column. At noon all confidence in everything seemed gone, and six banks and eighteen firms had "gone up," and the Clearing House and Stock Exchange finally shut up shop for the day, and advised everybody to go home till Monday.

Mr. Cooke and his family bear the new state of things with admirable fortitude, propriety, and good sense. At Mr. Cooke's request I have spent Sabbath at his home, and I have been deeply touched by the family life under the changed circumstances. Not the slightest impatience, false chagrin, mock heroics, or loss of faith in Providence is manifested.

Jay Cooke & Co., the bank that helped fund the Union cause in the Civil War, and in so doing played a crucial role during the modernization of the national finance system, had never made a great profit. Cooke's habit was to win contracts by agreeing to low commissions, betting that he would profit by investing the float—funds received but not yet transferred to the ultimate recipient. In those days, funds might not be payable for as long as a year, giving Cooke plenty of opportunity for gain. (Variations of this practice are common today. How many millions have flowed into the accounts of brokers promising low trading commissions? The brokers don't let the uninvested balances sit idle.)

To anyone looking at Cooke's business, which appeared to be bond sales, the enterprise seemed healthy. But its survival relied ultimately on its own investments, which were performing poorly. Perhaps more people should have seen the end coming. For instance, the firm had a lot of money tied up in the Northern Pacific Railroad, which was so cash-poor its workers were being paid in scrip.

Jay Cooke & Co. was merely the first domino. Others fell in the next days. The Panic of 1873 had begun. Lawyer George Templeton Strong recorded the bewilderment of its first days:

The secretary of the Union Trust Company, Carleton, son of a Methodist divine, is said to have vanished into Faery Land, like King Arthur, with $250,000 of the company's assets.

The street was not excited but faint, sick, prostrate, and resigned to the approach of some great indefinite calamity. My inquiries were answered: "Things look black"; "About as bad as they can look"; "No use trying to do anything," and so on.

Faith in financial agents is gone. Every treasurer and cashier is "suspect," and no wonder after the recent epidemic of fraud. The anticipated resumption of silver specie payments seems indefinitely postponed. Factories and employers throughout the country are discharging hands, working half time, or reducing wages. There is a prospect of a hard, blue winter. We read in the papers of a "shrinkage of values," but I see no sign of it in the bills I have to pay. Heaven help me!

The Cooke failure hadn't caused the panic; it had simply awakened people to the obvious: the hyperinflation of land values and stock prices, which had run far ahead of real economic gains, was a bubble; and the bubble had burst. The economy did not recover for six years, after about ten thousand businesses had failed.

Some notable "firsts" characterized the panic: it was international, spreading to London quickly via the Atlantic cable; and the Stock Exchange closed indefinitely. (It reopened ten days later.) Also, in a development George Templeton Strong called "queer, anomalous, and all wrong," people paid a premium to buy greenbacks instead of trusting only gold or silver. This last fact pointed to the almost complete acceptance of paper money as a legitimate part of the money supply. In 1879, when specie payment was resumed for the first time since its Civil War suspension, surprisingly little paper was redeemed. The mints had worked overtime to coin gold, but Americans had grown accustomed to the convenience of paper, and, most important, had confidence in it. The gold standard was still important—a panic would occur in 1893 when it seemed that the government would use both silver and gold to back the money supply—but gold was no longer necessary for individual transactions. (The government's flirtation with silver was a political sop to Western silver-mining states, whose output it had agreed to purchase, and to the widespread belief that inflation was good for farmers because it made prices rise. The 1893 panic hit when the silver dollar was worth less than two-thirds of a gold dollar, confusing investors, creating inflation fears, and causing foreign capital to be withdrawn.)

The collapse of Jay Cooke & Co. left the market open for competitors such as Drexel, Morgan & Co., the predecessor to the Morgan Bank. Some historians believe J. P. Morgan actually engineered the collapse. His firm had partnered with Cooke in that firm's last bond sale, and has been accused of holding back its efforts to create Cooke's cash shortage. In addition to market share, Morgan is said to have wanted higher commission rates from the government.

Whatever actually happened, Philadelphia lost more business to Wall Street. What had once been the financial center of the nation no longer played a leading role in any market. And, of course, commissions rose.

A Bucket-Shop Education, 1895–1901

Edwin Lefèvre

A bucket shop—the name may come from the buckets in which beer was delivered—essentially used stock prices for gambling. (The term is now sometimes confused with "boiler room"—a fly-by-night, hard-sell brokerage that pushes junk securities on marks.) A bucket-shop trader never owned stocks, and paid just 10 percent of the stock's value to place a bet. No shares were actually bought or sold. To "buy" was simply to bet that the price of a company's stock would rise. If it did, at the end of the day the virtual trade was "settled," with the house paying out a profit to the bettor. To "sell" one used a "put": if the price dropped, the house paid the difference between the closing price and the price at which it "bought" the put. If the customer bet wrong, as usually happened, the bucket shop simply kept the 10 percent that had been bet.

Historian Robert Sobel notes bucket shops filled a function similar to lotteries, offering dreams of a quick windfall. Some of the more successful operations were run by brokerages on the Curb Market—later the American Stock Exchange. These were nationwide operations.

In Reminiscences of a Stock Operator, Edwin Lefèvre, a well-known financial journalist of the early twentieth century, created the fictional character Larry Livingston to tell the story of the era's most famous speculator, Jesse Livermore, who began his career by observing that unforgiving world.

After studying every fluctuation in an active stock on Monday, and remembering past performances I would write down what it ought to do on Tuesday and Wednesday. Later I would check up with actual transcriptions from the tape.

Well, I kept up my little memorandum book perhaps six months. Instead of leaving for home the moment I was through with my work, I'd jot down the figures I wanted and would study the changes, always looking for the repetitions and parallelisms of behaviour—learning to read the tape, although I was not aware of it at the time.

One day one of the office boys—he was older than I—came to me where I was eating my lunch and asked me on the quiet if I had any money.

"Why do you want to know?" I said.

"Well," he said, "I've got a dandy tip on Burlington [Railroad]. I'm going to play it if I can get somebody to go in with me."

"How do you mean, play it?" I asked. To me the only people who played or could play tips were the customers—old jiggers with oodles of dough. Why, it cost hundreds, even thousands of dollars, to get into the game. It was like owning your private carriage and having a coachman who wore a silk hat. "That's what I mean; play it!" he said. "How much you got?"

"How much you need?"

"Well, I can trade in five shares by putting up $5."

"How are you going to play it?"

"I'm going to buy all the Burlington the bucket shop will let me carry with the money I give him for margin," he said. "It's going up sure. It's like picking up money. We'll double ours in a jiffy."

"Hold on!" I said to him, and pulled out my little dope book.

I wasn't interested in doubling my money, but in his saying that Burlington was going up. If it was, my note-book ought to show it. I looked. Sure enough, Burlington, according to my figuring, was acting as it usually did before it went up. I had never bought or sold anything in my life, and I never gambled with the other boys. But all I could see was that this was a grand chance to test the accuracy of my work, of my hobby. It struck me at once that if my dope didn't work in practice there was nothing in the theory of it to interest anybody. So I gave him all I had, and with our pooled resources he went to one of the near-by bucket shops and bought some Burlington. Two days later we cashed in. I made a profit of $3.12.

After that first trade, I got to speculating on my own hook in the bucket shops. I'd go during my lunch hour and buy or sell—it never made any difference to me. I was playing a system and not a favorite stock or backing opinions. All I knew was the arithmetic of it. As a matter of fact, mine was the ideal way to operate in a bucket shop, where all that a trader does is to bet on fluctuations as they are printed by the ticker on the tape.

It was not long before I was taking much more money out of the bucket shops than I was pulling down from my job in the brokerage office. So I gave up my position. My folks objected, but they couldn't say much when they saw what I was making. I was only a kid and office-boy wages were not very high. I did mighty well on my own hook.

The Cosmopolitan was the richest bucket shop in New England, and as a rule they put no limit on a trade. I think I was the heaviest individual trader they had—that is, of the steady, every-day customers. They had a fine office and the largest and completest quotation board I have ever seen anywhere. It ran along the whole length of the big room and every imaginable thing was quoted. I mean stocks dealt in on the New York and Boston Stock Exchanges, cotton, wheat, provisions, metals—everything that was bought and sold in New York, Chicago, Boston, and Liverpool.

You know how they traded in bucket shops. You gave your money to a clerk and told him what you wished to buy or sell. He looked at the tape or the quotation board and took the price from there—the last one, of course. He also put down the time on the ticket so that it almost read like a regular broker's report—that is, that they had bought or sold for you so many shares of such a stock at such a price at such a time on such a day and how much money they received from you. When you wished to close your trade you went to the clerk—the same or another, it depended on the shop—and you told him. He took the last price or if the stock had not been active he waited for the next quotation that came out on the tape. He wrote that price and the time on your ticket, O.K.'d it and gave it back to you, and then you went to the cashier and got whatever cash it called for. Of course, when the market went against you and the price went beyond the limit set by your margin, your trade automatically closed itself and your ticket became one more scrap of paper.

In the humbler bucket shops, where people were allowed to trade in as little as five shares, the tickets were little slips—different colors for buying and selling—and at times, as for instance in boiling bull markets, the shops would be hard hit because all the customers were bulls and happened to be right. Then the bucket shop would deduct both buying and selling commissions and if you bought a stock at 20 the ticket would read 20¼. You thus had only ¾ of a point's run for your money.

But the Cosmopolitan was the finest in New England. It had

thousands of patrons and I really think I was the only man they were afraid of. Neither the killing premium nor the three-point margin they made me put up reduced my trading much. I kept on buying and selling as much as they'd let me. I sometimes had a line of 5,000 shares.

I was only twenty when I first accumulated ten thousand dollars in cash. And you ought to have heard my mother. You'd have thought that ten thousand dollars in cash was more than anybody carried around except old John D. [Rockefeller], and she used to tell me to be satisfied and go into some regular business. I had a hard time convincing her that I was not gambling, but making money by figuring. But all she could see was that ten thousand dollars was a lot of money and all I could see was more margin. I soon made up my mind to go to New York, where I could trade in the office of some member of the New York Stock Exchange. I didn't want any Boston branch, where the quotations had to be telegraphed. I wanted to be close to the original source.

[In 1900] I came to New York with twenty-five hundred dollars. There were no bucket shops here that a fellow could trust. The Stock Exchange and the police between them had succeeded in closing them up pretty tight. Besides, I wanted to find a place where the only limit to my trading would be the size of my stake. I didn't have much of one, but I didn't expect it to stay little forever. The main thing at the start was to find a place where I wouldn't have to worry about getting a square deal. So I went to a New York Stock Exchange house. Well, it wasn't six months before I was broke. I was a pretty active trader and had a sort of reputation as a winner. I guess my commissions amounted to something. I ran up my account quite a little, but, of course, in the end I lost. I played carefully; but I had to lose. I'll tell you the reason: it was my remarkable success in the bucket shops!

I could beat the game my way only in a bucket shop; where I was betting on fluctuations. My tape reading had to do with that exclusively. When I bought the price was there on the quotation board, right in front of me. Even before I bought I knew exactly the price I'd have to pay for my stock. And I always could sell on the instant. I could scalp successfully, because I could move like lightning. I could follow up my luck or cut my loss in a second.

What was a perfect system for trading in bucket shops didn't work in [the New York broker's] office. There I was actually buying and selling stocks. The price of [American] Sugar on the tape might be 105 and I could see a three-point drop coming. As a matter of fact, at the very moment the ticker was printing 105 on the tape the real price on the floor of the Exchange might be 104 or 103. By the time my order to sell a thousand shares got to [the brokerage's] floor man to execute, the price might be still lower. I couldn't tell at what price I had put out my thousand shares until I got a report from the clerk. When I surely would have made three thousand on the same transaction in a bucket shop I might not make a cent in a Stock Exchange house. Of course, I have taken an extreme case, but the fact remains that in [the broker's] office the tape always talked ancient history to me, as far as my system of trading went, and I didn't realize it.

And then, too, if my order was fairly big my own sale would tend further to depress the price. In the bucket shop I didn't have to figure on the effect of my own trading. I lost in New York because the game was altogether different.

In short, I did not know the game of stock speculation.

To discourage stock market gambling, bucket shops were outlawed by the Securities Exchange Act of 1934. Sound sensible? Perhaps, but similar speculation quickly reappeared in respectable form. Option trading allows an investor to bet on the direction of a price without committing to purchase the underlying security. Stock index futures, introduced in 1982, allow an investor to bet on market moves with a margin as low as 5 percent.

PART FIVE

Trusts and Trustbusters

"These financial leaders are accused by the press of every sort of crime. . . ."

H. G. Wells, *1905*

Timeline

1900 — John Moody's first "Manual of RR and Corp. Securities"—
followed in 1909 by annual bond ratings

1901 — Morgan buys out Carnegie, organizes $1 billion U.S. Steel Corp.
headed by Charles Schwab

1901 — Morgan and Harriman battle for Northern Pacific RR, price
shoots from $100 to $1,000

1904 — Supreme Court orders Northern Securities RR trust dissolved

1906 — DJIA closes above 100 (100.25), January 12

1907 — Panic follows run on trust companies; Morgan organizes bailouts,
presaging Federal Reserve Act

1911 — Supreme Court dissolves Standard Oil

1912 — House Banking and Currency Committee investigates "money
trust," finds no conspiracy

1913 — Federal Reserve System est. with 12 regional banks

1913 — J. P. Morgan dies; estate worth $77 million—"not even a very rich
man," says surprised Rockefeller, worth $500 million

1913 — Ford's assembly line

1915 — Supreme Court says U.S. Steel combine unlawful

THE SCENE IN THE 1900S

Rockefeller and "The Chief Getters"

H. G. Wells

*B*etween the end of the Civil War and the close of the nineteenth century, immigration surged, especially in the 1880s and 1890s. America's population almost doubled, reaching more than 75 million. During this same period, control of the economy became concentrated in fewer and fewer hands. From about 1880 to 1901, companies in many major industries, rather than competing, combined their operations in "trusts." Standard Oil was the first, organized in 1879. General Electric and American Telephone and Telegraph, two other names familiar today, were once trusts. There were about fifty trusts in industries such as tobacco, meatpacking, whiskey, sugar, and beef. The steel trust, U.S. Steel, became the first billion-dollar enterprise.

The trusts promised economies of scale, with efficiencies being passed to the consumer. Their organizers claimed size was necessary for survival and beneficial to the working class. Skeptics saw monopolies that rigged prices and set wages at will.

"The big trusts," wrote Woodrow Wilson, while still a Princeton professor, "the big combinations, are the most wasteful, the most uneconomical, and, after they pass a certain size, the most inefficient, way of conducting the industries of this country. That is the difference between a big business and a trust. A trust is an arrangement to get rid of competition, and a big business is a business that has survived competition by conquering in the field of intelligence and economy. A trust does not bring efficiency to the aid of business; it buys efficiency out of business. I am for big business, and I am against the trusts."

The popular press fueled opposition. Ida Tarbell, whose father was ruined by Rockefeller, wrote The History of the Standard Oil

Company, *still considered one of the finest examples of investigative journalism ever produced. Upton Sinclair's novel* The Jungle *exposed the inhumanity of working conditions in the meatpacking business.*

But on a visit from England, H. G. Wells, author of The War of the Worlds, The Invisible Man, *and* The Time Machine, *saw another side of the trusts and the men who ran them.*

The group of people that attracts the largest amount of attention in press and talk, that most obsesses the American imagination, and that is indeed the most significant at the present time, is the little group—a few score men perhaps altogether—who are emerging distinctly as winners in that great struggle to *get*, into which this commercial industrialism has naturally resolved itself. Central among them are the men of the Standard Oil group, the "octopus" which spreads its ramifying tentacles through the whole system of American business, absorbing and absorbing, grasping and growing. The extraordinarily able investigations of such writers as Miss Tarbell and Ray Stannard Baker [author of *The Railroads on Trial*], the rhetorical exposures of Mr. T. W. Lawson [author of *Frenzied Finance*], have brought out the methods and quality of this group of persons with a particularity that has been reserved heretofore for great statesmen and crowned heads, and with an unflattering lucidity altogether unprecedented. Not only is every hair on their heads numbered, but the number is published. They are known to their pettiest weaknesses and to their most accidental associations. And in this astonishing blaze of illumination they continue steadfastly to get.

These men, who are creating the greatest system of correlated private properties in the world, who are wealthy beyond all precedent, seem for the most part to be men with no ulterior dream or aim. They are not voluptuaries, they are neither artists nor any sort of creators, and they betray no high political ambitions. Had they anything of the sort they would not be what they are, they would be more than that and less. They want and they get, they are inspired by the brute will in their wealth to have more wealth and more, to a systematic ardor. They are men of a competing, patient, enterprising, acquisitive enthusiasm. They have found in America the perfectly favorable environment for their temperaments. In no other country and in no other age could they have risen to such eminence. America is still, by virtue of its great Puritan tradition and in the older sense of the word, an intensely moral land. Most lusts here are strongly curbed, by public opinion, by training and tradition. But the lust of acquisition has not been curbed but glorified.

These financial leaders are accused by the press of every sort of crime in the development of their great organizations and their fight against competitors, but I feel impelled myself to acquit them of anything so heroic as a general scheme of criminality, as a systematic organization of power.

They are men with a good deal of contempt for legislation and state interference, but that is no distinction, it has unhappily been part of the training of the average American citizen, and they have no doubt exceeded the letter if not the spirit of the laws of business competition. They have played to win and not for style, and if they personally had not done so somebody else would; they fill a position which from the nature of things, somebody is bound to fill. They have, no doubt, carried sharpness to the very edge of dishonesty, but what else was to be expected from the American conditions? Only by doing so and taking risks is pre-eminent success in getting to be attained. They have developed an enormous system of espionage, but on his smaller scale every retail grocer, every employer of servants does something in that way. They have secret agents, false names, concealed bargains—what else could one expect? People have committed suicide through their operations, but in a game which is bound to bring the losers to despair it is childish to charge the winners with murder. It's the game that is criminal.

It is ridiculous, I say, to write of these men as though they were unparalleled villains, intellectual overmen, conscienceless conquerors of the world. Mr. J. D. Rockefeller's mild, thin-lipped, pleasant face gives the lie to all such melodramatic nonsense.

I must confess to a sneaking liking for this much-reviled man. One thinks of Miss Tarbell's description of him, displaying his first boyish account-book, his ledger A, to a sympathetic gathering of the Baptist young, telling how he earned fifty dollars in the first three months of his clerking in a Chicago warehouse, and how savingly he dealt with it. Hear his words:

"You could not get that book from me for all the modern ledgers in New York, nor for all that they would bring. It almost brings tears to my eyes when I read over this little book, and it fills me with a sense of gratitude I cannot express. I know some people, especially some young men, find it difficult to keep a little money in their pocket-book. I learned to keep money, and, as we have a way of saying, it did not burn a hole in my pocket. I was taught that it was the thing to keep the money and take care of it."

This is not the voice of any sort of contemptuous trampler of his species. This is the voice of an industrious, acquisitive, commonplace, pious man, as honestly and simply proud of his acquisitiveness as a stamp-collector might be. At times, in his acquisitions, the strength of his passion may have driven him to lengths beyond the severe moral code, but the same has been true of stamp-collectors. He is a man who has taken up with great natural aptitude an ignoble tradition which links economy and earning with piety and honor. His teachers were to blame, that Baptist community that is now so ashamed of its son that it refuses his gifts. To a large extent he is the creature of opportunity; he has been flung to the topmost pinnacle of human envy, partly by accident, partly by that peculiarity of American conditions that has subordinated, in the name of liberty, all the grave and ennobling affairs of statecraft to a middle-class freedom of commercial enterprise. Quarrel with that if you like. It is unfair and ridiculous to quarrel with him.

Early attempts by legislators to curb the trusts lacked bite. The Sherman Anti-Trust Act of 1890, for instance, even failed to define "trust" or "restraint of trade." As the new century began, even President Theodore Roosevelt called for action. When Northern Securities was formed as a holding company for railroad interests, Roosevelt instructed his Attorney General to seek its dissolution. In 1904, the government won. "The mere existence of such a combination," wrote Supreme Court Justice John Harlan in the majority opinion, "constitutes a menace" to free commerce. Northern Securities was broken up. In 1911, Standard Oil was ordered to dissolve. Even AT&T, which had been declared a "natural monopoly" in 1913, was broken into "Baby Bells" in 1984.

Charles Dow, 1901

William Peter Hamilton

Charles Dow, along with partner Edward Jones, founded the firm now synonymous with business journalism in 1882. Its first publication was the Customer's Afternoon Letter, *a two-page report of stock prices and news.*

Dow created the first "average" of stock prices for an 1884 issue. He believed the figure offered readers a measure of the stock market and the economy at large. His calculations did not include a single industrial company. The "components," as they are now called, were nine railroads, a steamship line, and the Western Union telegraph company. He added the first industrial stock, American Sugar, in 1894. By then the Customer's Afternoon Letter *had been renamed the* Wall Street Journal.

His scientific approach, novel for its time, derived from his personality. William Peter Hamilton, who came to know Dow when working at the Journal, *explained Dow's theory of market movements, and the importance of the "stock market barometer."*

Dow was a New Englander, intelligent, self-repressed, ultra-conservative; and he knew his business. He was almost judicially cold in the consideration of any subject, whatever the fervor of discussion. It would be less than just to say that I never saw him angry; I never saw him even excited. His perfect integrity and good sense commanded the confidence of every man in Wall Street, at a time when there were few efficient newspaper men covering the financial section, and of these still fewer with any deep knowledge of finance.

Dow also had the advantage of some years experience on the floor of the Stock Exchange. It came about in a rather curious way. The late Robert Goodbody, an Irishman, a Quaker and an honor to Wall Street, came over from Dublin to America. As the New York Stock Exchange requires that every member shall be an American citizen, Charles H. Dow became his partner. During the time necessary for Robert Goodbody to naturalize, Dow held a seat in the

Stock Exchange and executed orders on the floor. When Goodbody became an American citizen Dow withdrew from the Exchange and returned to his more congenial newspaper work.

Knowing and liking Dow, with whom I worked in the last years of his life, I was often, with many of his friends, exasperated by his over-conservatism. It showed itself particularly in his editorials in the *Wall Street Journal*, to which it is now necessary to allude because they are the only written record of Dow's theory of the price movement. He would write a strong, readable and convincing editorial, on a public question affecting finance and business, and in the last paragraph would add safeguards and saving clauses which not merely took the sting out of it but took the "wallop" out of it. In the language of the prize ring, he pulled his punches.

He was almost too cautious to come out with a flat, dogmatic statement of his theory, however sound it was and however close and clear his reasoning might be. He wrote, mostly in 1901 and the first half of 1902, a number of editorials dealing with methods of stock speculation. His theory must be disinterred from those editorials, where it is illustrative and incidental and never the main subject of discussion. It is curious also that in one of his earliest statements of the price movement he makes an indefensible claim. Under the caption "Swings Within Swings," in the Review and Outlook of the *Wall Street Journal* of January 4, 1902, he says:

> Nothing is more certain than that the market has three well defined movements which fit into each other. The first is the daily variation due to local causes and the balance of buying or selling at that particular time. The secondary movement covers a period ranging from ten days to sixty days, averaging probably between thirty and forty days. The third swing is the great move covering from four to six years.

Remember that Dow wrote this twenty years ago, and that he had not the records for analysis of the stock market movement which are now available. The extent of the primary movement, as given in this quotation, is proved to be far too long by subsequent experience; and a careful examination has shown me that the major swing before Dow wrote was never "from four to six years," rarely three years and oftener less than two.

But Dow always had a reason for what he said, and his intellectual honesty assures those who knew him that it was at least an arguable reason. It was based upon his profound belief in the recurrence of financial crises, at periodic intervals (as shown by recorded financial history), of a little more than ten years. Dow assumed for that period one primary bull market and one primary bear market, and therefore split the ten-year period in half. It was rather like the little boy who, being asked to name ten arctic animals, submitted "five seals and five polar bears"!

Dow first presented his average of industrial stocks in 1896. The twelve components were American Cotton Oil, American Sugar, American Tobacco, Chicago Gas, Distilling & Cattle Feeding, General Electric, Laclede Gas, National Lead, North American Company, Tennessee Coal & Iron, U.S. Leather, U.S. Rubber. Only General Electric exists today. It is still a Dow component.

Dow Jones increased the number of components in the Industrial Average to 20 stocks in 1916, and 30 stocks—its current number—in 1928. (That was also the year special calculations were introduced to offset the effects of stock splits and other vagaries. Thus the DJIA figure on any given day is not precisely the sum of the prices divided by 30.)

Wall Street trivia buffs may remember the DJIA figured prominently in a 1967 Broadway comedy that asked the musical question "How Now, Dow Jones?" The actual lyrics, however, are not as memorable as the review by Dorothy Parker: "Standard and Poor."

The Northern Pacific Corner
May 8, 1901

Bernard Baruch

Bernard Baruch was one of the century's most successful and influential investors. His carefully crafted mystique gave him a reputation as a stock market seer, which in turn gave him an influence with business leaders and politicians.

Early in his career he witnessed the extraordinary corner of Northern Pacific Railroad. The corner, which Baruch calls a "panic," grew out of a battle between two great egos. The belligerent was E. H. Harriman, who had climbed from the bottom of the Wall Street ladder to run the Union Pacific railroad empire. His opponent, banker J. P. Morgan, controlled most of the country's remaining railroads, including the Northern Pacific. The two men had fought before. Harriman, whom Morgan called "that two-dollar broker," was probably ahead on points.

This battle was sparked by Morgan's purchase of the Burlington Railroad, which had a valuable line in Chicago. Harriman had also been looking at the Burlington, so he asked Morgan if he could buy a one-third interest. Though Morgan was not usually averse to combinations, he refused Harriman.

Taking a less polite approach, Harriman quietly bought Northern Pacific stock, hoping to accumulate a majority of the $155 million of outstanding shares. He began his attack when Morgan was out of the country and James Hill, Morgan's partner in the railroad business, was in Seattle.

Eventually Harriman's efforts became obvious. Hill, ordering his engineers to clear the tracks, raced to New York, setting a new cross-country speed record. When he arrived, he was told by Harriman's broker, Jacob Schiff, that Harriman controlled a majority of shares. But Schiff was wrong. Because of a technicality, Harriman was actually just shy of a majority.

Both sides then bid to buy the few shares still available, and the battle became public knowledge.

In my entire career on the Stock Exchange, I do not recall another opening similar to this one. The first sale of Northern Pacific was at 114, or four points above its Saturday closing. On the second sale it jumped to 117. Thereafter the day was marked by spasmodic up-rushes as Eddie Norton, the floor member of Street & Norton, bought every share in sight at the market.

No one seemed able to fathom the cause of this rise. Directors of the Northern Pacific could not explain it. Bankers could not explain it. Eddie Norton, who was doing the buying, was not talking.

I was standing at the arbitrage desk where London cables were sent and received. Beside me stood Talbot Taylor, one of the better brokers and the son-in-law of James Keene, who was the man the Morgans usually turned to for difficult market operations.

I drew Taylor's attention to the fact that Northern Pacific could be bought in London several points below the New York price.

Taylor's brown eyes regarded me intently. His face was expressionless.

"Bernie," he said, tapping his lips with the butt end of his pencil, "are you doing anything in Northern Pacific?"

"Yes," I replied, "and I'll tell you how to make some money out of it. Buy in London, sell here, and take an arbitrage profit."

Taylor went on tapping his lips, then his forehead, with the pencil. At length he said, "I would not arbitrage if I were you. There is a terrific contest for control and Mr. Keene is acting for J. P. Morgan.

"Be careful," concluded Taylor, "and don't be short of this stock. What I buy must be delivered now. Stock bought in London will not do." With this priceless information, Eddie Norton's buying later that day was no mystery to me.

With Morgan and Harriman eager to acquire every possible share, the available supply of Northern Pacific stock was likely to be "cornered" rather quickly. Traders who had sold the stock short, anticipating its decline, would be unable to cover themselves. They would be forced to bid fantastic prices for Northern Pacific. To cover these losses they would have to dump other securities. A corner in Northern Pacific, in other words, would produce a general collapse in the market.

And so I decided to short in several other leading stocks in the market, to profit when these securities were dumped. I resolved not to do any trading at all in Northern Pacific. As it turned out, being on the sidelines proved the best place from which to observe the wildest situation the Stock Exchange had ever known.

On the following day, Tuesday, May 7, it was clear that the stock had been cornered. There was virtually no Northern Pacific stock that anyone wanted to sell. During the trading it touched 149 and closed at 143. But the really wild scramble came after the three o'clock gong.

Under the Stock Exchange's rules of that day, all stock bought or sold had to be delivered by the next day. If someone sold a stock short, the practice was to borrow the stock certificate from some broker, if necessary, paying a premium for its use. If a trader couldn't borrow the stock certificates he needed, the man to whom the stock had been sold could go into the market and pay any price for it. The trader who had been caught short would have to make good this price.

But in the case of Northern Pacific there simply weren't enough stock certificates to cover the needs of all the traders who had sold short. When the closing gong sounded the frantic traders surged around the Northern Pacific trading post bidding premium rates for any stock that might be available.

When one broker walked into the crowd, other traders, thinking he might have some Northern Pacific stock, charged him, banging him against the railing.

"Let me go, will you?" he roared. "I haven't a share of the d——d stock. Do you think I carry it in my clothes?"

Then, through the desperate crowd strode Al Stern, of Herzfeld & Stern, a young and vigorous broker. He had come as an emissary of Kuhn, Loeb & Company, which was handling Harriman's purchases of Northern Pacific. Stern blithely inquired: "Who wants to borrow Northern Pacific? I have a block to lend."

The first response was a deafening shout. There was an infinitesimal pause and then the desperate brokers rushed at Stern. Struggling to get near enough to him to shout their bids, they kicked over stock tickers. Strong brokers thrust aside the weak ones. Hands were waving and trembling in the air.

Almost doubled over on a chair, his face close to a pad, Stern began to note his transactions. He would mumble to one man, "All right, you get it," and then complain to another, "For heaven's sake, don't stick your finger in my eye."

One broker leaned over and snatched Stern's hat, with which he beat a tattoo on Stern's head to gain attention.

"Put back my hat!" shrieked Stern. "Don't make such a confounded excitement and maybe I can do better by you."

But the traders continued to push and fight and nearly climb over one another's backs to get to Stern. They were like thirst-crazed men battling for water, with the biggest, strongest, and loudest faring best.

Soon Stern had loaned the last of his stock. His face white, and his clothes disheveled, he managed to break away.

The next day, May 8, the corner in Northern Pacific was acknowledged and the panic spread. The shorts, knowing that they would have to acquire stock to cover themselves before the day's trading was over, bid wildly. The stock opened at 155, twelve points above the last quotation of the previous day. Soon it advanced to 180.

On the Exchange floor fear had completely taken the place of reason. Stocks were being dumped wildly, dropping from ten to twenty points. There were rumors of corners in other stocks.

Pandemonium reigned in the loan crowd from three until four-thirty. When Al Stern appeared again, he was shoved against a pillar as the traders surged upon him to renew the loans of the day before. Stern climbed on a chair and cried to the traders to keep off and listen to what he had to say.

When the crowd finally quieted, Stern broke the crushing news—those who had borrowed his stock would have to turn it in as he could renew no loans.

This action, I might explain, was not taken to squeeze the shorts to make them pay to the last dollar of ability as Jay Gould did in his Chicago & Northwestern corner of 1872. The reason for the action was that the Harriman and Morgan forces were at the showdown point in their struggle for control of the Northern Pacific. Neither could tell how much of the stock each side would be able to vote until the actual stock certificates were in hand.

That night the public rooms and corridors of the Waldorf [Hotel] were jammed, but by a far different kind of crowd than had peopled this palace of leisure and gaiety only a few days before. The ladies were gone. Men neglected the amenity of formal clothes.

Have you ever noticed how animals behave on a sunny day when no danger threatens? They lick their coats, preen themselves, strut and sing, each trying to put on a better show than the other fellow.

So with human beings. And like animals, when fear strikes their hearts, they forget their elegances and sometimes even the common courtesies.

One look inside the Waldorf that night was enough to bring home this truth of how little we differ from animals after all. From a palace the Waldorf had been transformed into the den of frightened men at bay. Men milled about from one throng to another, eager to catch the news of any change in the situation. Some men were too frightened to take a drink; others were so terrified they could only drink. It was, in short, a mob, swayed by all the unreasonable fears, impulses, and passions that play on mobs.

The next morning a tense, white-faced, almost silent band of men surrounded the Northern Pacific trading post. No word of compromise, no hope for truce had emanated from behind the guarded doors where sat the rival generals.

A babble of voices drowned the echo of the gavel. Within an hour Northern Pacific was selling at $400 a share. Before noon, it was $700. Shortly after two o'clock 300 shares were sold for $300,000 cash—$1,000 a share.

With Northern Pacific soaring, the rest of the list collapsed, losing up to 60 points as stocks were thrown over at any price. Call money loaned by banks to brokers opened at 40 per cent and touched 60. All sense of value and sanity was gone.

Eddie Norton stood with tears in his eyes at the thought of the imminent ruin of many of his friends. The wildest rumors sped to and fro. One report, which I later learned was cabled to London, was that Arthur Housman had dropped dead in our office. To contradict this he had to show himself on the floor of the Exchange.

Two-fifteen was the deadline when the shorts had to put up the stock certificates to cover their sales of the previous day. A few minutes before, Al Stern, the Kuhn, Loeb emissary, came onto the floor. Mounting a chair and shouting to make himself heard, he announced that his firm would not enforce delivery of Northern Pacific purchased yesterday.

Stern was followed by Eddie Norton, who announced that his firm also would not demand delivery of 80,000 shares due them.

The crisis was over. Northern Pacific sold off to 300. The general list steadied.

At five that evening the crowds at the Waldorf were relieved by a bulletin over the ticker that said Morgan and Kuhn, Loeb would provide stock for those short of it at 150. These were much more generous terms than most of the shorts had expected to get. The panic was ended.

When the smoke blew away there was some question as to who, after all, controlled the Northern Pacific. Harriman was a lion. He was ready to fight on. But Morgan and Hill had had enough. They were willing to compromise to avoid future hostilities. An agreement was reached whereby Harriman obtained representation on the boards of both the Burlington and the Northern Pacific, which was more than he had asked for in the first place.

Although the Panic of 1901 had no lasting effect on the economy, it revealed to Baruch a timeless lesson. "As with most financial panics," he concluded, "the stage had been set in advance by extravagant hopes and talk of a 'New Era.' Varied factors contributed to this surge of optimism. Our victory over Spain had stirred fantastic dreams of imperialism and dazzling predictions of new foreign markets. The public was in the stock market as never before. It was at this time, I believe, that women came into the market for the first time in any numbers. Over their teacups in the Waldorf's glass-enclosed Palm Room they talked knowingly of what U.S. Steel or Union Pacific or Amalgamated Copper was bound to do. Bellboys, waiters, barbers—everyone had a 'tip' to pass on. Since the market was rising, every bullish tip came true and every tipster seemed a prophet. Several times it seemed that the market had run its course and that a healthy reaction was on the way. Then a new stock would be brought forward and there would be another balloon ascension."

J. P. Morgan and the Panic of 1907

Frank A. Vanderlip

As Frank Vanderlip describes, the Panic of 1907 was caused by deficiencies in the banking and monetary system rather than economic trends or political news. Vanderlip, a senior executive of National City Bank (now Citibank), and previously Assistant Secretary of the Treasury, had a central role in the crisis and the events that followed, which would have lasting consequences.

The panic started with a run on the Knickerbocker Trust Company. (Trust companies may offer similar services to banks but are legally different and subject to different regulations.)

In our individualistic banking system of that time, the trust companies, operating under too-tolerant state laws, were engaged in some unsound banking practices. In that period none of the rapidly growing trust companies was a member of the Clearing House Association. A bank would send a trust company's daily accumulation of checks for collection to the clearing house, just as if those checks were a part of the bank's own business.

This parasitical device, akin to the habitual borrowing by an improvident neighbor of one's lawn-mower, finally tried the patience of the National Bank of Commerce, which had been performing this service for the Knickerbocker Trust Company. In a curt announcement, the public read that the National Bank of Commerce had declined any longer to clear the checks of the Knickerbocker.

The depositors of the Knickerbocker believed they read in this statement something of deeper significance. They began to pour into the trust company, determined to withdraw their deposits. The Knickerbocker did not have much cash. Trust companies were not required to keep cash reserves against their deposits at a ratio at all comparable with that of the National Banks, which had to have in their vaults cash equal to 25 per cent of their deposits. Lacking cash, the Knickerbocker quickly had to close its doors.

Immediately, an already timorous public grew suspicious of most of the other trust companies, and lines of depositors began to form in front of their doors. Extra editions of the newspapers, falling prices registered in the stock-market, wild rumors, these things contributed force to the wave of emotion that engulfed the banking system.

Oh, but we had a stern captain in 1907; it was during those days of strain that I discovered for myself what an admirable intelligence gleamed through the fierce eyes of J. Pierpont Morgan. He was our captain; he was literally the nation's captain. His leadership was something that was taken for granted when the banking mechanism was floundering in difficulties. The most important men responded to his call, eagerly, and usually were quick to do his bidding. Mr. Morgan could be savage when he was out of patience, and, when he was crossed, unrelenting.

One of the first moves that Mr. Morgan made, in an effort to quell the panic, was to summon the presidents of all the trust companies. Astonishingly enough, they never before had been brought together.

Well, Mr. Morgan, with his back to the fireplace, watched those men as they gathered in response to his call. In sharp contrast to the linkage of the bank presidents, through their Clearing House Association, and in other connections, was the complete lack of organization among the trust companies. In an angry undertone, Mr. Morgan complained to Mr. [James] Stillman [National City's president] that on this morning he had actually had to introduce to one another the presidents of some of the biggest trust companies. As was true of all bankers, Mr. Morgan had been going without sleep—hurrying from meeting to meeting; at the Morgan offices, at his home, at the Waldorf [Hotel], or in one or another of the banks. His nerves were raw that morning. He was using every fiber of his intelligence to encompass the problem of a nation. Moreover, he had, I think, a sound banker's contempt for the slovenly banking operations of some of those who were then gathering at his bidding.

Old Governor [Levi P.] Morton moved about clasping and unclasping inky-veined hands under the tails of his Prince Albert. As was his custom, he was wearing on his egg-bald skull a wig, one of a series of three that he owned, graded as to length of hair, and which he wore in succession. That old man—he was 83 in 1907—had been

Minister to France, he had been Vice-President of the United States when Benjamin Harrison was President, he had been Governor of New York; for eight years he had been the president of the Morton Trust Company. Presently he planted himself before Mr. Morgan, mouth partially opened as if he were carefully trying to select words for an important utterance.

"John," he said at last, "how old are you?"

Mr. Morgan's scowl would have blighted an oak. "Too old to waste my time talking to you," he growled as he strode away.

That particular morning Mr. Morgan had time only to urge upon the trust company presidents a need for united action. Hastily the New York Clearing House Association amended its by-laws so as to permit the admission of any trust company which agreed to keep a 15 per cent cash reserve. But it was clear to all of us, I think, that the big weakness was in the lack of coordination in the banking system as a whole.

Those weeks in October and November were a period of swift education for most bankers, and I was certainly an eager student. I was learning that the banking reforms which I had long been preaching would have to be expressed in the form of some sort of a central banking organization. We would have to invent a wholesale banking mechanism that would relieve our economic system from the intolerable strains to which periodically it was being subjected. I was learning also that banking is not a field for weaklings. If I was strong, I had need of all my strength and my own physical reserves were being drawn upon in the same way that we were having to take assets out of the bank's vaults.

I recall as if it were an act in a melodrama a day in November, when a group of us gathered for a meeting in a private office in the Trust Company of America Building. We were the directors of the Norfolk & Southern Railway. The road was in difficulties, as were most railroad corporations. The problem could be expressed always in one way: cash. We were there to go through the legal formalities necessary to authorize the issuance of a mortgage for $25,000,000. The shareholders had given their approval.

Among those present was Oakleigh Thorne, president of the Trust Company of America. He was as restless as a cat detained from its basket of mewing kittens; downstairs were many things demanding his attention. Who could say what bad news there might be coughing out of the stock-ticker? At any minute that menacing line of depositors might begin again to extend itself into the street to grow monstrously until it would be giving off a wave of hysteria, having repercussions all over the country.

As the lawyer lifted papers from his bag in preparation for the reading of the mortgage, there was a little talk of the latest gossip out of the Knickerbocker Trust Company mess. Most of us there knew, and had an affection for, John T. Barney who had been its president. Some were inclined to blame Charles Morse or Augustus Heintze for Barney's difficulties. Then the lawyer began his *pro forma* reading.

While he was in the midst of its dull phrases a telephone bell rang and, as Oakleigh Thorne answered it, the lawyer stopped reading.

"Barney has committed suicide," said Thorne. "Shot himself with a pistol."

No one commented. The lawyer went on reading. That was not callousness. We simply had no time to express our feelings. At that moment the battle was on; we were in it.

This panic led to the creation of the Federal Reserve. Although other countries, such as the United Kingdom, had central banks ready to act as a lender of last resort, the United States had avoided such an institution. This crisis, and Morgan's effectiveness in acting as a de facto central banker, proved the usefulness of a formal, full-time central bank. In 1910 Vanderlip met with Henry Davison of Morgan Bank, Paul Warburg of Kuhn, Loeb, and Senator Nelson Aldrich of Rhode Island, a powerful Republican considered an expert in finances, to devise an improved banking system. The men formulated the Aldrich Plan: "National Reserve Associations," to be owned and overseen by private bankers, would make loans to member banks and manage the money supply. The plan, though defeated in Congress, was the basis for the Federal Reserve Act of 1913, which created regional Reserve Banks. (Government involvement was the significant difference between the plans.)

PART SIX

Wall Street in World War I: Last Man Standing

"How little the Wall Street brokers and the financial experts realized that an Imperial Conference held in Potsdam, presided over by the Kaiser, was the real force that was then depressing the market!"

Ambassador Henry Morgenthau

Timeline

1914 — Fearing withdrawal of foreign capital due to conflict in Europe, on July 31 NYSE closes for 4½ months, longest ever

1914–18 — WWI

1914 — U.S. proclaims neutrality; will stay out of conflict for 3 years; will become leading lender and supplier of European belligerents, permanently growing economy and ending status as debtor nation

1915 — Charles Lynch and Peter Merrill found brokerage

1918 — U.S. heads "Over There"—helps end war in Europe

1919 — Keynes publishes opposition to Versailles Treaty

1919 — Bond ticker introduced

1920 — Bomb kills 40 outside Morgan & Co.'s headquarters

1920 — Collapse of Charles Ponzi's scheme to pay high returns to old investors with deposits from new investors

THE SCENE IN THE 1910S

"The Corner"

Elliott V. Bell

J. P. Morgan was far from being the richest man of his time. His estate was valued at about one-tenth of Andrew Carnegie's, one-twelfth of John D. Rockefeller's. Yet Morgan's control of the U.S. economy is unlikely to be matched. When Congress investigated the Morgan Bank in 1912, it discovered that the assets controlled by "the octopus," as the bank was called by critics, totaled $25 billion—more than five times the budget of the federal government.

Elliott V. Bell was business reporter for The New York Times, *and later the editor of* Business Week.

The position of the House of Morgan is unique and in those days its right to leadership was undisputed. The basis of the Morgan power is not easy to explain. It is not a large bank, as Wall Street banks go. A dozen other institutions have much larger resources. True, the firm exercises a strong influence over a number of these larger banks—the so-called Morgan banks—but it has never been established to what extent that influence is based on financial control. The sheer money power of "the Corner" [because the Morgan bank stood at the corner of Wall and Broad streets across from the Stock Exchange] is, of course, great; but my own belief is that this is a minor factor in the firm's leadership. What really counts is not so much its money as its reputation and brains.

Morally and intellectually Morgan's stands head and shoulders above the rest of the Street. I don't think many people would dispute that regardless of what they think of the morals and intellect of the Street in general. That the Corner has made its mistakes goes without saying; but institutions, like men, must be judged against the background of their time and environment and, as Wall Street goes, Morgan's stands pretty high.

It is not a mere bank; it is an institution. It has become a symbol of Wall Street itself, viewed variously as a predatory creature, exercising a "spider-web" control over most of the banking and business resources of the country, or, at the other extreme, as a semi-philanthropic organization whose benign ministrations cause great banks and corporations to flourish, giving employment to millions of workers and causing the stocks of "widows and orphans" to rise in value and give off dividends.

About it there is an extraordinary amount of romanticizing, friendly and hostile, which is participated in not merely by the financially ignorant but by a large part of Wall Street itself. Almost nothing happens in the Street that is not linked in some way with the Corner in the rumors and gossip with which Wall Street abounds. This is true even today when the firm's activities and influence have undoubtedly diminished.

This peculiar aura that surrounds the Corner is never openly acknowledged there, but it is tacitly recognized in the firm's relations with the press. The quality of this relationship may be conveyed by the old phrase *noblesse oblige*. It is a fixed policy.

Germany's Financiers Prepare for War
Potsdam, Germany, July 5, 1914

Henry Morgenthau

Morgenthau, later to be Secretary of the Treasury during Franklin Roosevelt's administration, was ambassador to Turkey when World War I began. There was no better spot from which to witness the struggle. Turkey's Ottoman Empire had been fighting the Balkan Wars (1912–13), which led to the larger conflict. It would eventually join the other two "Central Powers," Germany and Austria-Hungary, to fight against the Allies.

The German ambassador who boasted to Morgenthau in this account was Baron von Wangenheim.

The German Ambassador [had] left for Berlin soon after the assassination [on June 28, 1914 of Austria's Archduke Franz Ferdinand and his wife, Sophie], and he now revealed the cause of his sudden disappearance. The Kaiser, he told me, had summoned him to Berlin for an imperial conference. This meeting took place at Potsdam on July 5th. The Kaiser presided; nearly all the ambassadors attended. Moltke, then Chief of Staff, was there representing the army, and Admiral von Tirpitz spoke for the navy.

The great bankers, railroad directors, and the captains of German industry, all of whom were as necessary to German war preparations as the army itself, also attended.

Wangenheim now told me that the Kaiser solemnly put the question to each man in turn. Was he ready for war? All replied "Yes" except the financiers. They said they must have two weeks to sell their foreign securities and to make loans. At that time few people looked upon the Sarajevo tragedy as something that was likely to cause war. The conference took all precautions that no such suspicion should be aroused. It decided to give the bankers time to readjust their finances for the coming war, and then several members went quietly back to their work or started on vacations.

In telling me about this conference, Wangenheim, of course,

admitted that Germany had precipitated the war. I think that he was rather proud of the whole performance; proud that Germany had gone about the matter in so methodical and far-seeing a way.

Whenever I hear people arguing about the responsibility for this war or read the clumsy and lying excuses put forth by Germany, I simply recall the burly figure of Wangenheim as he appeared that August afternoon, puffing away at a huge black cigar, and giving me his account of this historic meeting.

The Imperial Conference took place July 5th; the Serbian ultimatum was sent on July 22nd. That is just about the two weeks interval which the financiers had demanded to complete their plans. All the great stock exchanges of the world show that the German bankers profitably used this interval. Their records reveal that stocks were being sold in large quantities and that prices declined rapidly. Germany was changing her securities into cash, for war purposes. There were astonishing slumps in quotations, especially on the stocks that had an international market. Between July 5th and July 22nd, Union Pacific dropped from 155½ to 127½, Baltimore and Ohio from 91½ to 81, United States Steel from 61 to 50½, Canadian Pacific from 194 to 185½ and Northern Pacific from 111⅜ to 108.

At that time the high protectionists were blaming [a] tariff act as responsible for this fall in values; other critics of the Administration attributed it to the Federal Reserve Act—which had not yet been passed. How little the Wall Street brokers and the financial experts realized that an Imperial Conference held in Potsdam, presided over by the Kaiser, was the real force that was then depressing the market!

War News Reaches Wall Street
July 31, 1914

The New York Times

A few minutes before the time for the opening of the New York Stock Exchange yesterday, when the most tumultuous session in its history was expected, members of the Governing Committee began gathering in the office of the President, H. G. S. Noble, on the sixth floor.

There had been no call for a meeting, and the understanding was that the Exchange would open as usual, but the successive shocks of the advance in the English bank rate to 8 per cent, the discovery that the market was loaded down with big selling orders, and almost bare of buying orders, and the news of the beginning of runs on banks in London and Berlin alarmed the brokers so much that they hurried upstairs to urge a reconsideration of the decision to remain open. Besides the pressure brought to bear on Mr. Noble from this source telegrams were pouring in on him from out-of-town banks and Exchanges calling on the New York market to remain closed.

New arrivals reported that suspension of the British Bank Act was imminent, and that Germany practically had declared war. By the time the Acting Chairman of the Exchange had mounted his little balcony to wait for the stroke of 10 o'clock, thirty-seven members of the Governing Board had gathered in the President's office. There was an insistent demand for a vote.

At ten minutes before the hour Mr. Noble hurried his associates across the hall to the Governors' room. An instant later and the crowd had voted almost unanimously to close the Exchange. At once word went out that for the third time in history the Stock Exchange had been compelled to close to protect the solvency of hundreds of firms. [A suspension of ten days had followed the Panic of 1873; a short closing, to allow clerks rest, had followed the Panic of 1893.]

Word was flashed through the country in time to catch the markets in other cities. Boston, Philadelphia, Pittsburgh, Baltimore, Detroit, Indianapolis, St. Louis, Chicago, Cincinnati, Columbus, Washington, and San Francisco immediately voted to close. In Cleveland the market nominally was open but no business of consequence was done. The Consolidated Exchange in New York, which had opened as usual at 9:30, suspended trading, and the New York Curb followed suit.

On the floor of the New York Stock Exchange, where hundreds of brokers were excitedly trying to shape their affairs for the expected crash at the opening, the announcement that the Governors had voted to close provoked a wild outburst of cheering. Men who had feared that the next hour would bring disaster to their firms ran about embracing one another, and the general feeling was one of great relief.

For an hour or two after the announcement from the rostrum, the floor of the Exchange presented an unnatural appearance. Where a gargantuan roar was wont to rise the quiet was so marked that men unconsciously subdued their voices. On the big black squares at the sides of the room hundreds of numbers showed as the operator left them when business ceased. Members of the Exchange walked about the room at a loss for something to do.

On August 1, Germany declared war on Russia. On August 4, it invaded Belgium. The Exchange remained closed until December 15. By then the United States had announced that it intended to stay out of the war. The stock market, rather than crashing, rose.

Charlie Chaplin
Learns to Sell Liberty Bonds, 1918

Charlie Chaplin

At the outbreak of war, the United States government chose neutrality. Wall Street was less certain of the right stance. Should it finance all the belligerents? Pick a side? Avoid involvement, as the government had?

Less than a week after fighting began, the J. P. Morgan Bank, which hoped to make a loan to France, requested guidance from Secretary of State William Jennings Bryan. An opponent of American involvement in the war, Bryan also objected to bankers. ("You shall not crucify mankind upon a cross of gold," he had said, arguing against the gold standard when running for President in 1896.) He referred the loan question to President Woodrow Wilson with a strong recommendation. "We are the one great nation which is not involved," he wrote, "and our refusal to loan to any belligerent would naturally tend to hasten a conclusion of the war. We are responsible for the use of our influence through example." The administration answered Morgan that: "There is no reason why loans should not be made to the governments of neutral nations, but in the judgment of this Government, loans by American bankers to any foreign nation which is at war are inconsistent with the true spirit of neutrality."

Wall Street kept pushing, arguing that much of the money borrowed by European governments would be spent in the United States. Eventually the administration permitted loans, and even made loans directly. Liberty Bonds were sold to the public to back the Allies. Rallies relying heavily on celebrities from the nascent world of movies traveled across the country.

At the beginning of the First World War, popular opinion was that it would not last more than four months, that the science of modern warfare would take such a ghastly toll of human life that mankind would demand cessation of such barbarism. But we were mistaken. We were caught in an avalanche of mad destruction and brutal slaughter that went on for four years to the bewilderment of humanity.

But in 1915 the United States alleged that it was "too proud to fight." This gave the nation its cue for the song "I Didn't Raise My Boy to Be a Soldier." This song went down very well with the public, until the *Lusitania* went down—which was the cue for a different song, "Over There," and many other beguiling ditties. By 1918, America had launched two Liberty Bond drives, and now Mary Pickford, Douglas Fairbanks and I were requested to open officially the third Liberty Bond campaign in Washington.

In Washington we paraded through the streets like potentates, arriving at the football field where we were to give our initial address.

The speakers' platform was made of crude boards with flags and bunting around it. Among the representatives of the Army and Navy standing about was one tall, handsome young man who stood beside me, and we made conversation. I told him that I had never spoken before and was very anxious about it. "There's nothing to be scared about," he said confidently. "Just give it to them from the shoulder; tell them to buy their Liberty Bonds; don't try to be funny."

"Don't worry!" I said ironically.

Very soon I heard my introduction, so I bounded onto the platform in Fairbanksian style and without a pause let fly a verbal machine-gun barrage, hardly taking a breath: "The Germans are at your door! We've got to stop them! And we will stop them if you buy Liberty Bonds! Remember, each bond you buy will save a soldier's life—a mother's son!—and will bring this war to an early victory!" I spoke so rapidly and excitedly that I slipped off the platform, grabbed Marie Dressler and fell with her—on top of my handsome young friend, who happened to be then the assistant secretary of the navy, Franklin D. Roosevelt.

Everyone knows that in wartime the big money is in the bond market. Even so, the volume of business during World War I surpassed all expectations. More than $20 billion in Liberty Loan bonds were sold to the public between 1917 and 1919. (Gross Domestic Product at the time was about $40 billion annually.) Total public debt rose from $1.3 billion to $26 billion. About three-quarters of the cost of the war was financed by borrowing.

Meanwhile, the United States, neutral for almost three years, profited as a source of supplies and capital. It had also been spared the devastation inflicted on the economies of other participants. Europe ceded to Wall Street an international dominance of financial markets that continues today.

"Economic Consequences of the Peace," 1919

John Maynard Keynes

Was World War II predetermined by the treaty that ended World War I? John Maynard Keynes, one of the greatest economists in history, believed a great disruption in European society—especially in Germany and Austria—was inevitable.

As official representative of the British Treasury to the Paris Peace Conference of 1919, Keynes tried to convince the Allies to consider the economic consequences of their demands. Some politicians were unconvinced of his analysis, others were unmoved by the prospect of Germany's economic destruction. France, especially, was determined to avenge its mistreatment in both the war just ended and the Franco-Prussian War of 1870, during which the Germans had occupied Paris until France paid a crippling "war indemnity" of five billion francs.

Frustrated, Keynes resigned his post and put his objections to the treaty in a book, from which comes this prescient account.

This chapter must be one of pessimism. The Treaty includes no provisions for the economic rehabilitation of Europe—nothing to make the defeated Central Empires into good neighbors, nothing to stabilize the new States of Europe, nothing to reclaim Russia; nor does it promote in any way a compact of economic solidarity amongst the Allies themselves; no arrangement was reached at Paris for restoring the disordered finances of France and Italy, or to adjust the systems of the Old World and the New.

The Council of Four paid no attention to these issues, being preoccupied with others—[French Premier Georges] Clemenceau to crush the economic life of his enemy, [British Prime Minister David] Lloyd George to do a deal and bring home something which would pass muster for a week, the President [Woodrow Wilson] to do nothing that was not just and right. It is an extraordinary fact that the fundamental economic problems of a Europe starving and disintegrating before their eyes, was the one question in which it was impossible to arouse the interest of the Four. Reparation was their main excursion into the economic field, and they settled it as a problem of theology, of politics, of electoral chicane, from every point of view except that of the economic future of the States whose destiny they were handling.

Europe consists of the densest aggregation of population in the history of the world. This population is accustomed to a relatively high standard of life, in which, even now, some sections of it anticipate improvement rather than deterioration. In relation to other continents Europe is not self-sufficient; in particular it cannot feed itself.

Internally the population is not evenly distributed, but much of it is crowded into a relatively small number of dense industrial centers. This population secured for itself a livelihood before the war, without much margin of surplus, by means of a delicate and immensely complicated organization, of which the foundations were supported by coal, iron, transport, and an unbroken supply of imported food and raw materials from other continents. By the destruction of this organization and the interruption of the stream of supplies, a part of this population is deprived of its means of livelihood.

Emigration is not open to the redundant surplus. For it would take years to transport them overseas, even, which is not the case, if countries could be found which were ready to receive them.

The danger confronting us, therefore, is the rapid depression of the standard of life of the European populations to a point which will mean actual starvation for some (a point already reached in Russia and approximately reached in Austria). Men will not always die quietly. For starvation, which brings to some lethargy and a helpless despair, drives other temperaments to the nervous instability of hysteria and to a mad despair. And these in their distress may overturn the remnants of organization, and submerge civilization itself in their attempts to satisfy desperately the overwhelming needs of the individual. This is the danger against which all our resources and courage and idealism must now co-operate.

Unfortunately, Keynes's predictions proved accurate. The German government tried to create wealth by printing money, only to impoverish its citizens with hyperinflation. Fascists promised order where there had been economic chaos.

After World War II, the United States took a different approach to economic reconstruction. Under the Marshall Plan, named for President Harry Truman's Secretary of State, George C. Marshall, the government helped rebuild Germany and restore its economy.

Today Keynes is best remembered for his 1936 book, The General Theory of Employment, Interest and Money. *In it he prescribes a "counter-cyclical" fiscal policy, telling governments to limit spending and raise taxes during booms, slowing the economy and building reserves to be spent during bad times.*

Bombing of the J. P. Morgan Bank
September 16, 1920

The New York Times *and B. F. Borsody*

Just before noon on this day, a horse-drawn cart filled with explosives and metal shrapnel stopped in front of the J. P. Morgan Bank. The driver disappeared among the passersby. A few minutes later the bomb exploded.

"It was a crash out of the blue sky—an unexpected, death-dealing bolt which in a twinkling turned into shambles the busiest corner of America's financial center and sent scurrying to places of shelter hundreds of the wounded, dumb-stricken, white-faced men and women, fleeing from an unknown danger."

A reporter for the Associated Press, who was the eyewitness to the explosion, thus described the scene. "I was just turning into Wall Street from Broadway," he said, "when I first felt, rather than heard, the explosion. A concussion of air similar to that experienced by a passenger on the subway when a train dashes into one of the under-river tubes was felt. Its force was sufficient to all but throw me off my balance. Instantly following the concussion came a sharp, resounding crash, which shook to their foundations the monster buildings facing either side of Wall Street. With the roar of the blast came the rattle of falling glass, and from the junction of Wall, Nassau and Broad streets—a block distant—screams of injured men and women.

"I dodged into a convenient doorway to escape falling glass and to reach a telephone and call the office. Looking down Wall Street later, I could see arising from the vicinity of the Sub-Treasury Building, and the J. P. Morgan and Company Bank, a mushroom-shaped cloud of yellowish green smoke which mounted to the height of more than 100 feet, the smoke being licked by darting tongues of flame.

"I reached the scene a few moments after the explosion took place. The smoke had partly cleared from the street, but from the Morgan building there was belching forth through the broken windows clouds of dust and white vapor. In the street an overturned automobile was blazing fiercely, and nearby, close to the body of a dead horse, was another fire, evidently among a pile of wreckage.

"Almost in front of the steps leading up to the Morgan bank was the mutilated body of a man. Other bodies, most of them silent in death, lay nearby. As I gazed horror-stricken at the site, one of these forms, half naked, and seared with burns, started to rise. It struggled, then toppled and fell lifeless into the gutter.

"On the opposite side of the street were other forms. One of them was that of a young woman—her clothing torn and burned away. It was moving, not in an effort to rise, but in the agony of death. I started toward her, but as I did it became still. Glancing down, I saw that the pavement was discolored with blood. In plain sight, within a radius of thirty to fifty feet, were nine lifeless forms.

"The body of the dead horse, in the middle of the street, showed plain evidence of having been in very close proximity to the center of the blast. It was literally torn to pieces.

"The windows of the Morgan building were blown out and through the opening I saw the smoke-blackened interior of what a few moments previous had been one of the handsomest banking rooms of the city. Opposite, the entrance to the newly completed white exterior of the Sub-Treasury annex was battered and torn as if having been subjected to a bombardment of machine-gun fire. The doorway, with its massive steel grillwork, was shattered, and the stone surrounding the door cracked and battered away.

"By this time, the crowd was pressing in, held in check by the hastily-gathering police. At the doorway of the Morgan Bank was a uniformed guard, apparently half-dazed, but sticking to his post and holding back those who sought to enter the structure.

"The crowd was strangely quiet, and over it seemed to hang a feeling of awe and horror. At the commands of the police, it moved and fell back silently. On the steps of the old Sub-Treasury building, the spot where years ago stirring scenes connected with the American revolution were enacted, stands a statue of George Washington. Looking down from its pedestal, between the massive granite columns, scarred by missiles from the explosion, the outstretched hand of the Father of his country seemed to carry a silent command to be calm.

"Then came the ambulances. Nearby, trucks and automobiles were first pressed into service. Volunteers, heeding not blood-smeared hands and clothing, tenderly lifted into the vehicles the bodies of the dying and the dead. The dead that remained for additional conveyances were charitably hidden from sight by coverings torn from awnings or robes from arriving motorcars.

"It was such a scene as I had pictured as a possibility during the war, should the enemy succeed in dropping on the financial district one of his deadly aerial bombs."

Forty people were killed, one hundred and thirty injured. The toll would certainly have been worse if the bomb had exploded just a few minutes later, during the lunch hour. In the archives of the Morgan Bank is an account from a former Western Union telegram operator, B. F. Borsody, who worked across the street from the bank:

At lunch time, noon, my usual route to the Childs Restaurant, on Pearl Street, near Wall Street, was past the site of the bomb. What saved my life was that the telegraph operator who relieved me for lunch that day was one minute late. Thus, I was just approaching the corner of Wall and Broad Streets, on the sidewalk before the J. P. Morgan offices, and around the corner from the bomb, when it exploded. The blast knocked me down, and, bruised and dazed, I picked myself up, looked around the corner of Wall Street, and saw an appalling scene. Before the Wall Street side of Morgan's the street was dotted with what looked like many clumps of rags, dead bodies strewn among several wrecked vehicles.

The day was sunny and bright: above the scene of the bombing the sun's rays filtered through a haze of tiny gleaming particles in the air. Still dazed, I sat down on the curb in front of Morgan's on the southeast corner of Broad and Wall Streets. Meanwhile, a dense crowd had gathered, but nobody noticed me sitting on the curb. A rivulet of blood, unnoticed by the crowds, trickled down the south gutter of Wall Street, and drained down the sewer-opening beside me.

The bombing remains Wall Street's deadliest mystery. Although various theories have been suggested, it is likely that anarchists, suspected at the time, were indeed responsible. Both the horrors and the profits rendered during World War I focused the energies of anarchist extremists. But no one was ever arrested or tried for the crime.

The Morgan Bank building still bears the scars of the bomb. David W. Wright, the bank's historian, says they have been left as a silent memorial.

PART SEVEN

Boom and Bust

"The rich man's chauffeur drove with his ears laid back to catch the news of an impending move in Bethlehem Steel; he held fifty shares himself on a twenty-point margin. The window-cleaner at the broker's office paused to watch the ticker, for he was thinking of converting his laboriously accumulated savings into a few shares . . ."

Frederick Lewis Allen

Timeline

1921 — Curb traders move indoors; New York Curb Exchange will become American Stock Exchange

1923 — 6-year bull market begins

1923 — Keynes was right: inflation and distress in Germany

1924 — Mass. Investors Trust and State Street Investment Trust, first mutual funds

1928 — Scudder introduces no-load funds

1929 — Dow hits high of 381.4, then crashes in October

1929 — October 29: "Black Tuesday" panic—DJIA falls 11 percent

1930 — Money tightened to reduce speculation; economy strangled

1932 — Dow low of 41.22, down 89 percent from 1929 peak

1933 — Glass-Steagall Act separates investment and commercial banking; creates Federal Deposit Insurance Corp.

1933 — State and federal bank "holidays" declared in March to end runs; FDR calms fears with first fireside chat

1934 — Graham and Dodd's "value investing" classic *Security Analysis* published

1934 — Securities and Exchange Commission est.

1934 — Congress limits margin loans

1935 — Federal Reserve Board granted more authority to set rates

1935 — Social Security Act

1936 — Keynes publishes countercyclical *General Theory of Employment, Interest and Money*

THE SCENE IN THE 1920S

Marxist Economics

Harpo Marx

In good times, as Bernard Baruch has observed, every bullish tip comes true and every tipster seems a prophet.

The market kept rising and we kept buying, on margin, to stay on top of the golden wave of prosperity.

I got my market tips from Groucho. Groucho got his from his friend Max Gordon, the New York theatrical producer, and passed them on to me. While we were in Boston with *Animal Crackers* Groucho lost touch, temporarily, with Max Gordon. So he settled for tips from an elevator operator in the Copley Plaza Hotel, which he duly and loyally passed on to me. We spent more time on the long-distance phone with our brokers than Chico did on the local phone with bookies.

Our stocks were rising like the price of whisky in a gold rush. I was now worth a quarter of a million dollars, at the rate of $68.50 per average invested share.

After the week in Boston the show moved to Baltimore. The Baltimore papers began to report strange rumors about the market. My broker was cautious on the phone, all of a sudden. Instead of chirping, "Buy, buy, buy," he began to say, "It might be wise to commence covering margins."

A bunch of scare-talk. This wasn't a boom that was going to go bust. The market was a solid institution and I was being advised by the country's best authorities: Max Gordon, Groucho Marx, and the elevator operator in the Copley Plaza Hotel. I kept on buying.

The Big Bull Market, 1927–1929

Frederick Lewis Allen

With the 1920s came irresistible technology: automobiles, movies, air-planes—air conditioning! The companies that sold these devices absolutely could not fail, right?

And don't forget wireless radio, greeted with the same enthusiasm (and frustration) as the Internet would be welcomed decades later. Children struggled to teach parents how to divine a clear signal with a flimsy crystal set. Adults philosophized about the medium's power to alter the world. Meanwhile, Wall Street hailed an industry with limitless growth. (Early charts of the Radio Corporation of America look remarkably similar to the charts of America Online.)

Also like the Internet, radio changed trading. Market news was now available everywhere, all the time. Brokers even set up shop on passenger ships.

The experts knew something wasn't right. Some took a breather, only to regret leaving the market too early. In March 1929, The New York Times *noted that "the people who know the least about the stock market have made the most money out of it in the last few months. Fools who rushed in where wise men feared to tread ran up high gains."*

As recalled by Frederick Lewis Allen, author of Only Yesterday, *the bull market that preceded the 1929 crash is a classic example of market mania. Perhaps most telling are the many warning signs obvious to us now.*

One day in February 1928, an investor asked an astute banker about the wisdom of buying common stocks.

The banker shook his head. "Stocks look dangerously high to me," he said. "This bull market has been going on for a long time, and although prices have slipped a bit recently, they might easily slip a good deal more. Business is none too good. Of course if you buy the right stock you'll probably be all right in the long run and you may even make a profit. But if I were you I'd wait awhile and see what happens."

While stock prices had been climbing, business activity had been undeniably subsiding. There had been such a marked recession during the latter part of 1927 that by February, 1928, the director of the Charity Organization Society in New York reported that unemployment was more serious than at any time since immediately after the war. During January and February the stock market turned ragged and unsettled, and no wonder—for with prices still near record levels and the future trend of business highly dubious, it was altogether too easy to foresee a time of reckoning ahead.

The financial editor of *The New York Times* described the picture of current conditions presented by the mercantile agencies as one of "hesitation." The newspaper advertisements of investment services testified to the uncomfortable temper of Wall Street with headlines like "Will You 'Overstay' This Bull Market?"

Anybody who had chosen this moment to predict that the bull market was on the verge of a wild advance which would make all that had gone before seem trifling would have been quite mad—or else inspired with a genius for mass psychology. The banker who advised caution was quite right about financial conditions, and so were the forecasters.

But they had not taken account of the boundless commercial romanticism of the American people, inflamed by year after plentiful year of Coolidge Prosperity. For on March 3, 1928, the very day when the *Times* was talking about hesitation, the stock market entered upon its sensational phase.

What on earth was happening? Wasn't business bad, and credit inflated, and the stock-price level dangerously high? Was the market going crazy?

What was actually happening was that a group of powerful speculators with fortunes made in the automobile business and in the grain markets and in the earlier days of the bull market in stocks— men like W. C. Durant and Arthur Cutten and the Fisher Brothers and John J. Raskob—were buying in unparalleled volume.

They thought that business was due to come out of its doldrums. They knew that with Ford production delayed, the General Motors Corporation was likely to have a big year. They knew that the Radio Corporation had been consolidating its position and was now ready to make more money than it had ever made before, and that as scientific discovery followed discovery, the future possibilities of the biggest radio company were exciting. Automobiles and radios—these were the two most characteristic products of the decade of confident mass production, the brightest flowers of Coolidge Prosperity: they held a ready-made appeal to the speculative imagination.

And so it went on, day after day and week after week. On March 16th the ticker was thirty-three minutes late [because it could not keep up with the volume of trades] and one began to hear people saying that some day there might occur a five-million-share day— which seemed almost incredible.

The speculative fever was infecting the whole country. Stories of fortunes made overnight were on everybody's lips. Wives were asking their husbands why they were so slow, why they weren't getting in on all this, only to hear that their husbands had bought a hundred shares of American Linseed that very morning.

Brokers' branch offices were jammed with crowds of men and women watching the shining transparency on which the moving message of the ticker tape was written.

Several times during the spring of 1928 the New York Stock Exchange had to remain closed on Saturday to give brokers' clerks a chance to dig themselves out from under the mass of paper work.

The Reserve authorities were disturbed. They had raised the rediscount rate in February from 3½ per cent to 4 per cent, hoping that if a lowering of the rate in 1927 had encouraged speculation, a corresponding increase would discourage it—and instead they had witnessed a common-stock mania which ran counter to all logic and all economic theory. They raised the rate again in May to 4½ per cent, but after a brief shudder the market went boiling on.

In the latter part of May, 1928, the pace of the bull market slackened. Prices fell off, gained, fell off again. The reckoning, so long expected, appeared at last to be at hand.

It came in June, after several days of declining prices. As selling orders poured in, the prophecy that the Exchange would some day see a five-million-share day was quickly fulfilled. The ticker slipped almost two hours behind in recording prices on the floor. Radio, which had marched well beyond the 200 mark in May, lost 23½ points.

But had the bull market collapsed? On June 13th it appeared to have regained its balance. On June 14th, the day of [Herbert] Hoover's nomination [as the Republican candidate for President], it extended its recovery.

Election Day came and Hoover swept the country. During that "Hoover bull market" of November, 1928, the records made earlier in the year were smashed to splinters. Had brokers once spoken with awe of the possibility of five-million-share days? Five-million-share days were now occurring with monotonous regularity; on November 23rd the volume of trading almost reached seven millions. Had they been amazed at the rising prices of seats on the Stock Exchange? In November a new mark of $580,000 was set. Had they been disturbed that Radio should sell at such an exorbitant price as 150? Late in November it was bringing 400. Ten-point gains and new highs for all times were commonplaces now. Montgomery Ward, which the previous spring had been climbing toward 200, touched 439⅞ on November 30.

The new era had arrived, and the abolition of poverty was just around the corner.

The Reserve authorities had waited patiently for the speculative fever to cure itself and it had only become more violent. Things had now come to such a pass that if they raised the rate still further, they not only ran the risk of bringing about a terrific smash in the market—and of appearing to do so deliberately and wantonly—but also of seriously handicapping business by forcing it to pay a high rate for funds. It almost seemed as if there were no way to deflation except through disaster.

The Reserve Board finally met the dilemma by thinking up a new and ingenious scheme. They tried to prevent the re-loaning of Reserve funds to brokers without raising the rediscount rate.

On February 2, 1929, they issued a statement in which they said: "The Federal Reserve Act does not, in the opinion of the Federal Reserve Board, contemplate the use of the resources of the Federal Reserve Banks for the creation or extension of speculative credit. A member bank is not within its reasonable claims for rediscount facilities at its Federal Reserve Bank when it borrows either for the purpose of making speculative loans or for the purpose of maintaining speculative loans."

The immediate result of the statement of February 2, 1929, was a brief overnight collapse in stock prices. Once again the Big Bull Market appeared to be on its last legs.

That afternoon several of the New York banks decided to come to the rescue. Whatever they thought of the new policy of the Federal Reserve Board, they saw a possible panic brewing—and anything, they decided, was better than a panic. The next day Charles E. Mitchell, president of the National City Bank, announced that his bank was prepared to lend twenty million dollars on call, of which five million would be available at 15 per cent, five million more at 16 per cent, and so on up to 20 per cent. Mr. Mitchell's action—which was described by Senator Carter Glass as a slap in the face of the Reserve Board—served to peg the call money rate at 15 per cent and the threatened panic was averted. Whereupon stocks not only ceased their precipitous fall, but cheerfully recovered!

The lesson was plain: the public simply would not be shaken out of the market by anything short of a major disaster.

As people in the summer of 1929 looked back for precedents, they were comforted by the recollection that every crash of the past few years had been followed by a recovery, and that every recovery had ultimately brought prices to a new high point. Two steps up, one step down, two steps up again—that was how the market went. If you sold, you had only to wait for the next crash (they came every few months) and buy in again. And there was really no reason to sell at all: you were bound to win in the end if your stock was sound. The really wise man, it appeared, was he who "bought and held on."

Time and again the economists and forecasters had cried wolf, wolf, and the wolf had made only the most fleeting of visits. Time and again the Reserve Board had expressed fear of inflation, and inflation had failed to bring hard times. Everybody heard how many millions a man would have made if he had bought a hundred shares of General Motors in 1919 and held on.

Mergers of industrial corporations and of banks were taking place with greater frequency than ever before, prompted not merely by the desire to reduce overhead expenses and avoid the rigors of cut-throat competition, but often by sheer corporate megalomania. And every rumor of a merger or a split-up or an issue of rights was the automatic signal for a leap in the prices of the stocks affected—

until it became altogether too tempting to the managers of many a concern to arrange a split-up or a merger or an issue of rights not without a canny eye to their own speculative fortunes.

Meanwhile investment trusts [i.e., mutual funds] multiplied like locusts. There were now said to be nearly five hundred of them, with a total paid-in capital of some three billions and with holdings of stocks—many of them purchased at the current high prices—amounting to something like two billions.

Branch offices of the big Wall Street houses blossomed in every city and in numerous suburban villages. In 1919 there had been five hundred such offices; by October, 1928, there were 1,192; and throughout most of 1929 they appeared in increasing numbers. The broker found himself regarded with a new wonder and esteem. Ordinary people, less intimate with the mysteries of Wall Street than he was supposed to be, hung upon his every word. Let him but drop a hint of a possible split-up in General Industries Associates and his neighbor was off hot-foot the next morning to place a buying order.

In September the market reached its ultimate glittering peak. It was six months, now, since Herbert Hoover had driven down Pennsylvania Avenue in the rain to take the oath of office as President of the United States.

Stop for a moment to glance at a few of the prices recorded on the overworked ticker on September 3, 1929, the day when the Dow Jones averages reached their high point for the year; and compare them with the opening prices of March 3, 1928, when, as you may recall, it had seemed as if the bull market had already climbed to a perilous altitude.

The rich man's chauffeur drove with his ears laid back to catch the news of an impending move in Bethlehem Steel; he held fifty shares himself on a twenty-point margin. The window-cleaner at the broker's office paused to watch the ticker, for he was thinking of converting his laboriously accumulated savings into a few shares of Simmons. An ex-actress in New York fitted up her Park Avenue apartment as an office and surrounded herself with charts, graphs, and financial reports, playing the market by telephone on an increasing scale and with increasing abandon.

Thousands speculated—and won, too—without the slightest knowledge of the nature of the company upon whose fortunes they were relying, like the people who bought Seaboard Air Line under the impression that it was an aviation stock. [It was a railroad in the Southeast.] Grocers, motormen, plumbers, seamstresses and speakeasy waiters were in the market. Even the rebellious intellectuals were there: loudly as they might lament the depressing effects of standardization and mass production upon American life, they found themselves quite ready to reap the fruits thereof. Literary editors whose hopes were wrapped about American Cyanamid lunched with poets who swore by Cities Service, and as they left the table, stopped for a moment in the crowd at the broker's branch office to catch the latest quotations; and the artist who had once been eloquent only about Gauguin laid aside his brushes to proclaim the merits of National Bellas Hess. The Big Bull Market had become a national mania.

	Opening Price	High Price (adjusted for splits)
	March 3, 1928	Sept. 3, 1929
American Can	77	181⅞
AT&T	179½	335⅝
Anaconda Copper	54½	162
Electric Bond & Share	89¾	203⅝
General Electric	128¾	396¾
General Motors	139¾	181⅞
Montgomery Ward	132¾	466½
New York Central	160½	256
Radio	94½	505
Union Carbide	145	413⅝
US Steel	138⅛	279 ⅛
Westinghouse	91⅝	313
Woolworth	180¾	251

Still the American could spin wonderful dreams of a romantic day when he would sell his Westinghouse common at a fabulous price and live in a great house and have a fleet of shining cars and loll at ease on the sands of Palm Beach. He saw a magical order built on the new science and the new prosperity: roads swarming with millions upon millions of automobiles, airplanes darkening the skies, lines of high-tension wire carrying from hilltop to hilltop the power to give life to a thousand labor-saving machines, skyscrapers thrusting above one-time villages, vast cities rising in great geometrical masses of stone and concrete and roaring with perfectly mechanized traffic—and smartly dressed men and women spending, spending, spending with the money they had won by being far-sighted enough to foresee, way back in 1929, what was going to happen.

CRASH!
March and October 1929

Elliott V. Bell

It didn't happen all at once. The Dow Jones Industrial Average, which had hit a high of 386 in September, had been falling steadily. On October 17 it closed just under 342. A week later it was under 306. Elliott V. Bell, who reported for The New York Times, *recalled the tragedy in this account written a few years later. He begins the story of October's crash with a revealing prologue about a famous and misunderstood incident. In March 1929, a well-known banker was thrust into a public battle with the Federal Reserve Board that had serious consequences. The authority of the Fed at that time, less than two decades after its creation, was not nearly as strong as today.*

MARCH 1929

One of the last examples, ill-fated as it turned out, of one strong individual attempting by a single-handed gesture to turn the course of financial events, occurred in March 1929, when Charles E. Mitchell, then President of the National City Bank of New York, hurled defiance at the Federal Reserve Board and, by throwing $25 million into the call-money market, postponed for seven months the stock market crash which was to usher in the great depression.

I feel a proprietary interest in this episode because it gave me my first big "exclusive" story and because, if I had not gotten the story, a great many other things which grew out of it might have been different.

A contest was then going on, between the Federal Reserve Bank of New York, of which Mr. Mitchell was a director, and the Federal Reserve Board in Washington, over what steps should be taken to check the stock market boom. In those early months of 1929 it was already apparent to sober-minded men in Wall Street that speculation had gotten out of hand and that sooner or later a crash was inevitable. The late Paul M. Warburg, head of the Bank of the

Manhattan Company, was the only important banker who publicly warned against the impending collapse, but many others held a similar view. No one, of course, even suspected that when the crash did come it would bring with it the worst depression in history.

The issue between the Federal Reserve Bank of New York and the Federal Reserve Board was not whether the boom should be checked; that had been agreed on for some time. The question was one of methods to be employed.

The Federal Reserve Bank of New York, which had been for years the tail that wagged the dog in the Federal Reserve System, wanted to tackle the problem along traditional banking lines. It wanted to raise its rediscount rate, thereby making credit dear so that speculation would become unprofitable. Such a course, it goes without saying, would have pinched not merely the stock market but business in general.

The Federal Reserve Board was reluctant to do anything that might hurt business. Having in mind the uproar which it had faced in 1921 when it was accused of having ruined the farmer by pricking the bubble of inflated commodity prices, it was fearful of stirring up popular resentment and of drawing down upon its head the wrath of politicians. It sought therefore to find a compromise, a means of making credit dear for the stock market while keeping it reasonable for business.

To this end the board issued in February 1929, its celebrated "warning" which said, in effect, that a member bank had no right to borrow from the Federal Reserve Banks for the purposes of making speculative loans. Inasmuch as all banks were at that time borrowing heavily from the Federal Reserve Banks and were at the same time lending heavily to the stock market, the board's warning, if followed literally, would have meant an immediate stoppage of the flow of funds to finance stock speculation. Not content with a mere warning, the board instructed its agents at the various Reserve Banks to call individual bankers upon the carpet and admonish them against overextension of stock-market loans.

This was the so-called "direct action" policy of the Reserve Board. While pursuing it, the board declined, week after week, to accede to the request of the Federal Reserve Bank of New York for permission to increase its rediscount rate. Wall Street bankers were solidly on the side of the local Reserve Bank, as was the accumulated tradition and doctrine of central-banking technique. In those days the head of a big Wall Street bank considered himself a much more important figure than any Federal Reserve Board member and it may be imagined how well such a policy of "direct action" went with the more important figures in the banking world.

Nevertheless, the policy did begin to take hold. Call money—money supplied to brokers by banks and subject to call at any time—began to get dearer. At first the stock market paid little attention. So long as stocks went up fast enough, 8 or 10 percent call money meant little. But finally there came a day in March when there was not enough money in the call market to go around. It was no longer a question of having to pay dear for money—money simply couldn't be had at any price. In the face of that there was nothing to do but sell. Stocks began to drop; call money soared to 20 percent; a panic developed, and the big bull market nearly came to an end right there, March 26, 1929.

I had not been a bank reporter very long at that time, and I found the events of that day pretty exciting. Irrespective of the merits of the stock market boom, I felt that it was a pretty high-handed, not to say undemocratic affair, that banks should suddenly refuse to lend money at any price, thereby deliberately precipitating a panic that was going to ruin a lot of people. This was my first experience of a "banking conspiracy." I kept going around to see bankers and suggesting to them that the public was going to be pretty sore when they found out about it. The bankers didn't have much to say. It was pretty plain that they didn't like it much themselves. Finally, about 5 P.M., when I should have been getting back uptown to my office, I went around to the National City Bank for one last effort to see Mr. Mitchell, who had been tied up in conference earlier in the day.

He was still tied up. His secretary assured me that I was wasting my time. Nevertheless, I waited. I waited an hour and a half. Finally, when I was about ready to give up, Mr. Mitchell sent out word that he was free and would see me.

I am afraid I pitched into him in a rather undiplomatic way. In effect, I asked him what the devil bankers meant by conspiring to bring on a panic. I have no way of knowing whether Mr. Mitchell had made up his mind in advance to make the statement he did or whether my naïve approach provoked him into it. Since then I have often heard and seen printed the statement that "Mitchell called in reporters" and "handed out" his statement. Nothing could be further from the truth. What he said was purely extemporaneous and was said to me alone.

He said that he had been in a series of conferences and had learned of the panic only late in the day, but that when he had found out what was going on, he had sent up to the Federal Reserve Bank and borrowed $25 million and thrown it into the call-money market. The dynamite was in a sentence that I carefully wrote down as soon as I had gotten outside his door. It was: "So far as this institution is concerned, we feel that we have an obligation that is paramount to any Federal Reserve warning, or anything else, to avert, so far as lies within our power, any dangerous crisis in the money market."

Next day the afternoon papers had picked it up and were carrying it on their front pages together with the news that the stock market was rallying sharply and that call money was going down as other banks followed Mitchell's lead. Carter Glass rose in the Senate to denounce the banker who had avowed his allegiance to a frenzied stock market, and Mr. Mitchell was already a marked man. As I walked along Wall Street, it seemed as though everyone was talking about my story. I kept hearing snatches of conversation: "And he said: 'So far as this institution is concerned . . .' " People took sides, and I found myself praised and blamed as though I had been an active agent in the matter. A money broker stopped me and asked me if I had written the story. "Well, you ought to be ashamed of yourself," he said. "The First National Bank lent more money yesterday than Mitchell did."

In the years that followed, the crash this statement was repeatedly used to bolster the charge that bankers in general had been "speculative-minded" and that Mr. Mitchell in particular was a ringleader of the bull movement in stocks. I do not presume to set myself up as a champion of Mr. Mitchell, but as far as this particular incident is concerned the charges are hardly just. His position was that banks had no right, even at the behest of the Federal Reserve Board, deliberately to precipitate a stock market panic by a concerted refusal to lend money at any price. Others certainly took the same stand, but they were not so frank as to let a reporter quote them.

Irrespective of the merits of his position, Mr. Mitchell's action meant the end of the Reserve Board's campaign of direct action.

The stock market took the bit in its teeth and ran away, fetching up finally with the breathtaking crash of October 24, 1929, which formally ushered in the great depression.

THE CRASH

October 24, 1929, was not the first day of the big break in stocks, nor was it the last. It was not the largest day in point of volume of stocks dealt in and, on balance, the decline of prices was not large. Nevertheless, it was the most terrifying and unreal day I have ever seen in the Street, and it constitutes an important financial landmark, for that day marked the beginning of the great decline in the prestige and power of Wall Street over national affairs.

The big bull market that had begun five years earlier with the election of Calvin Coolidge reached its peak in September of 1929. Stock prices turned downward in the latter half of that month and by the third week of October a spectacular decline was in progress.

On Monday, October 21, the market broke badly on 6,091,870 shares. Washington, according to the headlines of the day, viewed the situation as "sound." Professor Irving Fisher said stock prices were too low and "bankers" predicted a rally. The next day there was a rally, and Charles E. Mitchell, returning from abroad, opined the "decline had gone too far."

On Wednesday, October 23, stocks crashed again. The *New York Times* average of 50 stocks, which had reached 311.90 on September 19, fell to 261 that day, showing a loss of 16⅓ percent from the high of a month before. Washington was "surprised."

This, then, was the situation on the eve of October 24, 1929. Stocks had been falling for over a month; had lost, on the average, about one-sixth of their quoted value, and looked "cheap" according to the opinion of important bankers, economists, and government officials. Business was still good—the economic position of the country was "sound" and technically the stock market itself had been improved by a "healthy reaction." Practically everyone thought a good rally must be close at hand.

The day was overcast and cool. A light northwest wind blew down the canyons of Wall Street, and the temperature, in the low fifties, made bankers and brokers on their way to work button their topcoats around them. The crowds of market traders in the brokers' boardrooms were nervous but hopeful as the ten o'clock hour for the start of trading approached. The general feeling was that the worst was over and a good many speculators who had prudently sold out earlier in the decline were congratulating themselves at having bought back their stocks a good deal cheaper. Seldom had the small trader had better or more uniform advice to go by.

The market opened steady with prices little changed from the previous day, though some rather large blocks, of 20,000 to 25,000 shares, came out at the start. It sagged easily for the first half hour, and then around eleven o'clock the deluge broke.

It came with a speed and ferocity that left men dazed. The bottom simply fell out of the market. From all over the country a torrent of selling orders poured onto the floor of the Stock Exchange and there were no buying orders to meet it. Quotations of representative active issues, like [U.S.] Steel, Telephone [AT&T], and Anaconda [Copper and Mining], began to fall two, three, five, and even ten points between sales. Less active stocks became unmarketable. Within a few moments the ticker service was hopelessly swamped and from then on no one knew what was really happening. By 1:30 the ticker tape was nearly two hours late; by 2:30 it was 147 minutes late. The last quotation was not printed on the tape until 7:08 ½ P.M., four hours, eight and one-half minutes after the close. In the meantime, Wall Street had lived through an incredible nightmare.

In the strange way that news of a disaster spreads, the word of the market collapse flashed through the city. By noon great crowds had gathered at the corner of Broad and Wall streets, where the Stock Exchange on one corner faces Morgan's across the way. On the steps of the Sub-Treasury Building, opposite Morgan's, a crowd of press photographers and newsreel men took up their stand. Traffic was pushed from the streets of the financial district by the crush.

It was in this wild setting that the leading bankers scurried into conference at Morgan's in a belated effort to save the day. Shortly after noon Mr. Mitchell left the National City Bank and pushed his way west on Wall Street to Morgan's. No sooner had he entered than Albert H. Wiggin was seen to hurry down from the Chase National Bank, one block north. Hard on his heels came William C. Potter, head of the Guaranty Trust, followed by Seward Prosser of the Bankers Trust. Later George F. Baker, Jr., of the First National, joined the group.

The news of the bankers meeting flashed through the streets and over the news tickers—stocks began to rally—but for many it was already too late. Thousands of traders, little and big, had gone "overboard" in that incredible hour between eleven and twelve. Confidence in the financial and political leaders of the country, faith in the "soundness" of economic conditions had received a shattering blow. The panic was on.

At Morgan's the heads of six banks formed a consortium—since known as the bankers' pool of October 1929-pledging a total of $240 million, or $40 million each to provide a "cushion" buying power beneath the falling market. In addition, other financial institutions, including James Speyer and Company and Guggenheim Brothers, sent over to Morgan's unsolicited offers of funds aggregating $100 million. It was not only the first authenticated instance of a bankers' pool in stocks but by far the largest concentration of pool buying power ever brought to bear on the stock market—but in the face of the panic it was pitifully inadequate.

After the bankers had met, Thomas W. Lamont, Morgan partner, came out to the crowd of newspaper reporters who had gathered in the lobby of his bank. In an understatement that has since become a Wall Street classic, he remarked:

"It seems there has been some disturbed selling in the market."

It was at the same meeting that "T.W." gave to the financial community a new phrase—"air pockets"—to describe the condition in stocks for which there were no bids, but only frantic offers. (Mr. Lamont said he had it from his partner, George Whitney, and the latter said he had it from some broker.)

After the meeting, Mr. Lamont walked across Broad Street to the Stock Exchange to meet with the governors of the Exchange. They had been called together quietly during trading hours and they held their meeting in the rooms of the Stock Clearing Corporation so as to avoid attracting attention. Mr. Lamont sat on the corner of a desk and told them about the pool. Then he said:

"Gentlemen, there is no man nor group of men who can buy all the stocks that the American public can sell."

It seems a pretty obvious statement now, but it had a horrid sound to the assembled governors of the Exchange. It meant that the shrewdest member of the most powerful banking house in the country was telling them plainly that the assembled resources of

Wall Street, mobilized on a scale never before attempted, could not stop this panic.

The bankers' pool, in fact, turned out a sorry fiasco. Without it, no doubt, the Exchange would have been forced to close, for it did supply bids at some price for the so-called pivotal stocks when, because of the panic and confusion in the market, there were no other bids available. It made a small profit, but it did not have a ghost of a chance of stemming the avalanche of selling that poured in from all over the country. The stock market had become too big. The days that followed are blurred in retrospect. Wall Street became a nightmarish spectacle.

The animal roar that rises from the floor of the Stock Exchange and which on active days is plainly audible in the Street outside, became louder, anguished, terrifying. The streets were crammed with a mixed crowd—agonized little speculators, walking aimlessly outdoors because they feared to face the ticker and the margin clerk; sold-out traders, morbidly impelled to visit the scene of their ruin; inquisitive individuals and tourists, seeking by gazing at the exteriors of the Exchange and the big banks to get a closer view of the national catastrophe; runners, frantically pushing their way through the throng of idle and curious in their effort to make deliveries of the unprecedented volume of securities which was being traded on the floor of the Exchange.

The ticker, hopelessly swamped, fell hours behind the actual trading and became completely meaningless. Far into the night, and often all night long, the lights blazed in the windows of the tall office buildings where margin clerks and bookkeepers struggled with the desperate task of trying to clear one day's business before the next began. They fainted at their desks; the weary runners fell exhausted on the marble floors of banks and slept. But within a few months they were to have ample time to rest up. By then thousands of them had been fired.

Agonizing scenes were enacted in the customers' rooms of the various brokers. There traders who a few short days before had luxuriated in delusions of wealth saw all their hopes smashed in a collapse so devastating, so far beyond their wildest fears, as to seem unreal. Seeking to save a little from the wreckage, they would order their stocks sold "at the market," in many cases to discover that they had not merely lost everything but were, in addition, in debt to the broker. And then, ironic twist, as like as not the next few hours' wild churning of the market would lift prices to levels where they might have sold out and had a substantial cash balance left over. Every move was wrong. The market seemed like an insensate thing that was wreaking a wild and pitiless revenge upon those who had thought to master it.

The DJIA fell as low as 272.30 that day, but rose to close at 299.50. It stayed near that level for a few days before all support disappeared. On Monday, October 28, it fell to 260.60. October 29 was "Black Tuesday." More than 16 million shares were traded—33 percent more than on October 24. The DJIA closed at 230.10 that day. In the Times, *Bell wrote, "Groups of men, with here and there a woman, stood about inverted glass bowls all over the city yesterday watching spools of ticker tape unwind and as the tenuous paper with its cryptic numerals grew longer at their feet their fortunes shrunk. Others sat stolidly on tilted chairs in the customers' rooms of brokerage houses and watched a motion picture of waning wealth as the day's quotations moved silently across a screen. It was among such groups as these, feeling the pulse of a feverish financial world whose heart is the Stock Exchange, that drama and perhaps tragedy were to be found . . . the crowds about the ticker tape, like friends around the bedside of a stricken friend, reflected in their faces the story the tape was telling. There were no smiles. There were no tears either. Just the camaraderie of fellow-sufferers. Everybody wanted to tell his neighbor how much he had lost. Nobody wanted to listen. It was too repetitious a tale. . . ."*

After a short-lived rally in the spring of 1930 pushed the Dow close to 300, its level just before the Crash, a steady two-year decline began. It hit a low near 42 in June 1932, having dropped 89 percent from its 1929 high.

The decline was more than just the collapse of a speculative bubble. The government reacted to the crisis in exactly the wrong way: hoping to limit speculation, it tightened credit. By raising interest rates and reducing liquidity it restrained business, pushing firms and individuals toward failure.

Congress also erred by passing the toughest tariff protections in the history of the country. Other countries responded by raising their tariffs, reducing the foreign market for U.S. goods.

In the 1932 presidential campaign, Democratic Party nominee Franklin Roosevelt called for government to play a stronger role in the economy. Republican President Herbert Hoover called Roosevelt's ideas "a radical departure" from America's system of free enterprise. Roosevelt received 22.8 million votes; Hoover received just 15.7 million. The reforms proposed by the Roosevelt administration and enacted by Congress led to a transformation of Wall Street.

Ben Graham Calls the Bottom, 1932

Benjamin Graham

"This series is one of the timeliest and most significant which could be proposed," gushed Forbes *magazine when presenting the first of three articles by a young and relatively unknown investment manager. "The author, a lecturer at Columbia University, and with many years of practical experience and study in business, finance and stock markets, will lead you through an amazing consideration of facts, to equally amazing conclusions."*

The hype was deserved.

Suppose you were the owner of a large manufacturing business.

Like many others, you lost money in 1931; the immediate prospects are not encouraging; you feel pessimistic and willing to sell out—*cheap*. A prospective purchaser asks you for your statement. You show him a very healthy balance sheet, indeed. It shapes up something like this:

Cash and U.S. Gov. Bonds	$8,500,000
Receivables and Merchandise	15,000,000
Factories, Real Estate, etc.	14,000,000
	37,500,000
Less owing for current accts	−1,300,000
Net Worth	36,200,000

The purchaser looks it over casually, and then makes you a bid of $5,000,000 for your business—the cash, Liberty Bonds and everything else included. Would you sell? The question seems like a joke, we admit. No one in his right mind would exchange 8½ million in cash for five million dollars, to say nothing of the 28 million more in other assets. But preposterous as such a transaction sounds, the many owners of White Motors stock who sold out between $7 and $8 per share did that very thing—or as close to it as they could come.

The figures given above represent White Motors' condition on December 31st last. At $7⅜ per share, the low price, the company's 650,000 shares were selling for $4,800,000—about 60 per cent of the cash and equivalent alone, and only *one-fifth of the net quick assets* [cash, marketable securities, and short-term receivables minus short-term debts]. There were no capital obligations ahead of the common stock, and the only liabilities were those shown above for current accounts payable.

The spectacle of a large and old established company selling in the market for such a small fraction of its quick assets is undoubtedly a startling one.

But the picture becomes more impressive when we observe that there are literally dozens of other companies which also have a quoted value less than their cash in bank. And more significant still is the fact that an amazingly large percentage of *all* industrial companies are selling for less than their *quick* assets alone—leaving out their plants and other fixed assets entirely.

This means that a great number of American businesses are quoted in the market for much less than their liquidating value; that in the best judgment of Wall Street, *these businesses are worth more dead than alive*.

For most industrial companies should bring, in *orderly* liquidation, at least as much as their quick assets alone. Admitting that the factories, real estate, etc., could not fetch anywhere near their carrying price, they should still realize enough to make up the shrinkage in the proceeds of the receivables and merchandise below book figures. If this is not a reasonable assumption there must be something radically wrong about the accounting methods of our large corporations.

A study made at the Columbia University School of Business under the writer's direction, covering some 600 industrial companies listed on the New York Stock Exchange, disclosed that over 200 of them—or fully one out of three—have been selling at less than their net quick assets. Over fifty of them have sold for less than their cash and marketable securities alone.

. . . Businesses have come to be valued in Wall Street on an entirely different basis from that applied to private enterprise. In good times the prices paid on the Stock Exchange were fantastically high, judged by ordinary business standards; and now, by the law of compensation, the assets of these same companies are suffering an equally fantastic undervaluation.

When Graham's first Forbes *article appeared, the Dow was at 42, its low following the 1929 crash. It had lost almost 90 percent of its value from its 1929 high.*

About the same time, Graham began work on a business textbook he had planned a few years earlier. Written with David Dodd, the book, Security Analysis, *laid the foundation for what has become known as "value investing," and became a bible for successful Graham disciples such as Warren Buffett. The book, which has appeared in five editions, has sold almost a million copies. The publisher still offers a reprint of the original edition for purists. (At a ceremony when David Dodd's daughter presented Buffett with her father's copy of the first edition, Buffett recalled a court case in which he was cross-examined by a lawyer who thought he had caught Buffett dissenting from the sacred text. As Buffett explained, the lawyer had quoted the third edition, which included the work of additional authors, rather than the first edition, which did not include the paragraph in question.)*

Roosevelt's "Banking Holiday," March 1933

President Franklin D. Roosevelt

More than five thousand banks shut down between the 1929 stock market crash and the March 1933 inauguration of Franklin Roosevelt. In the last lame-duck months of President Herbert Hoover's term, several states declared short banking suspensions.

The day after his inauguration, Roosevelt proclaimed a national four-day "banking holiday." In his first fireside chat, broadcast to the public by radio, he explained why.

I want to talk for a few minutes with the people of the United States about banking—with the comparatively few who understand the mechanics of banking but more particularly with the overwhelming majority who use banks for the making of deposits and the drawing of checks. I want to tell you what has been done in the last few days, why it was done, and what the next steps are going to be. I recognize that the many proclamations from State Capitols and from Washington, the legislation, the Treasury regulations, etc., couched for the most part in banking and legal terms should be explained for the benefit of the average citizen. I owe this in particular because of the fortitude and good temper with which everybody has accepted the inconvenience and hardships of the banking holiday. I know that when you understand what we in Washington have been about I shall continue to have your cooperation as fully as I have had your sympathy and help during the past week.

First of all let me state the simple fact that when you deposit money in a bank the bank does not put the money into a safe deposit vault. It invests your money in many different forms of credit—bonds, commercial paper, mortgages and many other kinds of loans. In other words, the bank puts your money to work to keep the wheels of industry and of agriculture turning around. A comparatively small part of the money you put into the bank is kept in currency—an amount which in normal times is wholly sufficient to cover the cash needs of the average citizen. In other words the total amount of all the currency in the country is only a small fraction of the total deposits in all of the banks.

What, then, happened during the last few days of February and the first few days of March? Because of undermined confidence on the part of the public, there was a general rush by a large portion of our population to turn bank deposits into currency or gold—a rush so great that the soundest banks could not get enough currency to meet the demand. The reason for this was that on the spur of the moment it was, of course, impossible to sell perfectly sound assets of a bank and convert them into cash except at panic prices far below their real value.

By the afternoon of March 3 scarcely a bank in the country was open to do business. Proclamations temporarily closing them in whole or in part had been issued by the Governors in almost all the states.

It was then that I issued the proclamation providing for the nation-wide bank holiday, and this was the first step in the Government's reconstruction of our financial and economic fabric.

The second step was the legislation promptly and patriotically passed by the Congress confirming my proclamation and broadening my powers so that it became possible in view of the requirement of time to extend the holiday and lift the ban of that holiday gradually. This law also gave authority to develop a program of rehabilitation of our banking facilities. I want to tell our citizens in every part of the Nation that the national Congress—Republicans and Democrats alike—showed by this action a devotion to public welfare and a realization of the emergency and the necessity for speed that it is difficult to match in our history.

The third stage has been the series of regulations permitting the banks to continue their functions to take care of the distribution of food and household necessities and the payment of payrolls.

This bank holiday while resulting in many cases in great inconvenience is affording us the opportunity to supply the currency necessary to meet the situation. No sound bank is a dollar worse off than it was when it closed its doors last Monday. Neither is any bank which may turn out not to be in a position for immediate opening. The new law allows the twelve Federal Reserve banks to issue additional currency on good assets and thus the banks which reopen will be able to meet every legitimate call. The new currency is being sent out by the Bureau of Engraving and Printing in large volume to every part of the country. It is sound currency because it is backed by actual, good assets.

As a result we start tomorrow, Monday, with the opening of banks in the twelve Federal Reserve bank cities—those banks which on first examination by the Treasury have already been found to be all right. This will be followed on Tuesday by the resumption of all their functions by banks already found to be sound in cities where there are recognized clearing houses. That means about 250 cities of the United States.

On Wednesday and succeeding days banks in smaller places all through the country will resume business, subject, of course, to the Government's physical ability to complete its survey. It is necessary that the reopening of banks be extended over a period in order to permit the banks to make applications for necessary loans, to obtain currency needed to meet their requirements and to enable the Government to make common sense checkups. Let me make it clear to you that if your bank does not open the first day you are by no means justified in believing that it will not open. A bank that opens on one of the subsequent days is in exactly the same status as the bank that opens tomorrow.

I know that many people are worrying about State banks not members of the Federal Reserve System. These banks can and will receive assistance from member banks and from the Reconstruction Finance Corporation. These state banks are following the same course as the national banks except that they get their licenses to resume business from the state authorities, and these authorities have been asked by the Secretary of the Treasury to permit their good banks to open up on the same schedule as the national banks. I am confident that the state banking departments will be as careful as the National Government in the policy relating to the opening of banks and will follow the same broad policy. It is possible that when the banks resume a very few people who have not recovered from their fear may again begin withdrawals. Let me make it clear that the banks will take care of all needs—and it is my belief that hoarding during the past week has become an exceedingly unfashionable pastime. It needs no prophet to tell you that when the people find that they can get their money—that they can get it when they want it for all legitimate purposes—the phantom of fear will soon be laid. People will again be glad to have their money where it will be safely taken care of and where they can use it conveniently at any time. I can assure you that it is safer to keep your money in a reopened bank than under the mattress.

The success of our whole great national program depends, of course, upon the cooperation of the public—on its intelligent support and use of a reliable system.

Remember that the essential accomplishment of the new legislation is that it makes it possible for banks more readily to convert their assets into cash than was the case before. More liberal provision has been made for banks to borrow on these assets at the Reserve Banks and more liberal provision has also been made for issuing currency on the security of those good assets. This currency is not fiat currency. It is issued only on adequate security—and every good bank has an abundance of such security.

One more point before I close. There will be, of course, some banks unable to reopen without being reorganized. The new law allows the Government to assist in making these reorganizations quickly and effectively and even allows the Government to subscribe to at least a part of new capital which may be required.

I hope you can see from this elemental recital of what your government is doing that there is nothing complex, or radical in the process.

We had a bad banking situation. Some of our bankers had shown themselves either incompetent or dishonest in their handling of the people's funds. They had used the money entrusted to them in speculations and unwise loans. This was of course not true in the vast majority of our banks but it was true in enough of them to shock the people for a time into a sense of insecurity and to put them into a frame of mind where they did not differentiate, but seemed to assume that the acts of a comparative few had tainted them all. It was the Government's job to straighten out this situation and do it as quickly as possible—and the job is being performed.

I do not promise you that every bank will be reopened or that individual losses will not be suffered, but there will be no losses that possibly could be avoided; and there would have been more and greater losses had we continued to drift. I can even promise you salvation for some at least of the sorely pressed banks. We shall be engaged not merely in reopening sound banks but in the creation of sound banks through reorganization. It has been wonderful to me to catch the note of confidence from all over the country. I can never be sufficiently grateful to the people for the loyal support they have given me in their acceptance of the judgment that has dictated our course, even though all of our processes may not have seemed clear to them.

After all there is an element in the readjustment of our financial system more important than currency, more important than gold, and that is the confidence of the people. Confidence and courage are the essentials of success in carrying out our plan. You people must have faith; you must not be stampeded by rumors or guesses. Let us unite in banishing fear. We have provided the machinery to restore our financial system; it is up to you to support and make it work.

It is your problem no less than it is mine. Together we cannot fail.

In the week after the holiday, about five thousand banks — three-quarters of the banks in the Federal Reserve System — opened their doors. Much of the currency that had been withdrawn in earlier bank runs was redeposited.

Matthew Josephson, an author who worked briefly at a brokerage, surveyed Wall Street a week after the holiday ended. "I went down to the Street," he recalled years later, "and found the financial district so quiet it seemed like a ghost town. Many brokerage firms had closed down; the rest functioned with skeleton staffs. Just before the opening bell at 10:00 A.M. I entered the board room of one of the leading firms founded by members of one of America's 'Sixty Families.' A younger scion of that family, whom I had known for some years, was now managing partner of the firm. He greeted me good-humoredly as an 'early bird.' In a spacious room that could have held a hundred or more persons, I saw only two or three gloomy customers, who watched the opening in silence. I had brought with me some government bonds, the fragments of my small estate, which had been well liquidated in 1931, and asked the broker to sell them and invest the proceeds in ten different 'blue chip' industrials. We bought some shares of General Electric, Union Carbide, and J. C. Penney Stores, ranging from $10½ to $20 per share, with a conservative margin of 50 percent. The broker looked at me as if I were quite a brave fellow."

"He Knows All the Tricks of the Trade," 1933

Matthew Josephson

The Securities Exchange Act, created to regulate and police financial markets, marks the beginning of modern Wall Street. Prior to that, the first rule of laissez-faire capitalism applied: Buyer Beware. Suddenly, with the Securities and Exchange Commission supervising the Street, sellers had a responsibility to disclose truthful information, and brokers were obliged to treat their customers fairly.

The new SEC offered something to anger everyone. Wall Street, of course, chafed under its new collar. New Dealers, delighted by the new laws, were shocked at President Roosevelt's choice of SEC chairman: Joseph Kennedy, father of the political clan. Kennedy, whose fortune had come from bootlegging during Prohibition, had ruthlessly exploited the Street's lack of regulation.

Matthew Josephson, best known as author of The Robber Barons *and* The Money Lords, *briefly had a job on Wall Street.*

Kennedy, who actually believed he had made Roosevelt President, had received no Cabinet appointment, but he had an inside line to what was going on in Washington. In the early spring of 1933 it was known that the end of prohibition was drawing near; bottles would be needed, at first for beer, later for whisky and gin. Kennedy therefore became a participant in an important pool that would operate in the stock of Libbey-Owens-Ford Glass Company.

In this case the cream of the jest was that Libbey-Owens-Ford manufactured chiefly plate glass, not bottles. But the gullible part of the speculative public, dreaming of "repeal" stocks, confused its business purpose with that of the Owens Illinois Glass Company (which did make bottles). Elisha Walker, the man whom A. P. Giannini had recently driven out of the Transamerica Corporation, noticed that Libbey-Owens-Ford was depressed in price, and on learning that the company needed cash, he arranged for the pool to take an option on 125,000 shares of its stock at a price well below the current market. Joe Kennedy's share was about one-fifth of that block. Amid tremendous trading generated by market riggers the stock of Libbey-Owens-Ford rose nearly 50 percent within a few weeks, and the pool made a substantial profit.

Joe Kennedy's reputation in Wall Street was that of a "loner"; he would take part in a pool of Smith and Bragg, but he also operated secretly on his own. In R. J. Whelan's informed biography of the elder Kennedy, it is demonstrated that he was one of the toughest operatives in the Street and regarded as a bit too ruthless even by his hard-boiled associates, Smith, Bragg, et al.

In his pool operations—though not in the Libbey-Owens-Ford business—he generally concealed himself by means of an agent or a dummy corporation, for he counted on receiving some high political appointment. In business, as in politics, Kennedy deployed all the arts of the born manipulator.

Roosevelt's liberal followers were astonished when, in June, 1934, only a few months after the little scandal of the Libbey-Owens-Ford pool, it was announced by the White House that Kennedy was to be appointed chairman of the newly established Securities and Exchange Commission! Most people had expected that [James L.] Landis [a law professor who helped draft Roosevelt's new securities laws] or [Judge Ferdinand] Pecora would have that office; but it was known that Wall Street hated Pecora, and Baruch, on being consulted, gave his approval to the choice of Kennedy, who was keen to have the job. One wag among the New Dealers remarked that "naming Joe Kennedy as chairman of the SEC was like setting a wolf to guard a flock of sheep."

To his intimates Roosevelt explained that the eminent plunger had made his pile and had promised to stay out of the market. He "knows all the tricks of the trade," Roosevelt added. There was also the political debt owing Kennedy for his donations to the Democratic Party chest, an important consideration. The Wall Street community was amused at finding Joe Kennedy in the role of reformer and cop, but made no objections. He was Irish, one of the Street's nouveaux riches; when he had once tried to do business with the younger Morgan, he had been snubbed; and it was known that he bore no love for the hierarchs of the financial community.

Up to the last moment [NYSE president Richard] Whitney had

fought for the autonomy of the Exchange and repeatedly declared that the SEC law would destroy the free market. But once the law came into force he reversed himself completely and announced that the New York Stock Exchange would cooperate "one hundred percent" with the Commission. (Some thought Whitney's abrupt reversal comic.)

The SEC marked a decisive change in the relationship of the Government to the economy. Some held that the provisions of the law were innocuous or depended on their application by the Commissioners and their being tested in the Courts. The law indeed moved into untrodden ground, legally speaking; its main purpose was to require "truth in securities," that is, in dealings in securities. Registration of all corporate securities listed on Exchanges—and later the unlisted as well—was requisite, and with it explicit information about the corporation, far more than ever published hitherto. Options to syndicates, or pools, on blocks of stock at prices more advantageous than the current market were prohibited; and insiders or directors were forbidden to use their knowledge of their company's affairs for short-term profits in trading. Pool operations and rigging were barred, and short selling was limited to sales of one-eighth of a point above the last sale. There were even clauses in the law that forbade a man's "claiming ignorance of what his wife was doing in the market," or, in other words, evading responsibility by transfer of shares to a wife or child. Finally, violators of the law were made subject to fines of up to $10,000 and/or terms of imprisonment. Thus it was expected that the free market would no longer go unbridled as before.

At the beginning of the new regime some old-timers sulked and growled. One man vented his bitterness at a law which would compel insiders of a corporation to turn over their market profits to their corporation treasuries, while they must bear any losses they sustained themselves. "That, I say," he exclaimed, "is downright confiscation, or our constitution is nothing but a scrap of paper!"

Others, however, who operated many-branched houses for small investors, said that the SEC law would be recognized in time as "the greatest thing that has ever happened to Wall Street."

Another law of great importance to Wall Street was the Glass-Steagall Act. It split investment banks, which sell stocks and bonds, from com-

mercial banks, which accept deposits from individuals. The idea was to separate the public's money from capital markets, preventing common abuses such as banks investing in high-risk stocks, sometimes as an original underwriter with responsibility for reselling the securities to the public; banks making questionable loans as a means of boosting the prices of stocks it owned; and bank salespeople pitching to customers the securities the bank most needed to sell. The insurance business was also separated from banking.

After a few decades, banks found ways around Glass-Steagall. In the 1970s, Merrill Lynch developed the "Cash Management Account," which allowed people to write checks against their funds at the brokerage; other firms soon copied that idea. Commercial retail banks later set up "independent" investment firms.

After several attempts, opponents of Glass-Steagall succeeded in repealing the act in 1999.

The Harder They Fall, 1938

Ferdinand Pecora and The New York Times

The bull market of the 1920s hid a multitude of management sins and a few outright crimes. The truth came out during the Depression. Ivar Kreuger, who built a billion-dollar empire out of a match company, committed suicide when his fraud was exposed in 1932. Joseph Harriman, president of Harriman National Bank and Trust, was convicted of embezzlement. Samuel Insull, who assembled a multibillion-dollar collection of public utility companies, fled to Greece to avoid trial for embezzlement and fraud. Extradited, he was tried and acquitted. Albert Wiggin, head of Chase National Bank, was found to have shorted the bank's stock before and during the 1929 crash, when he was in charge of maintaining its price. From September to November of 1929, he made more than $4 million.

And then there was Richard E. Whitney, president of the New York Stock Exchange. In 1933, when the Roosevelt administration was preparing the Securities Exchange Act, the Senate Committee on Banking and Currency called many witnesses from Wall Street. Ferdinand Pecora, counsel for the committee, recalled Whitney's arrogance in particular:

The official Stock Exchange point of view, as expressed by Mr. Richard E. Whitney, its President, held that it was a "perfect institution": its members were high-minded; its officers vigilant; its rules were adequate. . . . The Exchange bore no responsibility, and ought to have none, for the truth of statements in prospectuses and other information relative to the securities which were listed upon its board. Its sole function was to act as a market place for the sale and exchange of stocks and bonds, a place where the laws of supply and demand might play themselves out free of all extraneous interference.

The Exchange authorities not only defended their practices, but did so on the highest moral grounds. Said Mr. Richard Whitney: "The policies of the New York Stock Exchange have resulted from a century-old experience. The New York Stock Exchange has been fully aware of its serious responsibilities."

The Exchange's refusal to pay heed to popular demand for reform was, he declared, simply a manifestation of "courage to do those things which are right, regardless of how unpopular they may be for the time being. . . . The Exchange is a market place. . . . If a market place for securities is to fulfill its function in the economic order of things, it must fairly and honestly permit the forces of supply and demand to determine prices. The Exchange, as an institution, must be impartial."

It was admitted, of course, that there were some abuses, and these were condemned in principle, but it was not admitted that they obtained widely in practice. The officers indeed had heard rumors of wrongdoing, but only seldom had they actually discovered it.

In 1938, Whitney was no longer president of the Exchange, but he continued to influence its administration, meanwhile maintaining his haughty image of old-fashioned virtue. It was nothing more than a front.

Five minutes after trading at the New York Stock Exchange began on March 8, 1938, the gong announcing a halt was sounded. Traders looked toward the rostrum and fell quiet. A somber man read a brief announcement, after which the Exchange released a written statement:

In the course of an examination of the affairs of Richard Whitney & Company, the Committee on Business Conduct discovered on March 1, 1938, evidence of conduct apparently contrary to just and equitable principles of trade, and on Monday, March 7, 1938, at 1:30 p.m. presented to a special meeting of the Governing Committee charges and specifications. Hearing on the charges was set for March 17, 1938. This morning the firm of Richard Whitney & Company advised the Exchange that it was unable to meet its obligations and its suspension for insolvency was announced from the rostrum of the Exchange shortly after 10:00 a.m.

No doubt the New York Times *story of April 12 was read with some delight in Washington:*

Richard Whitney spent last night in a cell in the Tombs prison and will be taken in handcuffs to Sing Sing by train today in the company of two extortioners who used to be lawyers, a gunman and a man convicted of rape.

Immediately after he had been sentenced yesterday by Judge Owen W. Bohan to serve from five to ten years, he vetoed the suggestion made to the court by his counsel, Charles H. Tuttle, that he might at least be sent to prison alone. He said he wanted no favors, and thereby won the approval of Deputy Sheriff Matthew Larkin, who took him from the court room in General Session to lodge him in the Tombs for the night. The deputy sheriff would otherwise have had to make a special trip with him to Sing Sing.

It was learned this was the opening of Whitney's attempt to win good-behavior marks, after Mr. Tuttle explained to him that his sentence could thereby be shortened to three years and four months of actual servitude, if the Parole Board is satisfied he will not revert to crime.

He had already eliminated himself for life from the security business before he appeared for sentence yesterday morning, by signing consent to a permanent injunction by Attorney General John J. Bennett, Jr.

It was on this injunctive farewell to the business in which he had once ruled as president of the New York Stock Exchange and on a final appeal by Mr. Tuttle to Judge Bohan that Whitney depended to the last for leniency. He had staked everything in the security business until he was caught, and then he had thrown his hand in, staking everything once more on complete confession.

He stood with his feet planted, hands behind his back, listening attentively while Mr. Tuttle reminded the judge of this and added that Whitney had "neither avoided the law nor chosen the coward's course of flight from the country or from life."

"He still has courage," said Mr. Tuttle. "He still has character. Though his former prominence made confession inexpressibly hard and an unspeakable punishment in itself, nevertheless he has confessed. He has faced his friends, which perhaps is the hardest task of all. The strengthening and redemptive power of confession is a spiritual truth taught by every religion and all human experience.

"Fortunately the losses which his wrongdoing has caused have not fallen upon many persons and certainly upon none of slender means. Nor has there been claim that his acts were with any purpose of permanent spoliation. The spectacle of his fall constitutes in itself a deterrent which no one in like station will soon have the hardihood to defy; and the process of reconstitution and the material for it are already manifest.

"Save for his counsel, he stands here alone. He has chosen to drain this bitter cup by himself, without even the presence of those persons who sought the opportunity to intercede and who expressed the wish to be with him today.

"Even his own brother [George Whitney, partner of J. P. Morgan & Co.], who desired most earnestly permission to stand by him at this bar today, shoulder to shoulder, is at Mr. Whitney's own imperative wish now with the loyal wife and two daughters upon whom the shadow of grief and desolation today falls."

Mr. Tuttle spoke for half an hour and left no indication where, between a suspended sentence and the maximum of twenty years, he thought justice would be served.

Whitney's head advanced perceptibly as Judge Bohan addressed him directly, and he turned his right ear slightly, the better to hear. It was several minutes before he realized that the judge was reading, not talking, and that Mr. Tuttle's impassioned plea had fallen on a prepared manuscript. His face seemed to sag for a moment. Then he pulled himself back to the same impassive front. "The Court has carefully read the memorandum filed by the District Attorney (Thomas E. Dewey), the Probation Report and the Psychiatric Report," said the prepared judgment which the Court thereafter released. "Were you the ordinary type of cashier or other faithless employee, the Court might be disposed to temper justice with mercy. It is apparent, however, from the memorandum filed by the District Attorney, that your criminal conduct has extended over a period of six years.

"To cover up your thefts and your insolvency, you resorted to larcenies, frauds, misrepresentations and falsifications of books and financial statements causing losses of several millions of dollars. As a result of your misconduct you were caught, to use your own words, 'like a rat in a trap.'

"Your acts have been deliberate and intentional and were committed with an unusually full opportunity for understanding their effect upon others and the consequences to yourself. You have enjoyed the advantage of the best education in America; you had the fruits of business and financial success; you had bestowed upon you the confidence and trust of testamentary benefactors and were repeatedly chosen as spokesman of one of the largest financial markets in the world. All these you have betrayed.

"I can find nothing in your record to mitigate the sentence which I am about to pronounce."

Whitney barely waited to hear the judge declare the indeterminate sentence of five to ten years would cover both of his pleas of guilty, one for the theft of $109,000 in securities from the New York Yacht Club and the other for the theft of $105,000 in securities from the estate of George R. Sheldon, his father-in-law.

He picked up his blue topcoat and gray felt hat and grimly faced left, holding up one elbow slightly as if he expected it to be taken. It was. He was marched into the pen behind the court room.

By noontime he had first felt handcuffs, when Deputy Sheriff Larkin handcuffed him in order to take him across the Bridge of Sighs from the Criminal Building into the Tombs. Thereafter he sat motionless on the cot of the cell in which he was locked, alone.

Dr. Walter Bromberg, head of the [state's] psychiatric clinic, [had] appeared in the court room to verify the board's conclusion that Whitney's psychologic reactions are "urbane and sportsman-like."

The Bromberg report gave Whitney an "intelligence rating which could not be equalled by more than 1 per cent of the American population," but it adds: "He was sometimes stubborn and at no time did he believe he would run afoul of the law."

A further appraisal of Whitney's character in the report of Irving W. Halpern, chief probation officer, declared that "contributing factors in his delinquency are pride, obstinacy, unshakable belief in his own financial judgment and a gambling instinct."

From Sing Sing came word last night that Warden Lewis E. Lawes intended to put Whitney through the usual prison routine.

When he arrives there today, therefore, he will doff the double-breasted blue flannel suit of yacht club style which he wore when imprisoned and will get into gray shoddy. Richard Whitney will become a number.

Whitney's brother George repaid all the debts. Whitney was paroled in 1941.

PART EIGHT

Wall Street Goes to Main Street

"During the past few years we have been trying to readjust our-selves. Some of us have been a little slow in realizing that the readjustment has to be permanent . . ."

"A Declaration of Policy," Charles E. Merrill and

E. A. Pierce, 1940

Timeline

1939 — WWII begins

1940 — France falls to Germany in June; U.S. markets follow

1943 — With men at war, women work on NYSE floor

1944 — Bretton Woods (VT) Conf. pegs international currencies to U.S. dollar; creates International Monetary Fund and World Bank

1946–52 — Marshall Plan rebuilds Europe, in contrast to harsh policies following WWI

1948 — National Labor Relations Board lets unions demand pensions

1949 — 8-year bull market begins

1949 — U.S. brings antitrust suit against AT&T, previously denoted "natural monoply"

1951 — First cross-country direct long-distance

1952 — Saturday trading ends

1953 — NY Curb Exchange becomes American Stock Exchange

1954 — DJIA rises above 1929 peak

1954 — First proxy battle: Robert Young wins NY Central RR

1955 — Ike's heart attack sparks short sell-off, September 24

1956 — DJIA closes above 500 (500.24), March 12

1957 — European Economic Community (EEC, also "Common Market") est. to coordinate trade policy

1959 — 12.5 million Americans own stock

1960 — Organization of Petroleum Exporting Countries (OPEC) est.

1961 — Average daily NYSE volume 4+ million shares, nearly triple the level immediately following the war

1961 — SEC says insider trading illegal

1962 — 10-year bull market ends; stocks lose 25 percent

News from the Home Front

11 *Wall*

*In an editorial on December 8, 1941, the Wall Street Journal fore-
cast great economic changes: "War with Japan means industrial
revolution in the United States," it said. "The American productive
machine will be reshaped with but one purpose—to produce the
maximum of things needed to defeat the enemy. It will be a brutal
process. It implies intense, almost fantastic stimulation for some industries; strict rationing for others; inevitable, complete liquidation
for a few. War with Japan will be a war of great distances. Thus,
certainly in its preliminary stages and probably for the duration, it
will be a war of the sea and the air. This means unlimited quantities of ships and shells, bombers and bombs, oil, gasoline." Bull's-
eye.*

*And though fortunes were made on Wall Street as a result of
war spending, the Street's self-interest and cynicism also gave way
to patriotism and compassion. Men who swapped NYSE trading
posts for U.S. Army and Navy posts kept up with news from home
by reading 11 Wall, a mimeographed monthly. The items that follow were written after reports of D Day and V-J Day reached the
Exchange.*

JUNE 1944

Dear Fellows:

There weren't many letters this past month but, when
the reports of the actions on the different fronts came
in, we understood. We were thrilled as we learned just
what you were doing. Came the news from the Far East,
then the advance past Rome, and finally, at 12:39 A.M.

on June 6th, an announcer broke in on a music program with "The German D.N.B. news announces that allied troops have landed on the coast of France. This is an enemy broadcast and until we receive official confirmation this report must not be accepted on the basis of rumor. Programs will be interrupted to give you latest reports." Who slept? Lights shining through apartment and house windows made midnight seem like early evening. As the news spread, and it did with the speed of lightning, so shone more and more lights. For more than two hours nothing but news items from enemy broadcasts. Then, around 3 o'clock, the news was officially confirmed by General Eisenhower's headquarters. All of us were welded to our radios. We prayed.

New York wasn't New York on June 6th. Sure there were people here, their bodies, anyway, but all their thoughts were elsewhere. All churches were open for prayer. All sports events were canceled. Trinity [Church] received a constant stream of people, at all hours. At St. Patrick's Cathedral the crowds were so large that some worshipers knelt on the steps. At eleven sharp on the Exchange the bell rang, trading halted instantly, not even a 'phone rang, and John Coleman read General Eisenhower's order of the day. Two minutes of silent prayer followed. Everyone was visibly affected. Never in the history of the Exchange was there such powerful and deep silence. Prices that followed were firm and the market closed strong.

SEPTEMBER 1945

Dear Fellows:

Did you ever want to shake someone's hand, to slap them on the back affectionately, want them with you, to sing and exchange warm greetings . . . and talk excitedly . . . when they were miles away? That's what we wanted to do; that's how we felt, with the steam blow-ing the lid off the kettle amid the paper blizzard of August 14. Useless and lost, but ever so happy, is inadequate description of our emotions that day, wishing you were here to join with us in celebrating the end of a long and terrible war. To us, however, came poignantly the warm realization that we would be privileged to sit down with you soon. So, please, now that your major job is done, hurry home . . . hurry . . . hurry . . . hurry.

Bob Raymond, perhaps anticipating our plea, did just that, flew in the other day from Italy, and from the other direction came Clarence Buttenweiser, from Hawaii. The path has been beaten, from both directions, so come on along, all of you, as fast as you can.

We realize that many are already on the way, on the seas and in the air. We know it from those we see daily and, also, from the constantly growing bundles of returned news letters, for want of current addresses. Which suggests the thought that this may be our swan song, a last news letter which, because of what it signifies, we have been wanting to put together for a long time.

The absence of men during the war led to a historical first: The New York Stock Exchange allowed women on the Exchange floor. They were barred again after the men returned.

Wall Street Goes to Main Street, 1940

Charles E. Merrill and E. A. Pierce

Merrill Lynch, Pierce, Fenner & Beane was the most successful brokerage in the half century that followed the creation of the Securities and Exchange Commission.

Merrill's success with individual investors was a goal from the beginning. In a 1940 "policy statement" that also served as a savvy marketing cream puff, the managers outlined their philosophy.

That it needed to be described in detail reveals much about how brokers operated before the SEC and the public's distrust afterward.

In fact, during the entire 1940s Wall Street failed fully to benefit from the growth in the economy. Though the Dow Jones Industrial Average doubled, it fell short of the much greater growth in corporate profits. The public, remembering 1929, still had little taste for investing. Merrill and Pierce hoped to make stocks palatable again.

A DECLARATION OF POLICY

CHARLES E. MERRILL AND E. A. PIERCE

TO PARTNERS AND MANAGERS:

We are glad to be able, at last, to write you in some detail about this new firm of ours.

We think you will want to know more about what led to the consolidation of the three companies—E. A. Pierce & Co., Cassatt & Co., Incorporated, and Merrill, Lynch & Co., Inc.—and you will want to know where we go from here.

The first part of the story is simple. It deals with problems with which we are unfortunately all too familiar—problems of general business depression from which our industry has not even begun to recover. In the security business, as in others, the collapse shook our houses beneath us.

SECURITY BUSINESS PERFORMS AN ESSENTIAL SERVICE

During the past few years we have been trying to readjust ourselves. Some of us have been a little slow in realizing that the readjustment has to be permanent, and a few doubt the possibilities of any successful readjustment. Nevertheless, we are convinced that the buying and selling of stocks, bonds, and other evidences of liens and ownerships is a fundamental business that performs an essential service. . . . The sooner we recognize that the temper of living may never again be identical with what it was twelve or fifteen years ago, the sooner we shall gear ourselves for success under present and future conditions.

ALL MUST JOIN TO REESTABLISH FAITH

We've got a job to do—we in the security business—a job of reestablishing faith in the security market as a place for sound investment. . . .

OUR SUCCESS DEPENDS ON SERVICE TO THE PUBLIC

These policies rest on a conviction—not always uppermost in our minds, we'll grant you—that in order to win success we business men have to put the public's interest first. The customer may not always be right, but he has rights, and upon our recognition of his rights and our desire to satisfy them, rests our chance to succeed. It's not banal poppycock to say today that we've got to succeed through the service we can render the investing public. And it's only looking facts in the face to say that a legitimate, honest service is the only justification for success.

. . . Disturbing is the large percentage of potential investors and speculators in securities who are suspicious of the motives and operations of the security business and the people engaged therein. You and we know the reasons for this lack of confidence and we know that it won't be eliminated until we convince the public that our house is now in order.

CONFIDENCE, IN THE MAIN, IS ON THE INCREASE

. . . Our plan is based on our appraisal of what our firms ought to do to meet this situation. If we do the best we can, and if we have properly adjudged what the investing public wants, our plan will succeed.

Here are the ideas which we have developed, and have incorporated in a statement of policy which starts out by saying:

Policies and services of Merrill Lynch, E. A. Pierce & Cassatt were formulated in a spirit of enlightened self-interest. While based on the conviction that they constitute an important advance in both facilities and protection for the investor and speculator, they represent primarily the kind of a brokerage service that we believe will have the greatest chance for enduring success. It is our opinion, as well, that the customer is entitled to this modernized form of brokerage service.

FINANCIAL STABILITY AS THE KEYSTONE

The first specific matter set forth in this statement has to do with financial stability, the keystone of our entire operation.

... The firm will at all times maintain a working capital position well in excess of the requirements of the New York Stock Exchange.

The second objective will be attained by the issuance of a complete financial statement, in a form designed for maximum clarity and understanding.

Now in the matter of departmental policy: we operate a brokerage business in securities and commodities, and also underwrite and distribute securities. But these are two distinct businesses, with entirely separate functions. No conditions will be permitted which might create conflicts affecting the interests of our several types of customers.

TO HELP OUR CUSTOMERS APPRAISE
THE POSSIBILITY OF BIAS

In practically all transactions for account of customers the firm will act only as a commission broker. However, in transactions involving securities in which the firm acts as principal dealer, the customer will be notified in advance.

When supplying informative analytical printed reports concerning a security in which the firm is not acting as principal, the firm intends to indicate in such reports the extent of the aggregate direct and indirect ownership of such security. ...

This has been a general objective of brokers during recent years, but we intend to test this specific practical application as a part of our plans for the year 1940.

PLEDGE AID FOR STILL FURTHER PROTECTION

You may be interested in knowing how your senior partners feel about the SEC. We'll tell you. We are in full accord with the fundamental purpose of the Securities and Exchange laws—to give the investor adequate information, and to prohibit manipulation and fraud—and we pledge to our customers a complete cooperation with all future efforts designed to strengthen further these fundamental purposes.

No regulations or policies, however, can pretend to guarantee profits nor insure against loss. But we believe our customers can confidently use the Exchanges for investment and speculation with assurance that there are no stacked cards.

OUR RESEARCH DEPARTMENT WILL STICK TO FACTS—CLEARLY PRESENTED

Now as to the question of advising the customer on his investments: we don't believe we can run a brokerage firm and be a good investment counsel at the same time . . . In other words, we are going to provide facts, ungarnished with advice. Advice is going to be out—unless it is specifically asked for, and then only with the approval of one of our partners or managers.

RUMORS AND "HOT TIPS" ARE TABOO

Let's take a look at our registered representatives, or customer's men. They are going to represent an important phase of our new job, principally because we think we are going to make it possible for them to operate on a different and sounder basis than in the past. One of the troubles in our business has been a potential conflict of interest between the customer and the customer's man, created by compensation practices which we believe were wrong. We're going to minimize, perhaps even eliminate, that potential conflict of interest.

Between ourselves, we think the best name for these men is service representatives, because it best expresses what we would like them to be in our organization . . . [T]hey will assist their customers in getting all desired factual data; they will offer no advice as to the purchase or sale of securities or commodities except under restrictions mentioned a few paragraphs back; they will circulate no rumors, "confidential suggestions," or "hot tips" . . .

SECURITY BUSINESS IMPORTANT TO OUR WHOLE PEOPLE

In closing, we'd like to express our unshakable confidence in the future of our country, in the basic soundness of our type of economy—capitalism—and in the essential place that the security business has in that economy. . . .

In 1980, Citicorp chairman Walter B. Wriston, who had grown his institution to the limits of the Glass-Steagall Act, sketched "The Bank of the Future":

"It will take your funds for deposit and pay you close to money-market interest on them, up to the minute you take them out, by check or otherwise. It will give you medium- or short-term loans, or a mortgage on your home. It will invest your surplus funds in anything from gold and real estate to commercial paper, commodities futures, or the stock market. It will insure your life, your mortgage, or your business. It will underwrite stock issues for that business or negotiate a private placement, or arrange a merger. It will do all this electronically in most major cities of the world, and it will let you take your account with you wherever you go. In fact, the bank of the future will help you sell your old house and buy a new one somewhere else simultaneously. The bank of the future will do all this because the customer of the future will be satisfied with nothing less. And the customer already knows that he can demand all this because the bank of the future that I have described already exists.

"Don Regan runs it, and it's called Merrill Lynch, Pierce, Fenner & Smith."

The White Shark, 1954

Diana B. Henriques

Most coverage of the corporate raiders of the 1980s focused on the next big deal. Forgotten were their fascinating predecessors. For instance, during his successful 1954 battle for the New York Central Railroad, Robert Young introduced the proxy battle, in which appeals are made directly to shareholders rather than to management. In the next year more than thirty other proxy battles were fought. Raiders won six.

In her book The White Sharks of Wall Street, *reporter and author Diana B. Henriques tells the story of Wall Street players like Young, Louis Wolfson, and Thomas Mellon Evans—men who, though now obscure, were once greatly feared.*

In the business world of the late fifties—that hazy fax-free and pre-laptop era when a round-trip to the Coast took days and takeover battles took months—Thomas Mellon Evans was a widely recognized figure. A Daddy Warbucks lookalike, he was so familiar that business writers could use his name unexplained, just as the names of investment wizard Warren Buffett and entrepreneur Donald Trump would be used decades later. He was a controversial figure as well—a New Jersey congressman would later brand him "the white shark" and *Forbes* magazine called him "the man in the wolf suit." Long before Drexel's Michael Milken became a household name in the eighties by facilitating the use of junk bonds to finance hostile corporate takeovers, Tom Evans had used debt, cash, and the tax code to seize control of more than eighty American companies, small and large. Long before giant pension funds and other institutional investors began to lobby for "shareholder rights," Tom Evans was demanding that public companies operate only for their shareholders—not for their employees or their executives, not for their surrounding communities, but for the people who owned their stock. His view seemed selfish and harsh in the pallid institutional community of that day, but he preached it fiercely and effectively.

By 1959, Tom Evans already had become the leading practitioner of a strange new form of corporate ruthlessness, one that squeezed "fat" out of profitable corporations in the relentless pursuit of greater profit. By 1968, the *Wall Street Journal* had declared Tom Evans "something of a legend for his tough methods of operating the company once he wins control. He demands prompt profit performance from both assets and men; if he does not get it, he sells the assets or fires the men."

Yet, despite the swath that Tom Evans cut across America's corporate landscape in the fifties and early sixties, most of the people who poured into Wall Street in the eighties to practice "M&A"—mergers and acquisitions—had no idea they were standing on anyone's shoulders. They thought they were part of a new age, engaged in something history had never seen before. They were wrong. Everywhere they strode, Tom Evans had been there ahead of them.

Then, as now, raiders told shareholders a simple story: new, aggressive executives could "unlock the shareholder value" being ignored by self-satisfied and self-serving management. (Sometimes that story was accurate. Raider Lou Wolfson was rebuffed by Montgomery Ward's eighty-one-year-old chairman, Sewell Avery, a legend because he had been carried out of his office by two soldiers after refusing to comply with government regulations during World War II. Avery, convinced the country was due for a recession after the war, avoided expanding his chain at precisely the time his competitors were exploiting the growing suburbs. Montgomery Ward has since gone out of business.)

The empire of Thomas Mellon Evans was undone in part by nouveau raiders of the 1980s. Outbidding investor Robert Bass, who had put the company "in play," Robert Maxwell wrested the Macmillan publishing empire from Evans's son Ned in 1988. By then, Ned Evans was practically the Establishment. Few people remembered he had won control of Macmillan's board just eight years earlier.

"Securities Bazaar," October 1957

Carter Henderson

Chances are you have bought stock on the Nasdaq exchange. Chances are your parents or grandparents would have gasped at the thought. Before it became a high-tech operation known for even higher-tech companies, before it opened a Times Square headquarters with as many flashing lights as the nearby video game centers, the National Association of Securities Dealers was a place where people really had to hustle to make—literally—a dime.

In a cacophonic stock-trading room high in a skyscraper overlooking Wall Street's serene Trinity Church, a slim girl surrounded by Western Union teleprinters puts a red megaphone to her lips and bellows, "San Jacinto for Lundborg" at a shirt-sleeved, Napoleon-sized man seated a scant eight feet away.

"Thirty-one ah half two ah half," he yells back. He then swivels around, plugs a phone jack into a wildly buzzing switchboard and says, "You sold a hundred Food Mart at eleven three quarters." Seconds later, a lad tending two teletypes hollers, "Mick, Polaroid for Worchester." "Tell 'em thirty-eight-nine," the man fires back before gulping down a sip of lunchtime coffee and a mouthful of chicken soup.

The man in the midst of this madhouse is Milton "Mickey" Pauley, 51, a professional stock trader for Troster, Singer & Co., Wall Street specialists in buying and selling the thousands of stock issues traded outside America's 18 securities exchanges. His operations mirror the most varied, least known and zaniest securities bazaar in America—the over-the-counter stock market.

Mickey single-handedly trades more shares in a week than most investors do in a lifetime, knows which over-the-counter stocks the biggest brokers, banks and investment trusts are buying, and frequently picks up rumors of corporate developments—many right, some wrong—days before any news is released to the general public.

Mickey Pauley earns his living buying and selling unlisted stocks in competition with some of the smartest securities men in Wall Street—who often are better informed about market conditions than he is. Brokers, banks, dealers and other potential customers will do business with him only if his selling or buying price is as good or better than his competitors', whose quotations they also check.

Brokers buy and sell securities as agents for customers, charging a commission for the service. Dealers such as Troster Singer buy securities, maintain an inventory and try to sell their securities at a profit.

"During the past few weeks," says Mickey, "this over-the-counter market has been in an absolute turmoil. I've had to give up my usual custom of going out for an hour lunch with friends once or twice a week, and even canceled a trip to Canada. When the market is falling on its face, a stock trader like me has got to be in there trading stocks."

An estimated 50,000 to 60,000 different stocks are traded over the counter, compared with the roughly 3,000 listed on the New York Stock Exchange, American Stock Exchange, and the other formal trading arenas. The market is such a potpourri that $60,000 or so will get you one share of stock in the Los Angeles Turf Club, Inc., or some 3,500,000 shares in a penny stock such as Beehive Uranium Corp. If you like safe situations, the O.T.C. market offers shares in the Bank of New York and First National Bank of Boston, both of which have paid dividends continuously for 173 years. But if you're a bit of a gambler, you can buy shares of Tucker (Motor Car) Corp., which never paid a dividend, never sold a car, and went out of business in 1949.

The O.T.C. market deals in thousands of tightly held and rarely traded stocks such as Upjohn Co. that may go for a decade without more than a few dozen shares changing hands. But it also boasts stocks such as Tennessee Gas Transmission Co., Kaiser Steel Corp., Collins Radio Co., Anheuser-Busch, Inc., and Vitro Corp. of America, that are as actively traded as many stocks listed on the exchanges. This market, much to the chagrin of the New York Stock Exchange, also makes regular—if modest—markets in American Telephone & Telegraph Co., Standard Oil Co. (New Jersey), General Motors Corp. and many other Big Board darlings.

O.T.C. market trading primarily is conducted by nearly 4,000 dealers in cities and hamlets across the country who are members of the National Association of Securities Dealers, Inc. They range in size from small brokers who stand ready to buy or sell shares in a locally prominent firm, to Wall Street giants such as Merrill Lynch, Pierce, Fenner & Smith, Inc., Blyth & Co., Inc., Carl M. Loeb, Rhoades & Co., and Kidder, Peabody & Co. that deal in the shares of many of America's most famous firms. The latter four firms not only trade over the counter but, as members, deal in securities on most of the nation's major exchanges.

Troster Singer, which limits itself to the O.T.C. market, makes markets in some 535 stocks, handles 800 to 900 trades daily, and sometimes loses well over $10,000 a day, which puts it in the same league with the giants.

The trading room is divided by a worn wooden table, topped with telephone switchboards leading to some 150 Wall Street brokers and dealers. Along both walls there's a battery of teleprinters and teletype machines linking the room with a nation-wide network of other firms that trade with Troster Singer. Across the far end of the room, there's a green blackboard where a man wearing a telephone headset continuously chalks up the changing quotations on the most active stocks the company buys and sells.

Troster Singer has entrusted Mickey with a trading portfolio of stocks worth some $250,000, and from this base he battles to make a buck. In the course of a seven-hour working day, Mickey usually answers several hundred phone calls from customers asking him to quote his bid or offer on any stock he trades, but without disclosing whether they want to buy or sell. Mickey averages about one trade on every ten quotes he gives out, and considers a gross profit of one eighth of a point or 12½ cents on every share swapped to be a trading victory.

The NASD didn't become the institution we know today until the 1980s, when individual states relaxed the approval process for registering stocks for sale. It also helped that a few companies that didn't have the interest or the means to meet the requirements for listing on an exchange—companies like Microsoft and Intel, for instance—proved to be worthwhile investments.

Fidelity a-Go-Go
Boston, 1957–1965

John Brooks

Mutual funds are not native to Wall Street. "Investment trusts," as they used to be called, grew best in Boston. To investors who ranked reliability above returns, Boston's Puritan traditions were more comforting than the hurly-burly of Wall Street. Then along came Edward Johnson II, a Boston Brahmin with a gambler's heart.

John Brooks profiled Johnson and his protégé Gerald Tsai in his book about Wall Street in the 1960s, The Go-Go Years.

Although never a trustee by profession, Johnson was almost the Boston-trustee type personified. In the nineteen sixties, which corresponded roughly with *his* sixties, he was a spry, smallish, clean-cut man, proud of the hole-in-one he once made at La Gorce Country Club; in orthodox trustee style, he favored a battered hat and a bow tie.

The market bug first bit him in 1924 when he read a serialization in the old *Saturday Evening Post* of Edwin Lefèvre's *Reminiscences of a Stock Operator,* the story of the career of the famous speculator Jesse Livermore. "I'll never forget the thrill," he told a friend almost a half century later. "Everything was there, or else implied. Here was the picture of a world in which it was every man for himself, no favors asked or given. You were what you were, not because you were a friend of somebody, but for yourself. And Livermore—what a man, always betting his whole wad! A sure system for losing, of course, but the point was how much he loved it. Operating in the market, he was like Drake sitting on the poop of his vessel in a cannonade. Glorious!"

[In 1943] he was offered the opportunity to take over Fidelity Fund, another Boston mutual-fund operation that then managed only the unimpressive total of $3 million—and Johnson had an investment company of his very own.

It is particularly significant, in the light of subsequent events, that the man who turned the Fidelity organization over to him refused to take a nickel for it, in keeping with the traditional Boston concept of a trusteeship as a sacred charge rather than a vested interest to be bought and sold.

Right from the start, his approach to investing Fidelity funds was an unorthodox one that he would later describe in the following characteristically picturesque terms: "We didn't want to feel that we were married to a stock when we bought it. You might say that we preferred to think of our relationship to it as 'companionate marriage.' But that doesn't go quite far enough, either. Possibly now and again we liked to have a 'liaison'—or even, very occasionally, 'a couple of nights together.' "

His maverick operations as head of Fidelity, while they fell far short of creating a scandal on State Street, nevertheless caused a certain amount of talk there during the nineteen forties. What in Tophet had come over Edward Johnson, a good sound Boston and Harvard man if there ever was one? But what he was doing then was only the beginning, and the next stage in Fidelity's evolution began with Johnson's first encounter with Gerald Tsai, Jr.

This encounter occurred early in 1952, when Johnson received a telephone call from a friend of his at the investment counselling firm of Scudder, Stevens and Clark. "I've got a young Chinese here, a clever fellow, but we don't seem to have a place for him at the moment," the friend said. "Anything you can do for him?" Johnson asked his friend to send the young man around. When Tsai appeared, Johnson liked his looks and hired him on the spot as a junior stock analyst.

The young man, then twenty-four, had been born in Shanghai in 1928 to Westernized Chinese parents; his father had been educated at the University of Michigan and later become Shanghai district manager for the Ford Motor Company. In 1947, with the war over at last, the younger Tsai was sent to America to college.

The reader's attention need hardly be called to the similarity between Tsai's reason for liking the market and that of Edward Crosby Johnson II—"you were what you were not because you were a friend of somebody, but for yourself." Boston Yankee and Asian immigrant, they were kindred souls in appreciating the market's cool objectivity, which gave both a chance to escape any feeling of prejudice. That the polarity of the prejudice differed—differed, indeed, by precisely 180 degrees—was beside the point.

At Fidelity, Tsai was not long in making his mark. He showed himself to be a shrewd and decisive picker of stocks for short-term appreciation, and so swift and nimble in getting into and out of specific stocks that his relations with them, far from resembling a marriage or even a companionate marriage, were often more like those of a roué with a chorus line. Sometimes, to continue the analogy, the sheets were hardly cool when he was through with one and on to another. Johnson—"Mister" Johnson to Tsai, as he was to almost everyone else in his own organization and the mutual-fund business in general—was fascinated and ever so slightly scandalized.

By 1957 Tsai felt confident enough of his position at Fidelity to write Johnson a memo asking—indeed, very nearly demanding—permission to start his own growth fund. "It took him only half an hour to decide," Tsai recalled long afterward.

Fidelity Capital Fund was the company's first frankly speculative public growth fund. Right from the start, [Tsai] operated it in a way that was at the time considered almost out-and-out gambling. He concentrated Fidelity Capital's money in a few stocks that were then thought to be outrageously speculative and unseasoned for a mutual fund (Polaroid, Xerox, and Litton Industries among them). He bought in huge blocks of ten thousand shares or more at a time, coolly notifying his brokers that if they couldn't assemble the block without pushing the price up substantially—say, more than a point or two—the deal was off. The brokers grumbled, but usually assembled the large positions; with huge commissions at stake, if one broker wouldn't deal with Tsai according to Tsai's specifications another assuredly would. His annual portfolio turnover generally exceeded 100 percent, or a share traded for every one held—a rate of trading unheard of in institutional circles at the time. He got a well-deserved reputation for catlike quickness in calling a market turn. "It was a beautiful thing to watch his reactions," Johnson says. "What grace, what timing—glorious! Why, if he had been on the Stock Exchange floor, he'd have become its number one trader in no time."

After the Cuban missile crisis that October [1962] he suddenly turned decisively bullish. In six weeks, he put $26 million into stocks for Fidelity Capital; the market leaped upward, and by the end of the year the fund's asset value had risen nothing less than 68 percent within three months.

Tsai had now perfected his method, and over the following three years he had the ideal market in which to project it. Up and up went Fidelity Capital's asset value, and finally, for the vintage market year of 1965, the fund achieved a rise of not quite 50 percent on a turnover of 120 percent.

The go-go years had begun, and Jerry Tsai, more than any other one man, had brought them into being. Suddenly, he was nationally famous.

Once, more than a generation earlier, Johnson's hero Jesse Livermore had filled the same role, his every move and gesture studied by the hangers-on who hoped to ride to riches on his coattails. As once "Jesse Livermore is buying it!" had been the signal for a general stampede into any stock, so now it was "Jerry Tsai is buying it!" Like Livermore's, his prophecies by force of his reputation came to be to a certain extent self-fulfilling. His legend itself was self-perpetuating, and a move by him in or out of a stock could in itself add to, or subtract from, the market value of a given company by hundreds of millions of dollars in the space of a few hours. The federal securities laws, which had not been on the statute books to bother Livermore in his heyday, now categorically forbade manipulation of stocks. But what could the securities laws do about Tsai? Was it his fault that everyone else wanted to follow his bets?

Fidelity, as every investor knows, has dominated the mutual fund world for decades. Its Magellan Fund alone dwarfs most other mutual fund companies. Its former manager, Peter Lynch, though now "retired," still appears as the face of Fidelity in advertisements: a buttoned-down Bostonian with a passion for growth stocks.

PART NINE

Uneasy Street

"I said: 'Bob, I get the impression that you're involved in something that's kind of crazy. Do you want to go through life as a fugitive?' And he said, 'Well, if I'm going to be a fugitive, I'm going to be a very rich fugitive.' "

Bernard Cornfeld, chairman of the Investors Overseas Services mutual fund firm, to financier Robert Vesco, shortly before both men became fugitives.

Timeline

1963–1974 — Vietnam War

1964 — William Sharpe creates "beta" as risk measure

1965 — Warren Buffett buys textile co. Berkshire Hathaway

1966 — Electronic ticker displays introduced to NYSE

1966 — DJIA flirts with 1000, February 9 (will hit it in 1972)

1967 — Muriel Siebert first woman NYSE member, December 28

1967 — Yippies disrupt NYSE by tossing money on trading floor

1968 — First U.S. trade deficit since 1893

1968 — Go-Go stock market; but inflation looms

1968 — NYSE closes Wednesdays for paperwork

1969 — 29-year-old Saul Steinberg raids Chemical Bank

1969 — Jerome Pustilnik founds INSTINET, the first electronic trading network to link buyers and sellers anonymously

1970 — Joseph L. Searles III is first black NYSE member, February 12

1970 — Penn Central RR goes bust

1970 — NYSE's Donaldson, Lufkin & Jenrette goes public

1970 — Vietnam fears—stocks collapse briefly in May

1971 — Bretton Woods agreement ends, exchange rates float

1971 — International Monetary Market in Chicago est.

1972 — DJIA closes above 1000, November 14

1973 — Options-pricing theory published; its creators, Myron Scholes and Robert Merton, will win Nobel Prize

1973 — Chicago Board Options Exchange est.

1973 — Dollar devalued 10 percent to fight inflation, February 12

1973 — Equity Funding Corp. bankrupt

1973 — OPEC oil embargo following Middle East war

1974 — OPEC raises oil prices 400 percent

1974 — Inflation + stagnant economy = "stagflation"

1974 — Franklin National Bank admits largest failure ever

1974 — Fidelity Investments offers check writing

1974 — First modern hostile takeover, Inco vs. ESB

1975 — "May Day"—fixed commissions abolished on May 1

1975 — S&P has lost more than half its value since 1973

1976 — Vanguard offers first index fund for individuals

1976 — Designated Order Turnaround (DOT) system est.

1976 — Alice Jarcho is NYSE's first regular female floor trader

1977 — Peter Lynch named head of Fidelity's Magellan Fund

1977 — Merrill Lynch introduces Cash Management Account

1978 — Bankruptcy Reform Act—Chapter 11 est.

1978 — Intermarket Trading System (ITS) links NYSE and others

1979 — Paul Volcker named Federal Reserve chairman

1979 — "Saturday Night Massacre," October 6—tight money policy

1979 — Congress passes Chrysler bailout bill

THE SCENE IN THE 1960S

Pennies from Heaven
August 24, 1967

Stew Albert

Stew Albert, a founding member of the Yippies protest group, joined Abbie Hoffman, Jerry Rubin, and other comrades for this prank at the visitors' gallery of the New York Stock Exchange.

We lined up waiting for our turn to get out on the balcony. But then the private police tried to close us down. They knew why we were there and they weren't going to let us use the facilities for our demonstration. They said the balcony was now closed for repairs.

"Hey, the only reason you won't let us in is because we are Jewish," declared Abbie Hoffman, who looked and was dressed like a handsome Jewish cowboy.

"Yeah, I can tell he hates Jews. Just look at his hair. He's a Nazi for sure."

Reporters were taking notes. The guard's picture was being snapped again and again. We were calling him a Jew hater and surely the accusation would reach Jerusalem.

The guard retreated and we walked out on the Stock Exchange balcony. Below us the millionaire brokers, apparently tipped to our presence, took notice and began gathering. Abbie then handed out the money, mostly fives and ones, and we tossed them over the edge. They went slowly fluttering down into the brokers' greedy hands. And they piled on top of each other trying to grab a fiver.

Trading halted. The immense floor of hi-speed greed was now paying attention only to me and my new friends. I thought I had wandered into a surreal Italian film about modern alienation and charismatic despair. When we ran out of paper and started throwing coins we were greeted with boos and derision. The guards came out and told us to make way for the tourists.

Down on the sidewalk we burned money, danced, and gave millions of press interviews. We told the world we were from a new generation that laughed at money and lived free.

A few weeks later the NYSE enclosed the visitors' gallery in bulletproof glass.

In the 1980s, Jerry Rubin became a venture capitalist, which let journalists play with the words "Yippie" and "Yuppie." (Though it was reported he had made $600,000 in one of the years before his death, he continued to support social causes.)

Lady of the Club, 1967

Muriel Siebert

Wall Street was never an exclusive men's club; it was a locker room. The testosterone-charged atmosphere was the same at exchanges everywhere. Leo Melamed, chairman of the Chicago Mercantile Exchange, recalled there was "a big argument" in 1967 when he changed the rule barring women from being employees or members. "The question was: 'How much above the knee should the skirt be allowed on the floor?' — in case it would give the members problems, you know, distractions in this very, very businesslike atmosphere we have on the floor, God forbid."

That same year a young woman bought a seat on the New York Stock Exchange, which also prohibited women from the trading floor. Though feminism was gaining popularity, Muriel Siebert wanted to make money, not news.

It was Jerry Tsai [the former Fidelity fund manager who had recently founded the Manhattan Fund] who gave me the idea to buy a seat on the exchange. That was during an era when a lot of people would not let me work for them in their research department and go out of town representing the firm. That was the Street at that time. They just didn't have women going out representing them and they weren't going to.

I was in Jerry's office and I said to him, "Jerry, where can I go where I can get credit on the business I'm writing?" And he said, "Why don't you buy a seat?" And I said, "Don't be ridiculous." I knew there were no women on the exchange. And he said, "I don't think there's a law against it."

So I took the exchange's constitution home. You had to be over 21, you had to have a business purpose, and you had to be able to finance it. He was right. There was no law against it. But until Jerry mentioned it to me, I had never thought about it. And that idea became a challenge.

There was some hostility when it got out what I was doing. A lot of people were very unhappy. I couldn't get sponsored by anybody that was a member on the floor. Mine were all upstairs people. The people that I had asked, when the time came, they just ran out the door.

But Ed Merkle, who ran Madison Fund, was super when I bought the seat. He tried to get me a couple of sponsors. Jim O'Brien, who was an upstairs partner at Salomon Brothers, became one of my sponsors, and so did Ken Ward, who was one of the deans of the analysts at Hayden Stone. And they each told me that they were called over during interviews and asked, "Gentlemen, what do you know about Miss Siebert's personal life?"

So I learned you can't break a tradition that was 175 years old and have everybody love you. It's got nothing to do with me as a person. People just like things status quo. One governor of the exchange said to me, "And how many more are there behind you?" Like I was gonna lead a doggone parade onto the floor.

And twenty years later, where are they? I was determined. But I didn't run down to the floor 'til I was a member a year, year and a half. I was a trainee and I had to wear my square little badge, and I had to have my sponsor with me every time I executed a trade. I wanted to prove to people that I had bought the seat for business purposes, not for publicity. Then I passed the floor test. That meant I could execute any order that I wanted to down there.

Now that made a lot of people angry. They thought I shouldn't work the seat. I could own it, but they thought a man should be executing the trades. I had a couple of people come up and tell me that.

And some of it, some of it was not nice.

You just had to stand there and cry. All you could do was cry.

And yet for every one of those, there was somebody who was super nice. You know, there's always this balance. While you don't expect somebody that you know to turn out to be a real bastard, there's somebody that you don't know well that turns out to be a special, super person.

Thank God there's a balance. It would have been too much.

About the time I decided to buy a seat, [the advertising firm of] Albert Frank Guenther Law had bought a whole-page ad in the *Wall Street Journal* saying, "We've lost our biggest account, Merrill Lynch, and we're looking for business." So I called and said, "I'm buying a seat later this month, and I'm not Merrill Lynch." They sent me Jack Penninger. He said, "We'll use your picture." I said, "No. No member of the stock exchange has ever done anything like that." And he said, "You're *different* from other members of the stock exchange." So there was a picture. That was the Meet Miss Muriel Siebert ad.

But what really made people mad was the hundred-dollar-bill ad.

I went into May Day [May 1, 1975, the day fixed commissions were abolished] very professionally and silently. But about a year later, I put an ad in the *Wall Street Journal*—it was Jack's idea—a full page of me cutting a hundred-dollar bill in half. When we first shot it, he didn't like the expression. He said: "Mickey, you have to look like Ginnie Sweetest. You are cutting the bill, you are cutting their commissions." So I said, "Okay. Girl Scouts of America all the way."

But Wall Street didn't like it. Hey, it was a rough environment at the time. Not everybody loved it. But a girl's gotta make a living.

I still think it's a great business for women and I still encourage young women to go into it. Wall Street is still the place where you can make more money. I am a feminist, but in my own way. I've gone through a lot of not-niceness. After I was a member, on a visit to England I became the second woman to go onto the floor of the London Stock Exchange. The queen was the first. They had reciprocity with New York, so that's how I got in there. And they were shocked. They took me around, in their hats and tails, and then I started talking to a couple of specialists, and they were surprised, because I knew what I was talking about. Look, there was a period when that was not considered nice for a woman.

In October 1976 another woman, Alice Jarcho, became the NYSE's first regular floor trader. (Women had acted as temporary replacements during World War II.)

Siebert's successes have included five years as New York's Superintendent of Banks and a respectable finish in a U.S. Senate primary. She continues to head Muriel Siebert & Co., and to appear in its ads.

"Conglomerator": James Ling, 1969

Stanley H. Brown

In the 1960s, a strange kind of corporation developed. Called a "conglomerate," after the type of rock that contains bits of other stones, it was a collection of often deliberately mismatched companies. Unlike the trusts of the late 1800s, which sought to combine the operations of small companies within an industry, a conglomerate supposedly had the ability to weather varied economic conditions because at least one component would thrive for any given situation. In some cases it worked. One must wonder, however, if the success of a company like Gulf + Western (best known for Paramount Pictures) was due to the corporate structure or to the energies of its chairman, Charles Bluhdorn. The question is especially difficult to answer because conglomerates, confusing to investors and auditors alike, are often supported by accounting shenanigans understood only by their top executives. (As economist and humorist Ben Stein has said, "Everyone thinks accounting is boring, but what they're getting confused about is that accountants are often boring. Accounting, for those of a criminal turn of mind, is the absolutely most lucrative, exciting, adventurous, glamorous place to be.")

One of the largest conglomerates, Ling-Temco-Vought (the predecessor of today's LTV Corporation), was assembled by a Texas businessman starting from a small electronics company. James Ling, an electrician by training, was an artist with corporations and corporate securities. Journalist and author Stanley H. Brown revealed the inner working of Ling's creative mind in his 1972 biography Ling, *the best book ever written about conglomerates and the people who put them together.*

He was a very big man in Dallas and in America, and his Ling-Temco-Vought, the thing he had built from practically nothing, was still, even as it began to stumble, a spectacular assemblage of industrial power. In 1969, Wilson & Company sold nearly $1.3 billion worth of beef, lamb, pork, veal, and chickens. In just one plant, that subsidiary could kill and process more than a million hogs a year.

Jones & Laughlin poured and shaped more than five million tons of steel worth more than $1 billion. Its Pittsburgh works, ancient and inefficient as they may have been, were an American industrial landmark. When you looked out on the night in the steel city, the fiery sight that you first encountered was a mill owned by Ling's corporation. The planes of Braniff flew all over the country and to Hawaii, Canada, and South America, to the tune of more than $300 million in revenues. LTV Aerospace sold more than $700 million worth of planes and aerospace hardware, including the A-7 Corsair II attack plane for the Navy and the Air Force, the Scout spaceprobe rocket system for NASA, and the tail section of the Boeing 747. Wilson Sporting Goods turned out more than $100 million worth of baseball gloves, golf clubs, tennis rackets, and other products, and was the world's biggest manufacturer of sports equipment. Other LTV subsidiaries were making chemicals and drug products, high-fidelity and communications equipment (including the top-secret electronics on ships like the *Pueblo*), $200 million worth of wire, cable, and floor coverings from Okonite, and lots more in factories employing more than 120,000 people scattered all over the country.

Total sales of the whole complex would top $3.75 billion in 1969.

Even LTV's problems were spectacular, stemming mainly from a total consolidated corporate debt of more than $1.5 billion that required payment of more than $100 million a year in interest by the corporation and its subsidiaries.

The little electrical contracting company that Ling had started the whole thing with wasn't even part of the sprawling enterprise any more, and what he controlled had been established and built by other men. But he had put it all together, and there it was, however briefly, the fourteenth largest industrial corporation in the United States. It didn't work very well, and it didn't stay together. And a lot of the reasons why it didn't were Ling's own doing, even though it is possible—and even valid—to blame it on the stock market for collapsing, on the antitrust people for filing a baseless suit, and on his own supporters for turning against him when maybe they should have let him alone.

None of that really matters now. Nor does the fact that what is left of Ling-Temco-Vought is foundering and isn't very interesting any more. A lot of people lost a lot of money backing Ling's fantastic enterprise (though that has troubled him a great deal). But nobody made them do it. And plenty of money was made by investors along the way.

Ling led his army of executives, financiers, and investors through more than a decade of financial and psychic adventure. In the course of that march, he demonstrated remarkable creativity as he found the parts and discovered the processes for assembling them into a quite beautiful machine, however flawed it eventually became. Without meaning to, Ling used what was at hand to express himself, his drives, his private visions.

Long before the part of Los Angeles called Watts became notorious as the place of a bitter race riot, it was known to some people for what stood on a little piece of land there. An immigrant Italian laborer who could barely speak English or even Italian had appropriated a small part of a city block to build a series of fantastic towers. Made of steel rods, cement, bits of broken bottles (including the easily recognizable blue ones used to pack milk of magnesia), and assorted junk of all kinds, these Watts Towers of Simon Rodia are considered by many to rank among the world's great works of art.

In a sense, the thing that Ling built and the way he built it became a kind of Watts Tower.

. . . Maybe nobody should be permitted to use a business enterprise in that way. Almost certainly if Ling had not been able to do what he did, he would have found another way to create a tower out of bits and pieces. Jim Ling doesn't need a defender or a critic of his esthetics or his motives. What he did was worth the try and worth looking at in all its aspects, including the esthetics. Leverage may build shaky towers, but when it works, it has a palpably beautiful quality that demands respect. A lot of people paid through the nose to get a good seat. But they got to be a part of one dandy show. And it could have worked. Maybe the next one will.

Instinet, 1969

Jerome M. Pustilnik

Many people believe the next big idea in the financial markets is already here, and that it is only a matter of time before it becomes the next big reality. Electronic trading networks (sometimes referred to as ECNs— Electronic Communications Networks) link buyers and sellers directly and anonymously, frequently without the spread between the asking price and the offering price that would be pocketed by a market maker. The first of them, Instinet, was founded by Jerome Pustilnik in 1969, long before most of its customers were even automated.

A telephone call in the early 1960s from a friend, portfolio manager at a large Philadelphia-based mutual fund, was the genesis of Instinet and electronic trading networks. He asked me to try to find a seller of a block of PaperCraft Corporation. As the manager of a research department at a small NYSE firm, I had access to state-of-the-art techniques and resources, which amounted to reading through *Vickers*, a publication listing the portfolio holdings of mutual funds, which was updated a month or so after each fund's quarterly report had been released. I found the possible seller there. My firm crossed 250,000 shares—a pretty big deal in those days.

Using the same procedure I arranged several other block crosses, which were "formalized" on the NYSE floor. But each effort was arduous and very time consuming, as only a small percentage of my searches yielded a trade.

I began to wonder if there might be a better way. By coincidence, I was serving on the board of a company founded by two former MIT professors of electrical engineering. Their company had developed one of the early online real-time business services, providing automated bookkeeping and warehouse fulfillment services to liquor distributors too small to have full systems of their own. It occurred to me that a logical use of that technology would be to place a terminal, which in those days meant a big, bulky, olive green teletype machine, at mutual funds and investment organizations throughout the country. Each organization could then enter and update its portfolio holdings, creating a current and searchable database that would be easier to use than *Vickers*.

Then I gradually understood the most useful information was not a listing of the portfolios' holdings but, instead, what stocks did they want to buy, *now;* and what stocks did they want to sell, *now*. That was the really important information.

As a brokerage firm employee, I realized that such a database could produce substantial commissions. But it was also clear to me that the most efficient configuration of this data network would be for the participants to trade directly with each other, with only the host computer acting as intermediary, not a broker.

NYSE rules, however, prevented any member firm from implementing this kind of trading network because it bypassed the floor and the floor's brokers and specialists. My idea for an institutional network (hence the name Instinet) would be anathema to them, as well as to major brokerage firms doing an institutional commission business. These realities would prevent my employer from trying to exploit my idea.

After a long struggle with this dilemma, I left the company and founded Instinet. The targeted users were the nations' largest investing institutions, such as Fidelity, Prudential Insurance, Citibank, Wells Fargo, and Calpers.

Instinet went live in December of 1969 with just six subscribers, and did its first trade three days later—100,000 shares of Ford Motor Company. Instinet's benefits of anonymity, low cost, and minimal impact upon market price were acknowledged, but resisted. Potential users said they were reluctant to split the market; but it was evident that they did not want to risk altering their relationships with the brokerages, which had grown cozy. Instinet struggled against these obstacles until the early 1980s when the combined pressures of competitive rates, performance measurement, regulatory and legal decisions led to the beginnings of acceptance.

Today—thirty years later and after its acquisition by Reuters—it has become the dominant electronic marketplace for institutional trading and the progenitor of a multitude of ECNs, each clamoring for attention.

When Instinet was founded, it had to sell customers on the idea of hardware and software, not just the idea of trading directly with each other. Now that every brokerage has a computer network, and each is linked by the Internet, ECNs are easier to start. In fact, it wasn't until about thirty years after Instinet, by which time the Internet was thoroughly developed, that the second ECN appeared.

Many ECNs now compete with Instinet: Island and Archipelago are among those that focus on stocks; bonds can be traded on ECNs like Limi-Trader. Each new network hopes to reach critical mass, a point at which the number of customers and volume of business offers a truly liquid market.

As Pustilnik anticipated, ECNs led to another market development that followed naturally from their automated nature: customers can trade at all hours. Today, some traders, working counter to the conventional wisdom, use ECNs only after hours, because that is when volume is thinnest and prices can be manipulated. Individuals even use ECNs when they trade after hours in their online brokerage accounts. (Perhaps they should note that trader and journalist James J. Cramer calls the after-hours markets "the Badlands, the last great trading frontier." And he warns, "After-hours trading is an art form, one that exists at a level that rivals the most rigorous poker games for their bluffing and outrageous bidding. Your confidence in your hand must be supreme, and your judgment of your nameless and faceless opponents, both on the buy side and the sell side, must be perfect.")

Eyes on the Prize, 1970

Travers Bell

Travers Bell was chairman of the first black-owned New York Stock Exchange firm, Daniels & Bell. It was founded about eighteen months after Joseph Searles III, a former aide to New York mayor John Lindsay, became the first African-American member of the NYSE. (Preferring corporate finance to trading, Searles sold his seat about eight months later.)

My father was in the business, with the operations department of Dempsey Tegeler in Chicago, and he always tried to encourage me to see what the stock market was all about. One summer I needed some money, and he said, "Good, I've got a messenger's job for you." So I went down to Dempsey Tegeler in the Rookery Building on South Street the first day, and they gave me a briefcase and told me to make a delivery to a company called H. N. Billesby, which was in the Field Building right across the street. I unzipped the briefcase, looked at the raggedy papers in it, and I gave them to a guy, and he gave me a certified check for $175,000. My eyes went *boiiing!* The first thought that hit me was that this guy was paying me for paper!

I left Teachers College to stay on as a messenger. Then I got a job as a wire operator, then as an operations clerk. And in 1963, when I was 23 or 24, I got a break. Dempsey Tegeler acquired a firm called Straus, Blosser and McDowell in Chicago, with about fifteen offices. Out of the blue, they made me operations manager of the entire thing. I took courses in economics and business at Washington University in St. Louis, where Dempsey's home office was. You see, I had made a decision before I moved to St. Louis that I would wind up in New York because that was where the securities industry was. Essentially, what made the decision for me was that Jerry Tegeler, who my dad had worked for for fifteen years and who really liked my dad a great deal, came to me one day and said: "Travers, you know there was no way for me to help your dad. I really couldn't move him, because nobody's mind was ready for that."

But he said: "I'm past that point now. I think our people can re-act to the fact that you can deliver. And you're obviously good at what you do and you learn real fast. But I'm going to do something a lot of people aren't going to like—I really am. I'm going to teach you this business."

And he did. He taught it to me.

I learned it in the days when there were no computers. And at the end of the day you had to tie everything together. So while I was not buying or trading, I actually had to balance to the penny every day.

That was what made me make my decision. The one point that outweighed everything else was that as a black man I had had this unusual opportunity to learn the securities business and that knowl-edge just was not with anybody else black. I had an obligation to ex-ercise that knowledge. That was really the triggering point. I felt it was more than me.

I graduated in 1967 and got a job at Fusz Schmelzle. I became an officer and director in charge of operations and new computer fa-cilities. I knew that someday I would open my own firm, but I needed more trading and sales experience. I was at Fusz Schmelzle as chief operations officer for three-and-a-half years, until 1970, when I started Daniels & Bell.

There were other blacks in the securities industry at that time, and I'd been talking to them about organizing a black-owned securi-ties firm. I had liaisons with a fellow in Los Angeles, one in Chicago and one in New York. And finally in 1970, when I decided that it was time to do it, the people literally could not make the decision.

The fellow in New York—he had been in the securities industry for thirteen years himself—he said, "Listen, this is too much of a risk for me at this time. I've got a good history and family and chil-dren, and I just don't want to take the risk." But he said, "I know someone in New York who is trying to do the same thing. I'd like to introduce you to him. Willie Daniels." And he did. And that's how I met Mr. Daniels. Within about five or six months, we had organized Daniels & Bell.

It was Danny Lufkin of Donaldson, Lufkin & Jenrette who got Willie Daniels and me into business. Willie and I had cut a deal with the Small Business Investment Co. of New York for a million-and-a-half dollars. But two or three days before the trigger date, the

Small Business Administration ruled that investing in our firm could be construed as re-lending money and that, therefore, they couldn't do it. Myron Kandel, who used to write *Wall Street Letter*, wrote a story about it, and Danny Lufkin read it. He ran into Daniels walking across Chase Manhattan Plaza and said, "Come on up to the office." And they went upstairs, and I came over, and he said, "Okay, I'll help you." And he did. He put up some cash, and then the Myron Kandel letter filtered back to the S.E.C., and they gave us an exemption, reasoning that the intent of the law had been to encourage business that could create capital for other minority businesses.

In the summer of the following year, we bought a seat on the New York Stock Exchange. It was an industry event. We had just a fantastic party, up at 120 Broadway in the Bankers Club. That's how we started our first day of business, after being up all night. And there we were, the first black member firm of the New York Stock Exchange.

The stock exchange is a buy and sell institution. Some members may be prejudiced; some may not be. But it makes no difference to them when you come down there. It's what have you got to buy, what have you got to sell, and what's the market? But I think there was prejudice from municipal administrations, which were all white at the time. As a municipal firm, we would go to people who did business in the city of New York or the city of Chicago, and they would say, "You've got to be kidding. This is not an arena you can play in." But the fact was, there were small, regional firms doing business with various cities across the country.

We thought our best hope would be to try to find some black mayors. The only place we could find them was down in rural towns in the South. Mound Bayou, Mississippi, was a classic because it was the oldest black municipality in the U.S. It had never had a financing, and here we came, knocking on doors and saying, "We want to do a bond issue." And this guy says, "What's a bond issue?" So we did a housing issue there. As a result, Mound Bayou is a very progressive town today. Maynard Jackson was a lawyer in his own Atlanta law firm at that time, just a lawyer. We made him co-bond counsel in the Mound Bayou deal. It was the first time a black firm had ever been a bond counsel in a bond issue. And we made the Citizens Trust Co. of Atlanta co-trustee, which was the first time a black bank had ever been a trustee of a bond issue.

It wasn't until 1982–83 that there was a real turn on the municipal side. Prior to that, many black mayors had said: "Yes, we're going to put you in our deals. But we're getting feedback from the members of the financial community that it's okay if we give you a deal for, say, 15 or 20 million bucks, Travers, but when you're talking about $300 million or $400 million, it's hard for us." But Connecticut's treasurer, Henry Parker, eliminated the whole argument. After a lot of deliberation, he appointed us to a $5.5 billion transaction. Then anybody saying they couldn't put us on a $300 million deal had no argument. There was no longer any reason to say that we couldn't do it, because it had been done.

In bringing unknown black credits to the market, I've tried to convince people to forget whether this is a black municipality. We say, "This is the credit, this is the deterrent, and this is how we think it can be done." But I've run into literally hundreds of deals where people come to me and tell me, "Listen, don't you know that this deal will make history?" All the deals we've done have made history. But if the numbers weren't there, I'd put them on the shelf and say, "Not at that expense. I don't want to pay to make history."

Our interest is real clear and real simple: There must be independent financial investment banks in order to generate capital for minority financial institutions and minority businesses and to provide investment opportunities for the minority general public. But they have to compete in the overall marketplace. That's the key. I don't mind involving myself in issues that are charity, but I have to earn money to do that. My business is a profit-and-loss business. I've never lost sight of that.

The Rise and Fall of Bernie Cornfeld, 1970

Bernard Cornfeld

"I remember in those go-go days," said Fidelity Investments' Edward Johnson III, recalling the boom of the late 1960s, "that when I saw Bernie Cornfeld on the front page, in color, of Der Stern *magazine, with his favorite cheetah and in his velvet jacket, I knew we were in high territory."*

Few people today recognize the name of this former financial bellwether. For those unfamiliar with Cornfeld's story, he ran Investors Overseas Services, a Geneva-based mutual fund company with prominent American directors such as Pat Brown, the former governor of California. IOS ballooned as its outstanding returns were advertised by Cornfeld's ostentatious lifestyle. Eventually the company itself attracted investors — some legitimate, some not.

At the height, we had a total of eighteen funds with something over $2.5 billion under management. We had offices in 100 countries. We had 25,000 salesmen, virtually all of them full time. Toward the end, we had positive cash flow of between $15 million and, on one particular day in the middle of a sales contest, $100 million. Those numbers may not seem so large now, but at the time the whole U.S. mutual fund industry was less than $50 billion.

When we had company conferences, we had a United Nations setup, with earphones and translations into eight or ten languages. And there was a camaraderie that made the company unique, mostly because of our stock-option plan—which permitted everybody, from salesmen to ladies that served the coffee, to buy company stock at a fraction of what might be considered a realistic value. In a way, though, the stock-option plan led to our demise, because it became necessary to do a public offering. We couldn't maintain a plan where we were buying back option shares based on a formula that kept going up, because it related not to actual cash on hand but to book value, which was substantially higher. So we had to permit people to sell their shares outside the company.

A few things happened at the time of our public underwriting. One is that we created 143 millionaires in the company, some on paper, some in cash. No one except retiring shareholders sold more than 10 percent of their stock. A lot of people that suddenly discovered they were very rich decided to retire. That not only weakened the company but substantially weakened my position because it included some of our key board members, people I could count on for support.

Anyway, one day some German banks began a program of selling the stock short. Now, in the United States you've got to cover your shorts within seven days. This wasn't true overseas; they were simply bookkeeping transactions: They didn't have to deliver the stock. We knew it was short selling because in the underwriting, only six months earlier, no individual stockholder received more than 10,000 shares. So if a block of 500,000 shares hit the market, it had to be a short sale.

The stock went from something like 18 to 12 in the spring of 1970. Ed Cowett, who headed our banking operations and was also president of IOS at the time, went on a trip to Japan and left instructions that we were buyers at 12. He had put together a pool, just after the underwriting, of people who were prepared to buy at that price. I committed to $300,000. John King [head of King Resources], some of his associates and some other people I don't remember were in the pool. They were people Ed had contacted just in case we needed some support in the aftermarket.

When Cowett got back from Japan, he discovered that $11 million of our stock had been purchased. He told them to stop, and tried to raise money to cover the shortfall. He raised some by utilizing the money of the IOS Foundation, but we were still about $2.3 million short. So Ed borrowed the money from our bank and took down the rest of the stock in his family trust, for which he was very much criticized afterward.

Ed had a very serious flaw. He thought the market in any stock—including ours—could be manipulated. Just as soon as we stopped purchasing, the stock really began to drop—going from 12 to 2, when it recovered slightly. But within the company there was total panic. Individuals who one day were worth $28 million, the next day saw they were worth 25, the next day 23, the next day 20, the next day 16. By the end of the week, they wanted someone to come in and save them. They had a choice between the Rothschilds and John King. They chose King, primarily because the Rothschilds were very arrogant and, in exchange for lending credibility to the operation, really wanted control, which they weren't particularly prepared to pay anything for.

Eventually the SEC indicated that if [the deal] went ahead, they would stop U.S. trading in the stock, so King had to pull out.

Now, it was June or July 1970, and sales, strangely enough, continued to be good. But morale was very bad, particularly with our large stockholders, who were also directors and key people in the company. Now, Harold Lever, who had been a member of Parliament for many years and whose family owned a bank in Switzerland, he offered to lend the company $5 million at commercial rates with the proviso that I resume my post as chairman. And then there was Robert Vesco [head of the $100 million International Controls Corporation conglomerate]. He went around to the board and promised to cover their losses in tax shelter deals. One director was promised $50,000 a year for life as a consultant. Vesco beat Lever by one vote. A lot of the key people now indicate that there was a sort of hysteria then and that they don't know how they could have supported Vesco.

When it became evident in about 1972 what Vesco was up to, I flew down to the Bahamas, where he lived at that time, but he just wasn't taking calls from me. I knew that Jim Crosby, chairman of Resorts International, had a direct line to Vesco, because Vesco wanted to purchase Resorts' operations in the Bahamas and go into the casino business. Crosby thought it would be awkward to give me Vesco's number since they were in the middle of negotiations— though he did call Vesco and Vesco assured him that he would be contacting me. Crosby and I played backgammon for a couple of hours and eventually he had to go to the restroom, and I promptly jotted down Vesco's number from his address book, which was by the telephone.

I called Vesco and said, "Look, Bob, I've come all the way down here to see you, and I would appreciate your cutting out this screwing around and getting together with me." And he said, "Okay, I'm going to the casino tonight; meet me there at seven."

He came to the casino with his mother, his father and a handful of bodyguards, and we went off to a corner. And I said, "Bob, I get the impression that you're involved in something that's kind of crazy. Do you want to go through life as a fugitive?" And he said, "Well, if I'm going to be a fugitive, I'm going to be a very rich fugitive."

I said, "Yeah, that's great, except that some of the money that you have comes from people where that's all they got." And he said, "Well, they've got their problems. I've got my problems."

I said, "Bob, if you're not interested in anybody but yourself, hasn't it occurred to you that one of these people is going to become desperate enough to come around and blow your brains out?" And he said, "Bernie, they're not going to blow my brains out. They're going to blow your brains out. You're the one who sold them the funds."

Vesco certainly was up to something. He eventually misused between $250 million and $500 million of IOS assets to prop up his highly leveraged conglomerate. (The huge spread between the estimates indicates how much about the fraud remains unknown.)

He did become a fugitive. His last chance to return to the United States vanished when it was discovered his support from Attorney General John Mitchell had been bought with contributions to President Nixon's reelection campaign. He settled in Cuba after a long stay in Costa Rica, where he had bribed the president for a residence permit.

Cornfeld moved to Beverly Hills to become a movie producer. On a trip to Geneva he was arrested, and, though he protested that he had not been aware of Vesco's schemes, was jailed for a year.

Where Did the Go-Go Go? 1970

David L. Babson

The market's postwar bull run, which saw a 400 percent rise in the Dow Jones Industrial Average, came to an abrupt end in 1970. Between January 1 and May 26 of that year, the DJIA lost a third of its value, falling to its lowest level since the beginning of the 1960s.

Speaking to a conference of fellow money managers in 1971, David L. Babson, head of the investment firm that bears his name, offered a frank assessment.

Asking the performance investors of the late 1960s what went wrong is like someone in 1720 asking John Law what went wrong with the Mississippi Bubble.

Or in 1635 asking Mynheer Vanderveer what went wrong with the Dutch Tulip Craze.

Nevertheless, this panel interests me because if we can identify what really did go wrong it may help to avoid a future speculative frenzy.

And if we are serious about getting to the bottom of what went wrong then we ought to say what really did go wrong.

So let me list a dozen things that people in our field did to set the stage for the greatest bloodbath in 40 years.

First, there was the conglomerate movement and all its fancy rhetoric about synergism and leverage. Its abuses were to the late 1960s what the public utility holding companies were to the late 1920s.

Second, too many accountants played footsie with stock-promoting managements by certifying earnings that weren't earnings at all.

Third, the "modern" corporate treasurers who looked upon their company pension funds as new-found "profit centers" and pressured their investment advisors into speculating with them.

Fourth, the investment advisors who massacred clients' portfolios because they were trying to make good on the over-promises that they had made to attract the business in the first place.

Fifth, the new breed of portfolio managers who churned their customers' holdings on the specious theory that high "turnover" was a new "secret" leading to outstanding investment performance.

Sixth, the new issue underwriters who brought out the greatest collection of low-grade junky offerings in history—some of which were created solely for the purpose of generating something to sell.

Seventh, the elements of the financial press who promoted into new investment geniuses a group of neophytes who didn't even have the first requisite for managing other people's money, namely, a sense of responsibility.

Eighth, the security salesmen who peddled the items with the best "stories" or the biggest markups even though such issues were totally unsuited to their customers' needs.

Ninth, the sanctimonious partners of major investment houses who wrung their hands over all these shameful happenings while they deployed an army of untrained salesmen to forage among a group of even less informed investors.

Tenth, the mutual fund managers who tried to become millionaires overnight by using every gimmick imaginable to manufacture their own paper performance.

Eleventh, the portfolio managers who collected bonanza "incentive" fees—the "heads I win, tails you lose" kind—which made them fortunes in the bull market but turned the portfolios they managed into disasters in the bear market.

Twelfth, the security analysts who forgot about their professional ethics to become "story peddlers" and who let their institutions get taken in by a whole parade of confidence men.

These are some of the things that "went wrong." But for those who stuck to their guns, who tried to follow a progressive but realistic approach, who didn't prostitute their professional responsibilities, who didn't get seduced by conflicts of interest, who didn't get suckered into glib "concepts," nothing much really did go wrong.

... As in earlier periods of delusion most investors tried so hard to be "smart" that they lost the "common sense" that pays off in the long run.

Following his remarks, Babson was asked, "Do you think the decline was due to the professionals?"

"Of course it was due to the professionals," he replied. *"The big institutions and the people that ought to know how to manage investments got sucked into speculation. The 1969–1970 bear market was due to the professionals—nobody else."* His recommendation was blunt: *"I think a lot of the professionals ought to get out of the business."*

Paper, 1967–1970

Donald T. Regan

In the late 1960s, brokerages fell victim to the old joke: "We lose money on every sale, but we make it up in volume." Donald T. Regan, chairman of Merrill Lynch and later Ronald Reagan's Secretary of the Treasury and Chief of Staff, said the problem was too much of a good thing. "Particularly in 1967 and early 1968, the Street took on a golden glitter," he explained. "With all of this volume, individuals swarmed into the market." But the volume meant extra expenses. "All that business pouring in the front door was not flowing so smoothly out the back; before it got out the back, lots of time went by, and lots of mud was churned up. Pools of paper, figuratively, and I have no doubt in some cases also literally, were all over the floor."

At this time a new plural noun—"fails"—became part of the vocabulary of Wall Street followers. Brokers were taking in each other's laundry, but they were not delivering any clean shirts. In other words, they were failing to deliver securities on the fifth business day, and they were therefore often in violation of Rule 64 of the New York Stock Exchange. . . .

The sums involved were enormous. By December 1968, fails had reached the alarming level of $4.1 billion. . . .

Finally the New York Stock Exchange had no choice but to restrict the trading periods. In the last half of 1968 the Exchange closed down for one day each week. Later, the system was altered so that the Exchange was opened for five working days, but for only four hours a day instead of the usual five and a half. Yet, even though trading hours had been cut, working hours stretched as brokers attacked the formidable task of bringing the rate of fails under control. . . .

Brokerage firms were running three shifts a day, but the volume was still pouring in, and the new, inexperienced employees seemed to be accomplishing little except to move papers from one pile to another.

The Street was caught in a paper blizzard. Paper came in through the doors and windows, and sometimes seemed to come down through cracks in the ceiling and up through the floor as well. Fails were only one of the results. Serious as they are, most fails do get straightened out in time. The resolution of a fail may take weeks or months and may raise the blood pressures of broker, transfer agent and customer, but still, most fails are cleared up eventually, usually within 30 days.

A couple of other complications are graver and even harder to resolve. These are shortages of securities [on hand, compared to what accounts showed.] . . . No one will ever know the precise value of missing securities in these days of crisis and chaos. The record keeping was so complex and was so incredibly tangled at the time that the quantities of securities missing simply can't be determined.

But in my judgment there was at least one day in 1969 when, if you had taken all of the securities in all of the vaults in all of the member firms and banks on the Street and counted them, and checked the count against the records, you would have found differences in the range of half a billion dollars. . . .

The firms beset by these huge differences naturally launched intensive searches. But in a number of cases, some involving firms that no longer exist, no amount of this figurative turning of pockets inside out uncovered the missing certificates.

Where they went will remain one of history's mysteries.

Ironically, firms working the hardest to automate faced the greatest risks. Many such efforts failed because the innovative procedures didn't link smoothly with the methods used by the rest of the Street. Some forward-thinking firms, such as Goodbody & Co., the fifth-largest firm on the Street at the time, actually went bust because of their innovations.

The Nifty Fifty, 1972–1974

Forbes

In the doldrums of the early 1970s, when the overall market fell back to levels of ten years earlier, a few dozen stocks mysteriously kept advancing. They came to be called the Nifty Fifty. In 1977, Forbes *magazine recalled that fairy-tale phenomenon.*

Once upon a time there was something called a "two tier" market on Wall Street. Actually, it wasn't so very long ago, and it didn't last for very long, but the period had some of the same mythic quality as the Wild West. Short-lived in fact, it is long-lived in fantasy.

What happened was this: It was late 1972 and amid euphoria, the Dow Jones average had broken a thousand. OPEC had not begun to show its devastating power over petroleum pricing. Peace was at hand in Vietnam, according to Kissinger. Dick Nixon had been returned to the White House by a landslide margin, and price controls were about to come off, as administration economists declared that the tide had turned in the battle against inflation.

Inexplicably, however, as if it knew something the rest of the world didn't, the market began misbehaving. By early 1973, despite record earnings across the width and breadth of industry, stocks began dropping at astonishing rates. The entire Big Board seemed—against all reason—to be sliding, if not exactly crashing, down around investors' ears. By late 1974 the market had lost all its gains of the preceding decade.

But in the midst of this general decline, four dozen or so stocks stood out—by holding up relatively well. These were the favorites of the biggest institutions in the land—the banks, the pension funds, the mutual funds—and within a few months in late 1972 and early 1973 they acquired a striking common denominator: They were the stocks whose prices and price/earnings ratios fell very little. It was not as if this handful—this "Nifty Fifty," as they came to be called—rose suddenly from the ocean; it was as though all of the

U.S. but Nebraska had sunk into the sea. The "two tier" market really consisted of one tier and a lot of rubble down below.

What held the Nifty Fifty up? The same thing that held up tulip bulb prices in long ago Holland—popular delusions and the madness of crowds. The delusion was that these companies were so good that it didn't matter what you paid for them; their inexorable growth would bail you out. Men like James Needham, then chairman of the New York Stock Exchange, demurred. "The large institutions," he complained, "persist in tightening their concentration in a favorite [few] stocks while ignoring hundreds of other choice investment opportunities." But no matter, you couldn't argue with success.

Of course, you know the rest. It was inevitable. The Nifty Fifty were—in the words of *Forbes* columnist Martin Sosnoff—taken out and shot one by one. The oil embargo hit Disney: down 27 points in four weeks. Production problems at Polaroid: down 50 points in three months. A critical cover story in *Forbes*: Avon Products lost 46% in six months. But the real problem was never the particular deflating needle. It was the fact that a company like Kodak was selling for three times the value of Ford Motor, and that was just plain silly. Sooner or later, money men all over town were making second decisions, and the sound of institutions unloading on institutions—a sound not unlike human moans—filled the air.

"The Nifty Fifty just tore everybody's guts out," Edward Johnson III of Fidelity Investments remembered in 1987. "But it was a performance game, and if you didn't own the Nifty Fifty, you were behind. We may be going back into that now, but instead of its being the Nifty Fifty, it's the Nifty 500, whatever is in the S&P. All of the geniuses have figured out that the best way to have a glorious party is to all join the index, and, needless to say, the consultants recommend it, the clients feel comfortable with it, and the only problem is that all of the money is flowing into a limited number of securities and the index is no longer an index. It's making its own market." During this period one Wall Street veteran commented memorably that Xerox's price-to-earnings multiple "discounted not only the future but also the hereafter."

May Day
May 1, 1975

Robert Haack, Donald Weeden, and E. John Rosenwald, Jr.

The New York Stock Exchange enjoyed price-fixing for almost two hundred years after the 1792 Buttonwood Agreement, in which the members "solemnly" promised to charge all customers one quarter of 1 percent commission and also agreed to trade only with member firms. By the 1970s, as NYSE president Robert Haack observed, "there was no real recognition of the economies of scale. You know a 100,000-share order shouldn't cost as much per 100 as a 200-share order. It was unusually lucrative. Some firms were getting very, very rich."

Something called a "third market" grew to service institutional investors. The first market is the organized exchanges and the second is the over-the-counter market, such as Nasdaq, for stocks that aren't, for whatever reason, listed on an exchange. The third market is a combination of the other two. It exists when stocks listed on the exchange are bought and sold off it.

DONALD WEEDEN
WEEDEN & CO.

A lot of people say that the third market—and Weeden & Co. in particular—was the catalyst for much of the change that has taken place in the last ten or fifteen years. I think, to a great extent, that is true, if catalyst is understood as a stirring up that caused much larger things to take place.

The New York Stock Exchange's argument was that it was the best, most responsible, most organized market in the world and that to do business away from it was detrimental to the public interest. On the surface that's a very straightforward, easily accepted concept. But what it really meant was, don't do business with our competitors, even if they have a better price. Now, that was an old argument, like Mr. Rockefeller might have made in trying to concentrate all of the oil business in Standard Oil.

Still, there was enough business out there, and there were people who saw the advantages of dealing with Weeden & Co. and were willing to ignore the entreaties of the New York Stock Exchange. Institutions were becoming larger and larger buyers of listed stocks, particularly among the industrial stocks, and they were desperately looking for ways of buying in amounts that were not always available in the auction market without price changes.

A proportion of our business came from members of the New York [Stock Exchange] who found that we were willing to buy a block of 1,000 or 1,500 shares at a better price—net—than the specialists on the floor of the NYSE. And so they went off-board and sold to us because it was in the best interests of their shareholders to do so. By 1968 it had gotten up to 8 percent of the total amount of business done in listed stocks on the New York.

We were not trying to change the world. We were not necessarily protective of our role. We merely wanted to compete.

The law that ended the NYSE's advantages took effect May 1, 1975— May Day. You could hear the distress calls clear across the country.

E. JOHN ROSENWALD, JR.
BEAR STEARNS

Prior to May Day, one of the major firms had gone off for a weekend retreat to plan a pricing strategy. They came back and announced to the world that at the opening on May 1, 1975, they would offer an 18 percent discount. I don't know where they came up with that figure, but I'll tell you, it lasted all of 60 seconds. Major institutional firms, full-service firms, in order to keep market share quickly became major discounters, and the discount from the old rate jumped dramatically.

On May Day many institutions were so frightened of litigation they had lawyers sitting on the trading desk, watching the traders to make sure they were negotiating and getting the best possible price.

A month after May Day, The New York Times reported that most brokers had cut their fees 25–35 percent, while some were offering reductions as steep as 50 or 60 percent.

Those cuts, however, were reserved for large-volume, large-order clients—mutual funds and institutions. Commission charges for individuals increased in that month.

The Black Box, 1974–1980

William Batten and John Phelan, Jr.

Brokers made a lot of money selling technology in the 1960s. IBM, Texas Instruments, Xerox, Digital Equipment—these and others were the hottest stocks in the Go-Go years. Many had defied the general slump of the 1970s.

Surprisingly, Wall Street had done little to automate its own business.

There were a few reasons. First was fear that "the black box"—the computer—would replace brokers. (This fear would resurface and cause a similar lapse during the online trading boom.) Another concern was links between firms. The few brokerages that tried to automate found their expensive efforts wasted because others didn't follow.

The NYSE in particular was focused on matters that appeared more urgent. Antiquated procedures had increased costs, pushing many firms toward bankruptcy; the recession had led to a drop in volume; fixed commissions had been abolished by Congress; and the cornerstone of the Exchange's monopoly, the rule that required member firms to work only with each other, had been deemed an unfair restraint of trade.

Just when it seemed least able to handle the cost and angst, automation was practically forced upon the NYSE. Congress, ordering an end to restrictions on dealing with nonmember firms, demanded a national market system. "It wasn't the best time to change things," said NYSE vice-chairman John Phelan, Jr. "There was really a feeling that the Exchange probably only had a couple of years to go."

William Batten was the newly elected chairman of the NYSE.

BATTEN

My perceptions of the exchange were clearly affected by the fact that I was chief executive officer of the J. C. Penney Co. for almost seventeen years. I saw through the '60s and the early '70s that member firms had to reduce hours and couldn't handle volume. I couldn't imagine having to close the store because you had too much business. That seemed rather preposterous to me. The message I got was that somebody wasn't managing the business very well. The other view I shared, though perhaps not as extreme as some, was that the New York Stock Exchange was a private club. So I went to the exchange with those two perceptions.

The idea of survival never had even been in my mind. I'd always taken that for granted. And to have people ask that question shook me up. Of course, you must remember that was during the period when there were a lot of people who thought the black box would replace the exchange. Everything would go to automatic trading. That thinking was very prevalent then. And that, of course, was the reason why they were asking the question "Will the exchange survive?"

Although there was talk about the electronic linkage of markets, there were no specifications of the components of the new market. Nobody knew, not in Washington or in New York, what that market would look like. So we were all starting from scratch. The SEC wisely did not mandate a specific system but put the responsibility on the industry to come up with one.

We proposed what later became known as ITS, or the Intermarket Trading System. We requested a meeting in Chicago of the other exchanges to explain it to them as we visualized it, and we got their input as to how it might look. There was very great resistance in that meeting. There were fears—which, again, were understandable—of electronic linkage leading to the New York Stock Exchange draining business from their exchanges. That was a natural fear because of the difference in size and resources of the New York Stock Exchange vis-à-vis the other exchanges. So that Chicago meeting did not end up with any kind of agreement. In fact, we couldn't even get an agreement on a date to have another meeting. Now *that's* major disagreement!

So we scaled our thinking down to linking with one exchange, which would be more digestible. And also, if it worked, it might convince the other exchange we were not out to grab their business. So we started with an experimental linkage with the Philadelphia exchange. And after that was in existence for a while and the other exchanges saw that nothing really bad was happening to the Philadelphia exchange, we could start linking all the exchanges together.

Many times people would ask me, "Do you think the New York

Stock Exchange can be run like a business?" My answer to that was "Well, somebody better run it like a business, because that's what it is."

ITS was launched in 1978 with fifty stocks. Seventy thousand shares traded that year. The system required two and a half minutes to execute a trade. Five years later, when the system listed 1,200 stocks, executions required just half a minute and daily share volume had risen to millions.

PHELAN

It was fortunate that we had that slow period in 1980 and 1981, because we had to adjust to the changes on the floor. That period was really a period of adjustment as we began the next phase of automation, which really had to do with the [specialists' order] books and some more systems in the back office and updating DOT [the Designated Order Turnaround system for routing and executing orders] and working on the next generation of systems. That's when I tried to get people to talk about volume. We talked about doing 100-million-share days and then 150-million-share days and then 200-million-share days, when we were only doing 20 million shares a day. I would get people telling me, "You're ruining your credibility by talking about this."

People had a hard time figuring out how you were going to handle those larger volumes. We did set up a plan to work with the member firms and their operations in the back office, because we learned a good lesson from the late 1960s: The front end can't do it if the back end can't do it. If you can't service the customer right, then neither the front end nor the back end is going to work. And when the 100-million-share days and 150-million-share days came in the latter part of 1982 and continued through 1983, for the first time people really understood that they couldn't do the volume without the automation.

We live in a time where things will not calm down.

As this book goes to press, NYSE daily volume commonly tops one billion shares.

Futures
Chicago, 1971–1982

Leo Melamed

Before the opening bells ring to open the financial markets of New York, all eyes are on Chicago. That's quite a change from the old days, when Chicago was just a place to sell agricultural products. Now financial products are traded like pork bellies. "Innovation happened at the Merc because we were hungrier," said Leo Melamed, who became chairman of the Chicago Mercantile Exchange in 1967. "We had much more to gain with success than an institution that was already very successful, such as the Chicago Board of Trade (CBOT). The Merc was on the make."

In terms of agriculture, we had hit the limits. I mean, the CBOT had grain and all the grain by-products, so we were locked out of that. We already had meats and we were doing well, but, I mean, where could you go with that? You can't invent another meat.

So now we were all meat, and I said we must diversify. You cannot depend on meats. In my mind was another idea, entirely different: not agriculture, but currencies. I saw finance as a universe that was totally untouched, completely open, and the sky was the limit. I recognized this would be revolutionary, but it was there. If [University of Chicago economist] Milton Friedman's view that Bretton Woods [a 1944 international agreement that set currency exchange rates] would indeed come apart in the near future was anywhere near correct, then my ideas for a currency futures market could work. [Futures fix a price now for transactions that might occur at a later date. Traders watch the price of futures to gain a sense of a market's direction.] So the president of the exchange, Everett Harris, and I met with Friedman and asked him what he thought of the idea. Well, he loved it.

We set the date for May 1972. I said to the traders of the Merc, "Look, you've got to leave your cattle pit, your hog pit, your belly pit; you've got to come help us launch currencies." And they came and did it. But I also knew they had to make a living. These people would give me their time, but for how long?

At the Merc, we never were looking for vindication, but we sure were looking for business. But if I had to pick a date when we were vindicated, I would pick September 1, 1976. That was the day the Mexican peso was devalued 50 percent and the entire world was all shook up. Nowhere could you get a forward price in Mexican pesos—except where? At the Chicago Mercantile Exchange, our market was right there. It opened up. It never had to sweat. A hundred million dollars changed hands, and we were safe and secure. And the world took notice that the Chicago IMM [International Money Market] stayed in business and continued to trade Mexican pesos.

Stock market futures were not a new idea. I remember as a kid on the floor being cornered by Elmer Faulkner, a little guy who wore spats—that was the thing I remembered about him. He smoked a big cigar and he used to spit in a spittoon that was on the floor. He said to me, "Of course, the ultimate future is the stock market futures." And then he'd spit into a spittoon and say, "But you'll never see it in your lifetime."

Melamed's innovations created an entire market of currency and stock index futures. "Futures has always had a sordid history," he admitted. "It looks like a gambling casino." But, he added, "it's misunderstood."

T. Rowe Price, 1983

James W. Michaels

Merrill Lynch is often credited with bringing Wall Street to Main Street in the mid-twentieth century. For all of Merrill's deserved honor, they share that distinction with other firms—some not based anywhere near Wall Street. One such firm is T. Rowe Price of Baltimore. Unlike Merrill, a corporate empire, T. Rowe Price was an extension of its iconoclastic founder.

Thomas Rowe Price established his firm in 1937. In 1950 the company offered its first mutual fund, the Growth Stock Fund, becoming part of the revolution in no-load "investment trusts" (those which charge only management fees, not sales commissions). It later became an early proponent of discount commissions, retirement planning, and international investing.

Price was also a great stock picker. "I never took a course in economics or investments in school or college," he boasted after six decades of successful investing. "I graduated in chemistry. Fortunately, I learned in 1931 that I did not have the ability to guess the ups and downs of the stock market averages or the trends in individual stocks. I learned that most of the big fortunes of the country were made by people retaining ownership of successful business enterprises that continued to grow and prosper over a long period of years. The owners of such businesses as Du Pont, Merck, 3M, General Electric, Weyerhaeuser and countless others were long-term investors. They did not sell out and buy back their ownerships of the businesses every time there was a change in the business and stock market cycles. It was obvious that to be a successful investor it was not necessary to know what the stock market was going to do."

Shortly after Price's death in 1983, Jim Michaels, longtime editor of Forbes, *recalled his unique style.*

T. Rowe Price was probably the most interesting investment practitioner of recent times. Not the most famous; he never achieved the influence of the late Benjamin Graham, because, unlike Graham, Price was not an articulate man. He never spelled out his ideas in detail nor tried.

Rowe Price's accomplishments lay not in theory but in a finely developed ability to sense trends before anyone else was aware of them. He was a pioneer of growth stock investing in the 1930s and made lots of money for his clients out of that. By the late 1960s, when growth stocks had become a religion, Price was among the first to recommend cutting back on them while the institutions were buying eagerly. He was early into what are now called emerging growth stocks, with his brainchild, the T. Rowe Price New Horizons Fund. In the late 1960s and early 1970s he latched on, again early, to natural resource inflation hedges and cable TV. In *Forbes* of November 9, 1981, when mortgage money was unavailable and building stocks were untouchable, Price recommended 15 of them. They handily outperformed the averages.

I had the pleasure of knowing Rowe Price and speaking with him fairly frequently over a quarter of a century, but that pleasure wasn't unalloyed. He would snap out with things like: "You don't know anything, do you?" if I failed immediately to grasp some point he was making. But behind my back he said good things about me and this magazine.

Price was like that, hard on everyone he dealt with, but equally hard on himself. He was a rigid disciplinarian, tightly budgeting his time and practicing his trade almost to his last breath. Over the past few years, while painfully ill, he wrote a handful of columns for *Forbes*. Why? Not for the money certainly, because he was a wealthy man. Not to gain attention for his business, because he had long since sold control of the investment management firm that bears his name. Why, then? "Investors," he said, "need help in these confusing times."

The help that Price offered was, essentially, fundamentalist. You make money, he liked to say, by finding "fertile fields" and sowing your money there. He wasn't interested in trying to catch swings in the market or in the economy. By fertile fields he meant industries and companies that were likely to do better than the economy over a long period. Because he was a loner who little cared for conventional investment opinion, he could see what the crowd overlooked.

Price refused to move his firm to New York; Wall Street had nothing he wanted. A longtime associate recalls: " 'Don't talk with brokers,' he'd say. 'They just want you to buy or sell something. Talk to management.'" Price's view of what makes for business success was compatible with *Forbes*'s. Perhaps that is why he chose us to deliver some of his last messages to the investing public. Like this magazine, Price put primary emphasis on management, its drive, motivation, and experience. Howard (Pete) Colhoun, who helped found Emerging Growth Partners in 1982, tells how Price hired him nearly 20 years ago. "He asked me how I'd go about interviewing a company. Instead of talking about growth rates and price/earnings ratios, I told him about my recent interviews with Xerox and SCM—this was the early 1960s before Xerox was well known. I said I had been impressed with the people at Xerox but depressed by the people at SCM. He hired me on the spot."

Colhoun recalls that Price admonished young analysts: "Don't tell me what's good about a company. Tell me what's wrong with it." Until he knew the potential flaws, he couldn't judge a stock properly.

People who knew Price use words like "clairvoyant" and "intuitive" to describe him. I have my own theory, however. What struck some people as almost mystical foresight was simply the product of extremely hard work and a lifetime of concentration on investments to the exclusion of most other things. As a result of his hard work and concentration Price learned to see meaningful patterns where others saw only unconnected events. I say this not to diminish Rowe Price but to praise him. He was a self-made hero, not a born hero.

"Silver Thursday"
March 27, 1980

Jerry Knight and James L. Rowe, Jr.

"Come at once to the Federal Reserve Board!"

Obeying that succinct command, James M. Stone, chairman of the federal government's Commodity Futures Trading Commission (CFTC), immediately reported to the office of Paul Volcker, chairman of the Fed. There he found Harold M. Williams, chairman of the Securities and Exchange Commission, and other senior officials. The brain trust was watching the stock market, which had dropped sharply on reports that the richest family in America owed hundreds of millions of dollars to brokers. The margin call—certainly the largest in history—panicked investors who wondered what stocks would be dumped to raise the cash needed to meet the call.

Stone had been summoned because the speculators, Nelson Bunker Hunt and W. Herbert Hunt of Texas, thought to be perhaps the richest men in the world, had been borrowing to buy silver and silver contracts. For a while, they had achieved huge profits—on paper. Then came Silver Thursday.

When the tangled story was unraveled, a bold scheme was revealed.

Jerry Knight and James L. Rowe, Jr., wrote for the Washington Post.

The silver market collapsed yesterday, costing speculators hundreds of millions of dollars and forcing federal authorities to take emergency actions.

The cash price of silver in New York plunged from $16.25 an ounce to $10.85, down 33 percent in 24 hours. Less than three months ago, silver was selling for $50 an ounce.

The biggest losers were two Texas billionaires, Nelson Bunker Hunt and his brother Herbert, who bought tons of silver last year, forcing prices to record highs.

Forced to come up with $100 million yesterday to cover their losses in the last two days, the Hunts began selling not only their silver but also their government bonds and their stock in several companies.

The Hunts' massive losses—on paper close to $4 billion since January—caused a financial crisis for their brokers, The Bache Group.

The Securities and Exchange Commission halted trading in Bache stock shortly after noon and quickly began investigating the silver-trading activities of the firm, the nation's fifth-largest broker.

. . . The stunning crash in silver prices caused what veteran analyst Newton Zinder called "a classic panic" in the stock market.

The stock market quickly recovered, but the story didn't disappear.

How could anyone lose $4 billion in the silver market? Who needs that much silver in the first place? Was it true that the Hunts had owned or controlled (through contracts for delivery) 200 million ounces? That much silver would be worth anywhere from $10 billion (at the high of $50 per ounce) to $2 billion (at $10 per ounce).

To understand the Hunts' thinking, consider the economy in 1980: Bank loans cost more than 19 percent; the inflation rate was on its way to 17 percent. The United States hadn't endured those levels since the Civil War. By definition, the U.S. dollar wasn't holding its value. What would you have done if, like the Hunts, you had billions of them? Ever since paper money was introduced, savvy investors have tried to protect their wealth from inflation by converting paper currency to gold or silver. The precious metal, limited in supply, would hold its value. The Hunts started buying silver in 1974. Then they discovered an interesting fact about commodity contracts—something Jay Gould and his friends had exploited when they tried to corner the American gold market in 1869. The contracts call for only a small portion of the total value to be paid up front, so the cash one spends actually controls a much larger value of the commodity. That got the Hunts thinking. Just how much silver could they buy?

Eventually the public, noticing silver prices were rising, bought in, driving the prices higher still. An ounce that had cost $6 in 1979 cost more than $50 at the beginning of 1980.

And still the Hunts kept buying.

The public, eager to benefit, searched through coin collections and cupboards for silver to sell. Silver flooded the market as people sold rings, bracelets, trophies, tableware. More important, the government of India *allowed the export of silver, which—in the form of silver bracelets—was the favorite form of savings in that economy. The Hunts hadn't anticipated the effect of Indian silver coming to market. The price per ounce dropped to $10. The Hunts, who had bought on margin, received their $100 million margin call.*

Only then was it revealed what the Hunts really had in mind.

Knight and Rowe, continuing to follow the story, filed this report in late April:

Like an image developing on a sheet of silver-coated photographic paper, details of what happened have emerged gradually in the last month. It is a far different view than the instant picture popped out on the day the silver prices hit bottom:

The Hunts were not alone in bidding up the price of silver. They had a formal partnership with two Arab sheiks. Another group of investors worked anonymously through a Swiss bank to amass another massive stash of the metal. Not even federal investigators know who they are.

The group's plan was audacious: sell securities backed by their silver, creating a private currency that could withstand inflation.

Instead, the Hunts had to borrow almost $2 billion—more than the U.S. government was lending for the Chrysler bailout that same year. Federal Reserve chairman Paul Volcker, who strongly disapproved of large loans made to speculators, approved the loans for the Hunts to prevent a fire sale of the Hunts' other assets.

"The potential was catastrophic," James Stone said. "It was a close call."

It was also a fitting climax to the 1970s, when the fight against inflation escalated from sloganeering—President Ford wore a WIN button, exhorting Americans to "Whip Inflation Now"—to desperate measures like a monetary policy so strict the announcement was made on a weekend to avoid upsetting the markets. (It was promptly dubbed the "Saturday Night Massacre.")

PART TEN

Greed Is Good?

"Greed is all right, by the way. I want you to know that I think greed is healthy. You can be greedy and still feel good about yourself."

Arbitrageur Ivan Boesky,
speaking to business school students, 1985

Timeline

1979 — Theodore Benna creates 401(k) plan; IRS approves

1979 — Hunts attempt to corner silver as inflation hedge

1980 — Ronald Reagan elected President

1980 — Prime rate hits 21 percent in December; high unemployment

1981 — IBM introduces PC

1981 — "Golden Parachutes" become norm for top management

1982 — S&Ls deregulated—will lead to massive losses

1982 — Mexico defaults

1982 — AT&T agrees to break up into 22 Baby Bells

1982 — Penn Square fails; feds bail out Continental Illinois

1982 — Recession ends, longest bull market begins

1983 — "Poison Pill" takeover defense devised

1984 — Texaco takeover of Getty sets new record; others, such as Standard Oil & Gulf, and Beatrice Foods purchase of Esmark, soon follow

1984 — Apple introduces Macintosh computer

1984 — First state eases restrictions on Nasdaq listings

1985 — Federal deficit hits new high; U.S. a debtor nation

1986 — Ivan Boesky cuts deal to plead guilty, names Milken

1987 — Federal Savings and Loan Insurance Corp. insolvent

1987 — DJIA closes above 2000, January 8

1987 — Alan Greenspan named Federal Reserve chairman in June

1987 — "Black Monday," October 19: 508 point (23 percent) fall in DJIA

1988 — Philip Morris buys Kraft

1988 — Drexel Burnham pleads guilty to insider trading

1989 — Feds agree on S&L bailout bill

1989 — Bidding $25 billion, KKR wins RJR Nabisco

1989 — Time and Warner merge

1989 — Berlin Wall comes down on November 9; Wall Street goes up

1990 — Michael Milken pleads guilty; receives 10 years

1990	Drexel Burnham Lambert goes bust
1990	Iraq invades Kuwait on August 4; U.S. bombs fly, January–March 1991
1990	Germany reunified; East Germany will join EEC
1991	DJIA closes above 3000, April 17
1991	Salomon Bros reveals Treasury corner attempt
1991	Feds seize Bank of Credit & Commerce

THE SCENE IN THE 1980S

The Predators' Ball

Connie Bruck

In late 1984, Forbes reporters Allan Sloan and Howard Rudnit-sky declared to this editor, with what I assumed was just hyper-bole, that they had "found the man who runs America's economy." They weren't kidding; and they were right. Scooping other journal-ists by almost two years, they soon wrote about a little-known bond trader in California named Michael Milken.

As we now know, Milken promoted the sale of junk bonds— high-yield debt notes issued by high-risk companies. He often quoted academic analyses to prove junk bonds can outperform lower-yield-ing bonds, even after taking into account defaults. But the profits from Milken's schemes owed more to simple accounting fraud than to advanced calculus.

Sloan and Rudnitsky's investigation discovered something essen-tial about the way Milken and his firm, Drexel Burnham Lam-bert, did business with high-profile clients like Carl Icahn, Saul Steinberg, and Steve Wynn. "Customers bought one another's paper at original issue," they reported, "thus providing the issuer with an infusion of capital. Over and over, we found key Drexel customers buying one another's securities in the secondary market, too, as well as chipping in to buy issues that it was particularly crucial for Drexel to place. . . . You take in my washing and I'll take in yours, and we'll all end up richer."

That being the case, one has to ignore Drexel's academic equa-tions, which naively assume a company issuing the bonds will de-vote the proceeds to its own operations. Milken's pals invested the proceeds in companies also leveraged by high-risk bonds, which in-vested in other companies leveraged by yet more high-risk bonds, and so on. That real-life scenario requires a different formula—one with a larger risk factor. To solve the equation you will need a calculator that displays negative numbers.

The most colorful account of Milken's gang came from Connie Bruck, author of The Predators' Ball, *titled after the "junk bond convention" Drexel hosted each year. The first, held in 1979, was attended by only sixty people. By 1985 it was a wild party.*

In the third week of March 1985, the faithful, fifteen hundred strong, came to Beverly Hills to pay homage to Michael Milken, the legendary junk-bond guru of Drexel Burnham Lambert whom many of his followers called simply "the King." For the next four days, they would savor the world he had created for them.

Breakfast was served at 6 a.m., a concession to popular tastes by Milken, who was at his desk each day by 4:30 a.m. Then came the perpetual round of presentations, sometimes three simultaneously in different rooms, given by heads of companies. These were nearly all Drexel clients, typically the small and medium-sized companies—run by entrepreneurs with healthy ownership stakes with whom Milken had carved out his historic franchise when he started doing financings for them, back in the late seventies and early eighties.

Because of their small size, or their lack of credit history, or their leveraged capital structure, these companies had been rated below investment grade by the rating agencies and thus had not been able to raise money by issuing bonds in the public market. The only way for them to borrow money was in short-term loans from banks or in private placements with insurance companies, which carried covenants so restrictive that they made the money almost not worth having.

Then, one day, Drexel's investment bankers had come knocking at the door. Drexel would underwrite their bonds, low-rated though they were, for the public marketplace. Michael Milken, a most extraordinary junk-bond trader, could raise $50 million, $100 million or more—the kind of long-term, relatively covenant-free capital that was available to these companies nowhere else. All they had to do was pay the price: a high yield to the investors, and an enormous fee to Drexel.

Now hundreds of buyers were in the audience for these presentations. There were the players who had turned nondescript or failing financial companies into dazzling success stories, based on the yield of the bonds that Milken offered them. And there were the money managers—people who ran investment portfolios for thrift institutions, insurance companies, public and private pension funds, mutual funds, offshore banks, college endowments, high-yield funds.

Now, in March 1985 at the Beverly Hilton, on the eve of an assault that would shake corporate America to its roots, he declared that the combined buying power of his assembled guests was three trillion dollars.

It was a heady message, and made more so by events of the preceding two weeks. The junk-bond-financed takeover had not sprung, fully functioning, from the minds of Milken and his Drexel colleagues; it had needed crafting and fine-tuning. T. Boone Pickens Jr.'s peanut-sized Mesa Petroleum had made a run at mammoth Gulf Oil in early 1984. Pickens had ultimately driven Gulf into the arms of its white knight, Standard Oil of California. Then Steinberg's Reliance had mounted its raid against Disney. Carl Icahn had launched his bid for Phillips Petroleum, after Pickens' Mesa had taken its turn and been bought out. These raids—all financed by Drexel junk bonds, except for Pickens' run at Phillips—had thrown off hundreds of millions of dollars to the raiders and to Drexel. But not one had acquired its target. Corporate America, therefore, had been able to deride these bids as nothing more than stickup artists' bluffs.

They couldn't do that anymore. A week before this Predators' Ball, the first Drexel junk-bond-financed takeover had actually swallowed its target. In a deal that started hostile but turned friendly, the Coastal Corporation was acquiring American Natural Resources Company for $2.46 billion—$1.6 billion of it from bank loans and $600 million from Milken's junk (an amalgam of notes, or debt, with high-yielding interest and preferred stock with high-yielding dividends). Oscar Wyatt, chairman and CEO of Coastal, had become a sudden star.

There were lots of people at this conference who were shaking Wyatt's hand, wishing him luck—and picturing themselves in his shoes. One of them was Nelson Peltz. Just a week earlier, Triangle Industries, a company with a $50 million net worth run by Peltz and Peter May, two unknowns, had made a $456 million bid for National Can, to be wholly financed by Milken's junk bonds. Coastal was a substantial company, and Wyatt, while he was anathema to the corporate establishment, was an experienced operator. But if Triangle Industries, a vending-machine, wire and cable company with little to its name besides the cash raised from previous junk-bond offerings, could succeed in taking over a major industrial company like National Can, then that meant that no prey was too large and no predator too inconsequential—so long as Milken could tap into his magic pools of capital.

The honored guests of this conference, therefore, were the takeover artists and their biggest backers—men like T. Boone Pickens, Carl Icahn, Irwin Jacobs, Sir James Goldsmith, Oscar Wyatt, Saul Steinberg, Ivan Boesky, Carl Lindner, the Belzbergs—and lesser lights about to shine, such as Nelson Peltz, Ronald Perelman, William Farley. The names tend to meld into a kind of raiders' litany, but they are not all the same. For Milken, they would have separate roles during the coming months, performing discrete functions in a vast, interlocking machine of which he alone would know all the parts.

What all these men did share, of course, were enormous egos and appetites, and they did not think of themselves as Milken's functionaries. Each thought he was using Milken to attain his own goal. This was true. But the larger truth was that they were joined in an effort to satisfy an appetite that dwarfed all of theirs, so enormous that all that their deals would throw off to Drexel and to Milken—billions in fees and in equity stakes—would only whet it.

On the second night of the Predators' Ball, while the lower-ranking troops (money managers and executives of medium-sized companies) were sent in buses to a show at a movie lot, some one hundred of the real players—takeover entrepreneurs, major investors, arbitrageurs, deal lawyers—attended a cocktail party at a bungalow at the Beverly Hills Hotel. From there they were chauffeured to dinner in a private room at the swank Chasen's in Beverly Hills.

In addition to Drexel's female employees, there were a number of extremely attractive young women at this dinner—so good-looking, in fact, that one takeover lawyer, George Katz of New York's Wachtell, Lipton, Rosen and Katz, renowned for his naiveté, remarked to a companion, "I've got to hand it to these guys—I've never seen so many beautiful wives!"

In fact few if any wives attended this dinner. An assessment closer to the mark was made by arbitrageur Martin Weinstein, who, noting that Irwin Jacobs had been deep in conversation for hours with one of these women at the far end of the room, commented to a friend, "Tell Irwin he doesn't have to work so hard. She's already paid for."

Insider, 1985

Dennis Levine

Fortunately for him, Dennis Levine is now a relatively obscure character from the insider trading scandals of the 1980s. But his story, big news at the time, led to the investigation that brought down Wall Street's biggest players.

It began with an anonymous letter from, of all places, Caracas, Venezuela. Sent to the New York office of Merrill Lynch, the letter read:

Dear Sir: pleased be informed that two of your executives from the Caracas office are trading with inside information. A copie with description of ther trades so far has been submitet to the S.E.C. by separate mail. As is mantion on that letter if us customers do not benefit from their knoleg, we wonder who surveils the trades done by account executives. Upon you investigating to the last consequencies we will provide with the names of the insider on their owne hand writing.

The letter from Venezuela named two Merrill employees. The firm's compliance department did what all good investigators do: they followed the money. First, looking into the employees' cash management accounts, they discovered a payment to an ex-Merrill broker named Brian S. Campbell. Then, digging through Campbell's trading records, they noticed one of his clients, Bank Leu in the Bahamas, displayed an unlikely acumen for buying stock in companies just before takeovers were announced. Campbell, they guessed, had noticed the bank's string of winners, and was tipping friends and family members. That might not have been illegal. But, in any case, because Campbell was no longer an employee, Merrill could not investigate the matter further. They turned it over to the Securities and Exchange Commission. The SEC telexed the bank, requesting information.

A few days later, one of the bank's anonymous clients called to check *on his account. The caller was Dennis Levine, a director in the mergers-and-acquisitions department of Drexel Burnham Lambert. Levine, just thirty-two, was paid $1 million a year. Apparently that wasn't enough. Through his offshore account, he made millions more illegally by trading stocks using inside information gained on the job. Valuing simplicity and secrecy, he had involved few accomplices. Or so he thought.*

"There's a problem," he was told by his banker. "We should get together soon." Levine flew to the Bahamas to meet with Bernhard Meier.

Somewhat sheepishly Meier said, "The SEC is investigating one of the brokers with whom we have been executing trades."

"What are you talking about?"

"We have executed a lot of our trades through one brokerage firm."

"Stuff that I bought?"

"Yes."

"Weren't you instructed to always break up the orders, to trade through different firms?"

"Yes."

"Didn't you?"

"No. Not always." Meier explained that he did try to deal through several brokers, but he was concerned that a few of them had a tendency to talk too much, to pass tips on to their clients to show them that they had good information. Meier had tried to avoid these brokers, and had steered much of his business to Brian Campbell at Merrill Lynch. Campbell, he said, had a good sense of timing. He knew when it was acceptable and profitable to buy quickly, but he also knew when to slow the pace of his dealings, lest the SEC become suspicious. Furthermore, Campbell gave Bank Leu the best available break on brokerage commissions (which, I realized, Bank Leu had not bothered to pass on to me).

I still did not understand. "Why is this a problem?" I asked.

"Well," Meier replied evasively, "they questioned Campbell."

"Why would they question him?"

Meier was clearly uncomfortable as he explained, "It appears as though—this disappoints me a great deal—he was also buying the same stocks that you were. Now the SEC wants to talk to us."

"What are you going to talk to them about? You're a Swiss citizen working in a Bahamian bank."

"We have no intention of talking to them. We cannot, under the law."

In frustration I asked, "Then what's the problem? You're telling me there is an SEC investigation. You're telling me that your brokers in New York were buying the stocks that I was buying—obviously they spotted a winning pattern. But you can't tell the SEC anything. What's the problem?"

Uncomfortable silence followed. Then Meier whispered. "There's another problem. We also bought the stocks here."

"Who?"

"I did," [the bank's general manager Jean-Pierre] Fraysse admitted. Meier said he had, too.

After an uncomfortable silence, Meier added enigmatically, "Other clients of the bank." Meier was responsible for numerous managed investment accounts, and he had brought them into this busy arena, satisfying his customers by providing them with handsome trading profits and fattening his own commission and service-fee income.

"Let me get this straight," I said, feeling the level of my voice rise. "I place an order for stock. Now I am discovering that not only were my orders filled, but you bought the same stocks for your personal accounts and for other accounts here at the bank, and then your brokers in New York bought for themselves and other people." They had a cottage industry going here! They had piggybacked my trades and magnified the effects in markets around the world. I gulped and asked, "Well, how many of your so-called managed accounts did you make these trades in?"

"Twenty-five or thirty."

"Oh, my God! And you did most of this through one broker?"

Meier nodded.

It was too late for Levine to conceal the trail. Soon he was under arrest. Fortunately for Levine, there was something he could do to reduce his sentence. After all, what is an investment banker but a dealmaker? The prosecutors were happy to trade up from Levine to a more prominent criminal, and Levine had one: Ivan Boesky. Levine had sold insider information to Ivan Boesky in return for a cut of Boesky's profits. Levine confessed, implicating Boesky, and served a reduced sentence. He was out of jail before prosecutors had finished parlaying his testimony into indictments of Boesky, Michael Milken, and others at Levine's old firm.

Den of Thieves, 1986

James B. Stewart

After catching insider trader Dennis Levine, prosecutors followed the trail to Levine's occasional accomplice Ivan Boesky, and from there to Michael Milken. Wall Street Journal editor James B. Stewart unraveled the complex story in his book Den of Thieves.

Ivan Boesky may have been the most feared man on Wall Street in January 1985, but he jumped during a Friday morning staff meeting when his secretary interrupted to say, "Mike's on the phone." Everyone in the room knew that "Mike" was Michael Milken, the junk-bond impresario at Drexel Burnham Lambert Inc.'s Beverly Hills office. He was the only person who always got through to Boesky. Mr. Boesky put his fingers to his lips and looked around the table, ordering silence. Then he picked up the phone. There were no pleasantries. Mr. Boesky himself said little, mostly indicating agreement with whatever Mr. Milken was saying. When he hung up, his eyes were gleaming with excitement. "We're putting all engines on max," Mr. Boesky exclaimed to his assembled traders.

He ordered his staff to buy as much stock of Diamond Shamrock as possible, while selling short Occidental Petroleum, betting that Diamond Shamrock would rise in price and Occidental would fall. The Boesky staff was baffled. Neither stock had been on their research or trading lists that morning. What had Mr. Milken told Mr. Boesky?

In fact, the night before, Drexel Burnham Lambert's West Coast office had been told confidentially that Occidental Petroleum Corp. and Diamond Shamrock planned to merge in a stock swap that would probably cause Diamond Shamrock's stock price to rise and Occidental's to fall. Since Drexel was being retained by Occidental, Drexel's traders were barred by law and firm rules from trading in the stock. But that didn't stop Mr. Milken, a man so powerful that he seemed omniscient.

Mr. Boesky's staff members weren't the only witnesses to the phone call. Mr. Milken's top salesman, James Dahl, was sitting next to Mr. Milken at the trading desk when Mr. Milken called Mr. Boesky, and listened as Mr. Milken issued the trading orders and he and Mr. Boesky refined their strategy to capitalize on the still-secret information. Unknown to Mr. Milken, this was the conversation overheard on Mr. Boesky's end by his traders. And, in fact, under a secret arrangement, Mr. Milken and Mr. Boesky owned the positions 50-50.

Even now, after pleading guilty to six felonies, Mr. Milken insists that he never engaged in insider trading. His spokesmen deny the account reported here, which is based on numerous interviews, including eyewitnesses, and review of sworn testimony. As these previously unreported details show, Diamond Shamrock looks like a brazen example of Mr. Milken's and Mr. Boesky's joint insider trading.

But the scheme proved star-crossed. The following Monday, Diamond Shamrock's board unexpectedly rejected the deal. Told of the development, Mr. Milken grabbed the phone, called Mr. Boesky and, as Mr. Dahl again listened, practically screamed: "The deal didn't go through. We've got to get out of the position."

In New York, Mr. Boesky was apoplectic, frantically ordering his head trader to unload the positions before the news became public. But it was too late; the ticker soon carried the news of the scotched deal, and every arbitrager was trying to dump Diamond Shamrock. Over the next day Mr. Boesky's traders struggled to contain the loss. Mr. Milken screamed at Mr. Boesky for taking too long to get out of the positions. Mr. Boesky screamed at Mr. Milken for getting them into the mess. When it was all over, Mr. Milken brooded at his desk. When Mr. Dahl asked what the matter was, Mr. Milken incautiously explained that he had a position "off-line" with Mr. Boesky and that the deal's collapse had just cost them $10 million.

Even though the conspirators lost money (insider trading is a crime whether money is made or lost), the trading set the stage for Wall Street's most sweeping criminal conspiracy since the passage of the securities laws—in which crimes of far greater reach than insider trading would become routine.

Mr. Milken's crimes alone were massive: systematically robbing clients by trading on their confidential information for his own gain, manipulating securities prices to force deals on which he could make huge fees, gouging unsuspecting clients on junk-bond trades, and in at least two cases, taking for himself, his relatives and a few Drexel colleagues securities meant for his customers.

As their power grew and the volume of their deals skyrocketed, Mr. Milken's band of traders and salesmen headquartered in Beverly Hills took on a superhuman aura—a tight-knit group working 16-hour days under extreme pressure and loving every minute of it.

In fact, the ruthless quest for profits set by Mr. Milken in Beverly Hills was debilitating. Head trader Warren Trepp began smoking four packs of cigarettes a day. Bruce Newberg started taking blood pressure medicine. One day Mr. Newberg raved hysterically when his phone line went dead during an important client call. It turned out Mr. Newberg had chewed through the cord. Another employee, Gary Winnick, complained he was developing a brain tumor and other serious ailments, though he remained healthy. Cary Maultasch developed psychological problems, began seeing a psychiatrist, and asked to be transferred to Drexel's New York office.

Mr. Milken set the tone, badgering traders for not squeezing the most out of a trade, hectoring employees who tried to leave after only 12 hours of work. When Mr. Dahl told Mr. Milken he was leaving early one day after learning his mother had cancer, Mr. Milken's only response was, "When are you going to be back?" Even when Mr. Milken himself briefly keeled over at his desk on the trading floor in 1981, his brother and co-worker Lowell came over, viewed the unconscious body, and simply returned to his office. The message was clear: Keep working.

As early as 1982, Mr. Milken was making $45 million a year, but his aides were struck by how obsessed he was with enhancing his wealth and power. Chatting with Mr. Winnick one day, Mr. Milken looked at the view across Century City and West Los Angeles to the coast and asked, "What do you think it'd cost to buy every building from here to the ocean?"

Once Mr. Milken discovered how his vast network of junk-bond buyers could be harnessed to hostile takeovers, he told his colleague Mr. Trepp in a tone of grim determination that "We're going to tee up GM, Ford and IBM, and make them cringe."

Mr. Boesky was the ideal partner in crime. For despite his fearsome reputation, he had neither Mr. Milken's market acumen nor his access to funds. Like so many of the clients that accepted Mr.

Milken's millions, Mr. Boesky became dependent. Drexel was supplying most of his financing—and charging him a whopping 17% interest.

Mr. Boesky exhibited his own eccentricities, especially when the subject was food. When he met stock trader John Mulheren for the first time at a dinner party at Manhattan's elegant Café des Artistes, Mr. Boesky was asked for his order. "I'll have every entrée," Mr. Boesky said. The waiter's pen stopped in midair. Mr. Boesky repeated, "I'll have every entrée." When the food arrived, the waiter had to wheel a table next to them. On it were that day's eight featured entrées. Mr. Boesky circled the table, looked them over closely, and took one bite of each. He selected one, and sent the rest back.

Mr. Boesky ran his office with an intensity similar to Mr. Milken's. When Mr. Boesky took a rare day off, he harassed his employees with calls to ensure that everyone else was still there working. He had remote control television installed in the office so he could watch each employee from his own control panel. Mr. Boesky's head of research, Lance Lessman, once complained to Mr. Boesky's son, Billy, that "Your dad's really been beating up on me."

"Seriously understand my father," Billy said in a somber tone. "He is stark raving mad."

When Mr. Milken enlisted Mr. Boesky in his schemes, Mr. Boesky was predisposed toward crime. He was already trading illegally on secret information from one of Wall Street's brightest young stars, Martin Siegel. The Kidder Peabody investment banker seemed to have it all: a beautiful wife, a spectacular Connecticut oceanfront estate, glowing press. But Mr. Siegel came to feel he couldn't live on his earnings of more than half a million dollars a year. The Connecticut house had cost $750,000. His wife needed full-time help with their baby. Their Manhattan apartment was too small, and what they considered an appropriate one would cost another $1 million. He was haunted, irrationally, by the bankruptcy of his father.

So Mr. Siegel convinced himself that he needed to provide Mr. Boesky with inside information. The payoff would be cash delivered by an Iranian courier who, Mr. Siegel came to learn, always seemed to skim something off the top. Otherwise, the payoffs went smoothly. On two occasions Mr. Siegel met the courier in the lobby of the Plaza Hotel. After the courier gave the Boesky-dictated password—"red light"—and Mr. Siegel responded, "green light," the briefcase containing the cash, neatly tied in Caesars Palace casino ribbons, was handed over.

But in 1985, Mr. Boesky decided he didn't want to risk another handoff in the Plaza lobby. He told Mr. Siegel to be at a phone booth on 55th and First Ave. precisely at 9 a.m. Mr. Siegel would pick up the receiver and pretend to be making a call. While he was on the phone, the courier would stand behind him as though he were waiting to make a call. He would place a briefcase by Mr. Siegel's left leg, then disappear.

Mr. Siegel arrived at the pay phone early on the appointed date. To kill time, he sat down at a table in the window of a coffee shop across the street. As he sipped his coffee, he spotted someone who had to be the courier: a swarthy man wearing a black peacoat.

Then Mr. Siegel saw someone else. About a half-block up the street, he spotted another dark-skinned man keeping an eye on the man Mr. Siegel suspected was the courier. Mr. Siegel started to panic. What was going on? Suddenly all of Mr. Siegel's fears about Mr. Boesky's reputed ties to the C.I.A. came to the fore. "They're going to kill me," Mr. Siegel thought. He fled.

Mr. Boesky called him later that day. "How did it go?" he asked.

"Nothing went," Mr. Siegel answered. "There was more than one person there."

"Of course," said Mr. Boesky. "There always is. I want to make sure they deliver." Mr. Siegel was amazed that Mr. Boesky didn't trust his own courier. Mr. Boesky insisted that Mr. Siegel repeat the exercise at the phone booth. This time the plan went without a hitch, and Mr. Siegel collected that year's "bonus" of $350,000.

But the frightening experience caused Mr. Siegel to pull away from Mr. Boesky, and eventually to stop giving him inside information. His attention was increasingly absorbed by his efforts to use insider trading profits to prop up a faltering Kidder Peabody. To this end, he launched an even broader insider trading scheme with Goldman, Sachs & Co. partner and chief arbitrager Robert Freeman.

While Mr. Freeman would later plead guilty to a single count of insider trading and his defenders would go on to vigorously assert his innocence and mistreatment by overzealous prosecutors, Messrs. Freeman and Siegel stole information from their firms and their clients to trade illegally on numerous deals. These included: Champion International's bid for St. Regis paper; Kohlberg, Kravis, Roberts & Co.'s purchase of Beatrice Cos.; and T. Boone Pickens's raid on Unocal. As Mr. Freeman once cynically joked to Mr. Siegel: "I've got to hand it to you. You really know how to trade information."

For the Milken/Boesky team, insider trading was a mere way station toward bigger goals and bigger crimes. They were willing, for example, to lose money on their insider trading when a broader goal was sought. In 1984, when Milken client Stephen Wynn of Golden Nugget Inc. found himself stuck with a big position in MCA, Mr. Milken simply directed Mr. Boesky to buy MCA shares until he had driven up the price sufficiently that Mr. Wynn could sell his stake at a profit. There is no evidence that Mr. Wynn knew of this illegal arrangement.

Mr. Boesky lost money selling his own shares, of course. Mr. Milken now owed Mr. Boesky $10 million. Paying him with something so simple as a check was out of the question: It would create a paper trail, and, more important, it would cost Mr. Milken money. Instead, Mr. Milken would get his own junk-bond customers to pay.

He directed Mr. Boesky to buy junk bonds from Milken clients, sell them back to Drexel at inflated prices, generating profits for Mr. Boesky. Then Drexel would convince other clients to buy the bonds at even higher prices. Some of the clients weren't smart enough to realize what was happening; others simply owed Mr. Milken for the many favors he did for them. In less than six months, Mr. Milken repaid Mr. Boesky more than $10 million. And in doing so, he generated further trading profits for his own operation.

The double threat of Milken information and Boesky buying power may have reached its apogee with the 1985 takeover by Drexel client Maxxam Group of Pacific Lumber. Pacific Lumber was gearing up to resist, but then Mr. Boesky started buying the company's shares on Mr. Milken's orders. Mr. Milken, of course, was privy to Maxxam's confidential plans, including the price it would ultimately be willing to pay. As usual, Mr. Milken shared ownership of Mr. Boesky's positions and promised to cover any possible losses. Mr. Boesky's SEC filings, of course, made no mention of Mr. Milken's secret interest.

Maxxam raised its offer, and, feeling under pressure from two raiders, Pacific Lumber capitulated. Mr. Milken's scheme netted

Drexel more than $20 million in fees and generated over $1 million in insider trading profits on the stock owned jointly by Messrs. Milken and Boesky. Pacific Lumber under Maxxam control soon aroused the ire of conservationists by felling tracts of redwood forest to meet its junk-bond payments.

But Mr. Milken's most lucrative ploy may have been his taking Beatrice Cos. warrants in connection with the leveraged buy-out of the company by KKR. Mr. Milken had extracted the warrants (the right to buy Beatrice stock at a low price) from KKR by arguing that he needed to offer them to clients as an inducement to buy the Beatrice junk bonds. Instead, Mr. Milken kept almost all the warrants for Drexel, lodging the bulk of them in his and his family's partnerships. The warrants eventually proved to be worth an estimated $650 million.

Mr. Milken's Beverly Hills colleagues believed they were all sharing in the profits generated by the high-yield department, both in their bonuses and through interests in investment partnerships set up by Mr. Milken. Mr. Milken refused, however, to give details of the partnerships. One day, Gary Winnick called Jim Dahl into his office and said, "I'm going to show you something that will make you sick." Mr. Winnick had gotten a master list of the partnerships. It showed that while most Milken deputies had an account, there were more than 40 accounts for Mr. Milken, his wife, his children and other relatives. In total, Mr. Milken had created more than 500 investment partnerships. One of them, named Otter Creek, paid out an astounding total of $473.4 million, most of it to Mr. Milken and his family members. And that was just one of the partnerships.

But no amount of money, legal or illegal, seemed to be enough for Mr. Milken. At the end of 1986, Drexel allocated $700 million in bonus payments to Mr. Milken's high-yield department. Under his arrangement with Drexel, Mr. Milken was free to allocate those payments to himself and his colleagues. Most of his employees thought Mr. Milken was generous with them. They had no way of knowing that that year, Mr. Milken kept $550 million—nearly 80% of the total—for himself.

Even that wasn't enough. The year before, Mr. Milken felt that Drexel Chief Executive Fred Joseph had cheated him on a finder's fee. Mr. Milken agreed that another department also deserved credit, but argued that his personal contact with the client had locked up the deal. Mr. Joseph disagreed and refused to give Mr. Milken the money. He thought the matter was over. But now, a year later, Mr. Milken again complained about the fee. He called Mr. Joseph repeatedly, arguing strenuously for hours about this one fee. In a year when he had just made $550 million (not counting the Beatrice warrants and other earnings), and when a conservative estimate of his net worth and that of his family would be $3 billion, Mr. Milken never stopped griping that he had been cheated. The amount in dispute: $15,000.

Using testimony from Dennis Levine, the Securities and Exchange Commission pursued insider trader Ivan Boesky, who confessed to a variety of crimes in 1986.

Drexel Burnham Lambert and Michael Milken sat in purgatory for almost two years while the SEC used Boesky's confession to prepare charges against them. Although everyone on Wall Street anticipated some penalty, DBL continued to be involved in major deals such as the takeover battle for RJR Nabisco. Their public relations machine worked overtime, straining to portray Milken as a compassionate philanthropist. For instance, arrangements were made for him to be photographed hosting sick children at baseball games. Those saccharine efforts only made DBL look ridiculous when charges were finally announced. There was no question of Milken's extensive fraud and DBL's involvement.

Prosecutors offered Milken a deal to plead guilty to only two felonies. Milken waited too long to answer, so the prosecutors filed a 98-count indictment. A year later, Milken pleaded guilty to six felonies. Still, he didn't do badly. His fine, though a staggering $600 million, was only a portion of his fortune. He was still worth at least hundreds of millions. Though sentenced to ten years, he served only 22 months. Also, despite being barred from the securities business for life, he has found a way to act as an "advisor" to some of his old clients.

Drexel's reputation, built over 152 years, never recovered. When it filed for bankruptcy protection in 1990, it had more than five thousand employees and $3.6 billion in assets, making the failure the worst in Wall Street history.

The Confessions of Ivan Boesky, 1990

Court Transcript

To much of the public, Ivan Boesky, a central figure in the insider trader scandals, was a cipher. He never stood trial. Nor did he appear before Congress, like the players responsible for Black Friday in 1869 or the Wall Street titans called to explain the 1907 panic and the 1929 crash. He had told his story to government lawyers, who kept the details to themselves for as long as possible while preparing indictments against his associates.

Boesky had already served his jail term by the time Drexel Burnham Lambert, the investment bank with which he had arranged many of his illegal deals, finally went bankrupt in 1990. Even then, he wasn't talking, or at least not saying anything interesting. Veteran Wall Street reporter Gene Marcial, from whom Boesky had little left to hide, couldn't get more than a few pseudo-religious insights from Boesky when he interviewed the ex-convict in 1994. Boesky simply didn't want to look backward.

Unfortunately for Boesky, a court compelled him to testify in the 1990 trial of a former associate, John Mulheren, who was charged with more than 40 counts of conspiracy and fraud.

Boesky was testifying on behalf of the government. Mulheren's lawyer, Thomas Puccio, hoped to discredit him as a witness.

Thomas Puccio: *Mr. Boesky, do you recall taking an oath yesterday when you appeared in this courtroom?*

Ivan Boesky: Yes, indeed.

That was an oath to tell the truth?

Only the truth, sir. . . .

Prior to coming into this courtroom to appear in this case, have you ever taken such an oath, Mr. Boesky?

Yes, I have.

On many occasions, is that correct?

A good deal.

Have you violated that oath before? And have you lied under oath?

I have.

How many times have you lied under oath prior to your appearance in this case, Mr. Boesky?

Several times. I cannot tell you the number.

Well, okay, let's start with the first time you lied under oath. When was that, sir?

Why don't you refresh my recollection, sir?

I don't have a crystal ball, Mr. Boesky.

Why don't you try first . . .

As you sit here, Mr. Boesky, can you think of one lie that you've told under oath?

Refresh my recollection, sir.

Well, without my refreshment of your recollection, is it your testimony that you can't think of one lie you've told under oath? Is that your testimony?

What is your question, sir?

. . . Mr. Boesky, do you agree with the following proposition: greed is healthy? Do you agree with that?

No.

Do you agree with the following proposition: greed is all right and one can be greedy and still feel good about one's self. Do you agree with those propositions?

I would have to see the context in which they're written.

Well, do you recall giving a speech to some students at the University of California at Berkeley?

Yes, I do. . . .

And in that speech that you gave, did you say greed is healthy?

I would have to see the context in which it was written, sir.

Without seeing the context, as you sit here right now, do you ever remember saying to an assemblage of students, "Greed is healthy"; do you remember it, yes or no?

Not out of context, I do not remember it.

Did you ever say to this assemblage of students that greed is all right and even if you're greedy you can still feel good about yourself, something to that effect?

If you have a copy of the speech, I'll be glad to refresh myself, sir. But without a copy of that speech, then I don't recall.

Bearing in mind that in the summer of 1986, according to your testimony, you were worth over $100 million, but less than $1 billion, how were you virtually wiped out about 15 months later?

Well, I think you know that I paid a substantial fine, did I not, sir, to the United States government.

How much was the fine that you paid?

$50 million in disgorgement, $50 million in penalty.

Was that every cent that you had at the time?

No.

How much did you have over and above that $100 million?

I don't recall.

Well, give us an approximation within $100 or $200 million, how much did you have over that?

I would have to see a financial statement, sir.

As you sit here right now, Mr. Boesky, you would have to see a financial statement to tell me within $100 or $200 million how much more you were worth than $100 million back in 1986, is that your testimony?

It is quite obvious that—

Can you answer my question?

Yes.

Yes or no?

I'll answer your question very gladly.

Can you tell me now?

I don't round off to the nearest $100 or $200 million. I would like to see a financial statement, sir.

As you sit here right now, you don't have an approximation you can give us within $100 or $200 million, is that right?

I know that my lawsuits alone exceeded a billion dollars, sir. . . .

Your lawsuits on which no one has collected one cent to date, Mr. Boesky, is that correct?

Claims exceed significantly more than a billion dollars. No judgments have been entered to my knowledge.

And you were fully prepared to turn over to the government every illegal cent that you earned by way of disgorgement, is that correct?

I was fully prepared to give the government what they asked for, sir.

Are you saying that the government only asked for $50 million in disgorgement and nothing else?

Don't minimize that amount, sir. That's not only, that's $50 million, a substantial amount. I think it's a record. I don't think that an amount, until recently, has ever been paid higher than that. . . .

You were a man who, over a period of years, dealt in very large sums of money, isn't that correct?

I think that's accurate.

I am going to assume, correct me if I am wrong, that you're the kind of man who is concerned about how much money you have and how much money you don't have, am I right?

Less than you think.

Or have I misjudged you?

I think you probably have.

Liar's Poker, 1986

Michael Lewis

The excesses of the 1980s were captured by many extraordinary journalists and authors. Looking back, two books are touchstones: Tom Wolfe's novel Bonfire of the Vanities *and Michael Lewis's stranger-than-fiction* Liar's Poker, *a memoir of his brief career trading bonds at Salomon Brothers.*

It was sometime early in 1986, the first year of the decline of my firm, Salomon Brothers. Our chairman, John Gutfreund, left his desk at the head of the trading floor and went for a walk. At any given moment on the trading floor billions of dollars were being risked by bond traders. Gutfreund took the pulse of the place by simply wandering around it and asking questions of the traders. An eerie sixth sense guided him to wherever a crisis was unfolding. Gutfreund seemed able to smell money being lost.

He was the last person a nerve-racked trader wanted to see. Gutfreund (pronounced *Good friend*) liked to sneak up from behind and surprise you. This was fun for him but not for you. Busy on two phones at once trying to stem disaster, you had no time to turn and look. You didn't need to. You felt him. The area around you began to convulse like an epileptic ward. People were pretending to be frantically busy and at the same time staring intently at a spot directly above your head. You felt a chill in your bones that I imagine belongs to the same class of intelligence as the nervous twitch of a small furry animal at the silent approach of a grizzly bear. An alarm shrieked in your head: Gutfreund! Gutfreund! Gutfreund!

Often as not, our chairman just hovered quietly for a bit, then left. You might never have seen him. The only trace I found of him on two of these occasions was a turdlike ash on the floor beside my chair, left, I suppose, as a calling card. Gutfreund's cigar droppings were longer and better formed than those of the average Salomon boss. I always assumed that he smoked a more expensive blend than the rest, purchased with a few of the $40 million he had cleared on the sale of Salomon Brothers in 1981 (or a few of the $3.1 million he paid himself in 1986, more than any other Wall Street CEO).

This day in 1986, however, Gutfreund did something strange. Instead of terrifying us all, he walked a straight line to the trading desk of John Meriwether, a member of the board of Salomon Inc. and also one of Salomon's finest bond traders. He whispered a few words. The traders in the vicinity eavesdropped. What Gutfreund said has become a legend at Salomon Brothers and a visceral part of its corporate identity. He said: "One hand, one million dollars, no tears."

One hand, one million dollars, no tears. Meriwether grabbed the meaning instantly. The King of Wall Street, as *Business Week* had dubbed Gutfreund, wanted to play a single hand of a game called Liar's Poker for a million dollars. He played the game most afternoons with Meriwether and the six young bond arbitrage traders who worked for Meriwether and was usually skinned alive. Some traders said Gutfreund was heavily outmatched. Others who couldn't imagine John Gutfreund as anything but omnipotent—and there were many—said that losing suited his purpose, though exactly what that might be was a mystery.

The peculiar feature of Gutfreund's challenge this time was the size of the stake. Normally his bets didn't exceed a few hundred dollars. A million was unheard of. The final two words of his challenge, "no tears," meant that the loser was expected to suffer a great deal of pain but wasn't entitled to whine, bitch, or moan about it. He'd just have to hunker down and keep his poverty to himself. But why? you might ask if you were anyone other than the King of Wall Street. Why do it in the first place? Why, in particular, challenge Meriwether instead of some lesser managing director? It seemed an act of sheer lunacy. Meriwether was the King of the Game, the Liar's Poker champion of the Salomon Brothers trading floor.

On the other hand, one thing you learn on a trading floor is that winners like Gutfreund always have some reason for what they do; it might not be the best of reasons, but at least they have a concept in mind. I was not privy to Gutfreund's innermost thoughts, but I do know that all the boys on the trading floor gambled and that he wanted badly to be one of the boys. What I think Gutfreund had in mind in this instance was a desire to show his courage, like the boy who leaps from the high dive. Who better than Meriwether for the purpose? Besides, Meriwether was probably the only trader with both the cash and the nerve to play.

The whole absurd situation needs putting into context. John Meriwether had, in the course of his career, made hundreds of millions of dollars for Salomon Brothers. He had an ability, rare among people and treasured by traders, to hide his state of mind. Most traders divulge whether they are making or losing money by the way they speak or move. They are either overly easy or overly tense. With Meriwether you could never, ever tell. He wore the same blank half-tense expression when he won as he did when he lost. He had, I think, a profound ability to control the two emotions that commonly destroy traders—fear and greed—and it made him as noble as a man who pursues his self-interest so fiercely can be. He was thought by many within Salomon to be the best bond trader on Wall Street. Around Salomon no tone but awe was used when he was discussed. People would say, "He's the best businessman in the place," or "the best risk taker I have ever seen," or "a very dangerous Liar's Poker player."

Meriwether cast a spell over the young traders who worked for him. His boys ranged in age from twenty-five to thirty-two (he was about forty). Most of them had Ph.D.'s in math, economics, and/or physics. Once they got onto Meriwether's trading desk, however, they forgot they were supposed to be detached intellectuals. They became disciples. They became obsessed by the game of Liar's Poker. They regarded it as *their* game. And they took it to a new level of seriousness.

John Gutfreund was always the outsider in their game. That *Business Week* put his picture on the cover and called him the King of Wall Street held little significance for them. I mean, that was, in a way, the whole point. Gutfreund was the King of Wall Street, but Meriwether was King of the Game. When Gutfreund had been crowned by the gentlemen of the press, you could almost hear traders thinking: *Foolish names and foolish faces often appear in public places.* Fair enough, Gutfreund had once been a trader, but that was as relevant as an old woman's claim that she was once quite a dish.

At times Gutfreund himself seemed to agree. He loved to trade. Compared with managing, trading was admirably direct. You made your bets and either you won or you lost. When you won, people— all the way up to the top of the firm—admired you, envied you, and feared you, and with reason: You controlled the loot. When you managed a firm, well, sure you received your quota of envy, fear, and admiration. But for all the wrong reasons. *You did not make the money for Salomon. You did not take risk*. You were hostage to your producers. They took risk. They proved their superiority every day by handling risk better than the rest of the risk-taking world. The money came from risk takers such as Meriwether, and whether it came or not was really beyond Gutfreund's control. That's why many people thought that the single rash act of challenging the arbitrage boss to one hand for a million dollars was Gutfreund's way of showing he was a player, too. And if you wanted to show off, Liar's Poker was the only way to go. The game had a powerful meaning for traders. People like John Meriwether believed that Liar's Poker had a lot in common with bond trading. It tested a trader's character. It honed a trader's instincts. A good player made a good trader, and vice versa. We all understood it.

The Game: In Liar's Poker a group of people—as few as two, as many as ten—form a circle. Each player holds a dollar bill close to his chest. The game is similar in spirit to the card game known as I Doubt It. Each player attempts to fool the others about the serial numbers printed on the face of his dollar bill. One trader begins by making "a bid." He says, for example, "Three sixes." He means that all told the serial numbers of the dollar bills held by every player, including himself, contain at least three sixes.

Once the first bid has been made, the game moves clockwise in the circle. Let's say the bid is three sixes. The player to the left of the bidder can do one of two things. He can bid higher (there are two sorts of higher bids: the same quantity of a higher number [three sevens, eights, or nines] and more of any number [four fives, for instance]). Or he can "challenge"—that is like saying, "I doubt it."

The bidding escalates until all the other players agree to challenge a single player's bid. Then, and only then, do the players reveal their serial numbers and determine who is bluffing whom. In the midst of all this, the mind of a good player spins with probabilities. What is the statistical likelihood of there being three sixes within a batch of, say, forty randomly generated serial numbers? For a great player, however, the math is the easy part of the game. The hard part is reading the faces of the other players. The complexity arises when all players know how to bluff and double-bluff.

The game has some of the feel of trading, just as jousting has some of the feel of war. The questions a Liar's Poker player asks himself are, up to a point, the same questions a bond trader asks himself. Is this a smart risk? Do I feel lucky? How cunning is my opponent? Does he have any idea what he's doing, and if not, how do I exploit his ignorance? If he bids high, is he bluffing, or does he actually hold a strong hand? Is he trying to induce me to make a foolish bid, or does he actually have four of a kind himself? Each player seeks weakness, predictability, and pattern in the others and seeks to avoid it in himself. The bond traders of Goldman Sachs, First Boston, Morgan Stanley, Merrill Lynch, and other Wall Street firms all play some version of Liar's Poker. But the place where the stakes run highest, thanks to John Meriwether, is the New York bond trading floor of Salomon Brothers.

The code of the Liar's Poker player was something like the code of the gunslinger. It required a trader to accept all challenges. Because of the code—which was *his* code—John Meriwether felt obliged to play. But he knew it was stupid. For him, there was no upside. If he won, he upset Gutfreund. No good came of this. But if he lost, he was out of pocket a million bucks. This was worse than upsetting the boss. Although Meriwether was by far the better player of the game, in a single hand anything could happen. Luck could very well determine the outcome. Meriwether spent his entire day avoiding dumb bets, and he wasn't about to accept this one.

"No, John," he said, "if we're going to play for those kind of numbers, I'd rather play for real money. Ten million dollars. No tears." *Ten million dollars.* It was a moment for all players to savor. Meriwether was playing Liar's Poker before the game even started. He was bluffing. Gutfreund considered the counterproposal. It would have been just like him to accept. Merely to entertain the thought was a luxury that must have pleased him well. (It was good to be rich.)

On the other hand, ten million dollars was, and is, a lot of money.

If Gutfreund lost, he'd have only thirty million or so left. His wife, Susan, was busy spending the better part of fifteen million dollars redecorating their Manhattan apartment (Meriwether knew this). And as Gutfreund was the boss, he clearly wasn't bound by the Meriwether code.

Who knows? Maybe he didn't even know the Meriwether code. Maybe the whole point of his challenge was to judge Meriwether's response. (Even Gutfreund had to marvel at the king in action.) So Gutfreund declined. In fact, he smiled his own brand of forced smile and said, "You're crazy."

No, thought Meriwether, just very, very good.

"Salomon Brothers' response to the publication of this story," Lewis later recalled, *"boggled my mind almost as much as it inflated my royalties. Acting under instructions from Mr. Gutfreund, the Salomon Brothers public relations man told reporters that the game occurred, but that it had been a practical joke. He was widely disbelieved. A few weeks later the Salomon spokesman mysteriously changed his story: The game had happened, and was presumably serious, but it had not involved Mr. Gutfreund. It had involved another managing director, who had recently died, and so was unavailable for comment. The Salomon spokesman was again ridiculed. Months later I opened a newspaper to find Mr. Gutfreund himself claiming that the story was pure fiction."*

In 1991 John Gutfreund resigned from Salomon after it was disclosed the firm tried to corner the market in U.S. Treasury notes. Gutfreund, who had decided to hide the firm's fraud, lost all credibility when he refused to acknowledge it even after it had been disclosed. "The firm's real crime," Lewis wrote at the time, *"was its curious attitude toward the truth. . . . Why did Mr. Gutfreund tell such stupid stories? The first answer is that he thought, not unjustifiably, that they would be believed."*

The Keating Five
April 8, 1987

William Black

*"This is shaping up to be the biggest financial disaster of the postwar era,"
Nathaniel C. Nash of* The New York Times *said about the savings and
loan crisis of the 1980s. He blamed "a confluence of error and ineptitude, at
times compounded by fraud. Congress, regulators and the industry all failed."*

*Misstep by misstep, the story went like this: S&Ls had been prevented
by law from making variable-rate loans, so when interest rates rose
quickly in the late 1970s the thrifts had to pay a higher rate to depositors
than they were charging for their old mortgages. Even then, the thrifts were
limited by law to paying less than the rates other institutions could offer,
so deposits disappeared. Congress, avoiding the cost of bailing out hundreds
of failing thrifts, instead propped them up by making them attractive to
cash-rich owners. It relaxed regulations on both who could own an S&L
and how an S&L could lend money. Previously, an S&L had to have 400
owners; now it could have one. Previously, no real estate developer could
even sit on an S&L board, to prevent the thrift from improperly approving
loans for that developer's property; now the single owner could actually be
a developer; previously, S&Ls were limited to making home loans; now they
could loan money to an entrepreneur in almost any field.*

*S&Ls may have been bound too tightly before the regulations were
eased; suddenly they were allowed to run wild, which is what they did.*

*After all, what did they have to lose? Most deposits were insured by
the federal government, thanks to the Banking Act of 1934. So why not
bet the farm—and everything else in sight? If the bets paid off, the S&L
would profit. If the bets lost, Uncle Sam would make things right with
the depositors.*

Unfortunately, too many of the bets lost.

*Government bank examiners noticed that the S&Ls were covering up
the truth with fraud. William Black, a lawyer with the San Francisco
branch of the Federal Home Loan Bank, estimated that fraud was "a
contributing factor" in three-quarters of the S&Ls that went bust.*

One of the S&Ls Black investigated became the most famous failure: Lincoln Savings and Loan, headed by Charles Keating, which invested two-thirds of its $6 billion of federally insured deposits in junk bonds and other high-risk ventures. ("The junkiest of the junk," as one regulator described it.) Lincoln also perpetrated massive accounting fraud, including swapping empty lots with other companies then adjusting their bookkeeping as if the lots had been sold at a profit.

But while few of Keating's investments returned a profit, he certainly got his money's worth when he went to Washington to buy politicians.

Four government regulators, including William Black, learned of Keating's influence when they were ordered to Washington to meet with five senators who had received campaign contributions from Keating and Lincoln. Those senators, later called "the Keating Five," did their best to stymie the regulators.

Not surprisingly, the most hostile senator was Dennis DeConcini of Arizona, where Keating was based. His associates had significant financial entanglements with Keating and Lincoln, including $50 million in personal loans to the senator's campaign aides. Though the state's junior senator, John McCain, would later admit that his involvement in this meeting was a blot on his record, he would also stick to an unconvincing claim that he was unaware of Keating's full influence. (His wife and father-in-law had made an investment of almost $360,000 in a Lincoln shopping center a year before the meeting, and the senator, along with his family, had taken nine trips at Keating's expense, including three to Keating's vacation compound in the Bahamas.)

Senator Alan Cranston, who barely stuck his head into the meeting, but who made clear that he agreed with the others, raised $1 million from Keating at practically the same moment.

The harassment of the regulators by some of the senators was noted by Black. He wrote the following memo to his boss, Federal Home Loan Bank Board chairman Ed Gray.

To: Edwin J. Gray

April 9, 1987

At your request I am providing you this memorandum, which reflects the substance of yesterday's meeting with Senators [Alan] Cranston, [Dennis] DeConcini, [John] Glenn, [John] McCain and [Don] Riegle.

The Federal Home Loan Bank of San Francisco (FHLB-

SF) personnel who attended the meeting were James Cirona (President and Principal Supervisory Agent), Michael Patriarca (Director of Agency Functions), myself (general counsel) and Richard Sanchez (the Supervisory Agent for Lincoln S&LA of Irvine, Calif.).

. . . DeConcini: Thank you for coming. We wanted to meet with you because we have determined that potential actions of yours could injure a constituent. This is a particular concern to us because Lincoln is willing to take substantial actions to deal with what we understand to be your concerns. Lincoln is prepared to go into a major home loan program— up to 55% of assets. We understand that that's what the Bank Board wants S&Ls to do. It's prepared to limit its high risk bond holdings and real estate investments. It's even willing to phase out of the insurance process if you wish. . . .

Lincoln is a viable organization. It made $49 million last year, even more the year before. They fear falling below 3 percent (net worth) and becoming subject to your regulatory control of the operations of their association. They have two major disagreements with you. First, with regard to direct investments. Second, on your reappraisal. They're suing against your direct investment regulation. I can't make a judgment on the grandfathering issue. We suggest that the lawsuit be accelerated and that you grant them forbearance while the suit is pending. I know something about the appraisal values [Senator Glenn joins the meeting at this point] of the Federal Home Loan Bank Board. They appear to be grossly unfair. I know the particular property here. My family is in real estate. Lincoln is prepared to reach a compromise value with you.

Cranston: [He arrives at this point.] I'm sorry I can't join you but I have to be on the floor to deal with the bill. I just want to say that I share the concerns of the other senators on this subject. [Cranston leaves.]

. . . McCain: Thank you for coming. One of our jobs as elected officials is to help constituents in a proper fashion. ACC [Keating's American Continental Corporation, parent company of Lincoln] is a big employer and important to the

local economy. I wouldn't want any special favors for them. It's like the Apache helicopter program that Dennis and I are active on. The Army wants to cut back the program. Arizona contractors make major components of the Apache helicopter. We believe that the Apache is important to our national defense. That's why we met with General Dynamics and tried to keep the program alive.

I don't want any part of our conversation to be improper. We asked chairman Gray about that and he said it wasn't improper to discuss Lincoln. I'd like to mention the appraisal issue. It seems to me, from talking to many folks in Arizona, that there's a problem. Arizona is the second fastest growing state. Land values are skyrocketing. That has to be taken account of in appraisals.

Glenn: I apologize for being late. Lincoln is an Ohio chartered corporation, and . . .

Cirona: Excuse me. Lincoln is a California chartered S&L.

Glenn: Well, Lincoln is wholly owned by ACC.

DeConcini: You said Lincoln was Ohio chartered. It's California.

Glenn: Well, in any event, ACC is an Ohio chartered corporation. I've known them for a long time but it wouldn't matter if I didn't. Ordinary exams take maybe up to 6 months. Even the accounting firm says you've taken an unusually adversary view toward Lincoln. To be blunt, you should charge them or get off their backs. If things are bad there, get to them. Their view is that they took a failing business and put it back on its feet. It's now viable and profitable. They took it off the endangered species list. Why has the exam dragged on and on? I asked Gray about this. Lincoln has been told numerous times that the exam is being directed to continue by Washington. Gray said this wasn't true.

. . . *Glenn:* I'm not trying to get anyone off. If there is wrongdoing I'm on your side. But I don't want any unfairness against a viable entity.

Cirona: How long do we have to speak to you? A half-hour, an hour?

DeConcini: As quickly as possible. We have a vote coming up soon.

... *Cirona:* This meeting is very unusual. To discuss a particular company.

DeConcini: It's very unusual for us to have a company that could be put out of business by its regulators. ...

(The senators left to vote. We resumed when Senators DeConcini and Riegle returned.)

Sanchez: Lincoln had underwriting problems with all of their investments, equity securities, debt securities, land loans and direct real estate investments. It had no loan underwriting policy manual in effect when we began our 1986 exam. When the examiners requested such a manual they were informed that it was being printed. The examiners looked at 52 real estate loans that Lincoln had made since the 1984 exam. There were no credit reports on the borrowers in all 52 of the loan files.

DeConcini: I have trouble with this discussion. Are you saying that their underwriting practices were illegal or just not the best practice?

Cirona: These underwriting practices violate our regulatory guidelines.

Patriarca: They are also an unsafe and unsound practice.

DeConcini: Those are two very different things.

Sanchez: You need credit reports for proper underwriting.

(Senator Glenn returns at this point.)

... *Patriarca:* They're flying blind on all of their different loans and investments. That's what you do when you don't underwrite.

Glenn: How long had these loans been on the books?

Sanchez: A fairly long time.

Glenn: How many loans have gone belly-up?

Sanchez: We don't know at this point how many of the 52 have defaulted. These loans generally have interest reserves.

Glenn: Well, the interest reserves should run out on many of these.

Cirona: These are longer term investments.

Patriarca: I know that Lincoln has refinanced some of these loans.

Glenn: Some people don't do the kind of underwriting you want. Is their judgment good?

Patriarca: That approach might be okay if they were doing it with their own money. They aren't; they're using federally insured deposits.

Riegle: Where's the smoking gun? Where are the losses?

DeConcini: What's wrong with this if they're willing to clean up their act?

Cirona: This is a ticking time bomb.

Sanchez: I had another case which reported strong earnings in 1984. It was insolvent in 1985.

Riegle: These people saved a failing thrift. ACC is reputed to be highly competent.

Patriarca: Lincoln was not a failing thrift when ACC acquired it. It met its net worth requirement. It had returned to profitability before it was acquired. It had one of the lowest ratios of scheduled assets in the 11th District, the area under our jurisdiction. Its losses were caused by an interest spread problem from high interest rates. It, as with most other California thrifts, would have become profitable as interest rates fall.

DeConcini: I don't know how you can't consider it a success story. It lost $24 million in 1982 and 1983. After it was acquired by ACC it made $49 million in one year.

McCain: I haven't gotten an answer to my question about why the exam took so long.

Sanchez: It was an extremely complex exam because of their various investments. The examiners were actually in the institution from March to October—8 months. The asset classification procedure is very time consuming.

McCain: What's the longest exam you ever had before?

Cirona: Some have technically never ended, where we had severe problems with a shop.

McCain: Why would Arthur Young say these things about the exam—that it was inordinately long and bordered on harassment?

. . . *Patriarca:* I'm relatively new to the savings and loan industry but I've never seen any bank or S&L that's anything like this. This isn't even close. You can ask any banker and you know about these practices. They violate the law and regulations and common sense.

Glenn: What violates the law?

Patriarca: Their direct investments violate the regulation. Then there's the file stuffing. They took undated documents purporting to show underwriting efforts and put them into the files sometimes more than a year after they made the investment.

Glenn: Have you done anything about these violations of law?

Patriarca: We're sending a criminal referral to the Department of Justice. Not maybe; we're sending one. This is an extraordinarily serious matter. It involves a whole range of imprudent actions. I can't tell you strongly enough how serious this is. This is not a profitable institution. Prior year adjustments will reduce that reported $49 million profit. They didn't earn $49 million. Let me give you one example. Lincoln sold a loan with recourse and booked a $12 million profit. The purchaser rescinded the sale, but Lincoln left the $12 million profit on its books. Now, I don't care how many accountants they get to say that's right. It's wrong. The only thing we have as regulators is our credibility. We have to preserve it.

DeConcini: Why would Arthur Young say these things? They have to guard their credibility too. They put the firm's neck out with this letter.

Patriarca: They have a client. The $12 million in earnings was not unwound.

DeConcini: You believe they'd prostitute themselves for a client?

Patriarca: Absolutely. It happens all the time.

. . . *Glenn:* Have they [Lincoln] been told what you've told us?

Patriarca: We provided them with our views and gave them every opportunity to have us hear what they had to say. We gave them our classification of asset materials and went through them loan by loan. This is one of the reasons the exam has taken so long. . . . We didn't use in-house appraisers. We sent the appraisals out to independent appraisers. We sent the reappraisals to Lincoln. We got rebuttals from Lincoln and sent them to the independent appraisers. I don't think there was any case that Lincoln agreed with the reappraisal.

Sanchez: None where the reappraisal indicated insufficient collateral.

Patriarca: In every case, after reviewing the rebuttal, the independent appraiser has stood by his conclusion.

DeConcini: Of course. They had to.

Patriarca: No. The rebuttals claim specific problems with the independent appraisers' reappraisals: "You didn't consider this feature or you used the wrong rental rate or approach to value." The independent appraiser has come back to us and answered those specific claims by saying: "Yes, I did consider that, and here's why I used the right rate and approach."

DeConcini: I'd question those reappraisals. If you want to bend over backwards to be fair I'd arbitrate the differences.

The criminality surprises me. We're not interested in discussing those issues.

Keating was never shy about his political connections. After regulators took control of Lincoln in April 1989, Keating boasted to reporters about his bribery: "One question, among many raised in recent weeks, has to do with whether my financial support in any way influenced several political figures to take up my cause. I want to say in the most forceful way I can: I certainly hope so." About the Keating Five, he said, "I would rate their performance pretty darn high. They should be congratulated."

Eventually, Keating was indicted and tried in California. Though convicted at his first trial, he was released because Judge Lance Ito, who would later oversee the trial of O. J. Simpson, gave the jury incorrect instructions. Convicted at the second trial and sentenced to twelve and a half years, he was freed after less than five. He still maintains his innocence.

The five senators who harassed the bank regulators received harsh treatment from the Senate Select Committee on Ethics. Only Cranston, however, received a formal rebuke. His long career essentially ended because of the $1 million he received from Keating.

The bailout of Lincoln cost taxpayers $2.6 billion. To bail out all the S&Ls, taxpayers paid more than $165 billion.

Black Monday
October 19, 1987

Steve Coll

"So much for the good life," Steven Swartz warned in the Wall Street Journal *a few days before Black Monday, the worst crash in New York Stock Exchange history, when the Dow Jones Industrial Average lost 22.6 percent in a single day. "For the first time in more than five years, many securities-industry professionals see a significant reversal in the stock market's direction. Already, the plunging bond market and some enormous trading losses over the past few months have exposed dirty linen some firms didn't know they had: unprofitable business lines, monstrous overhead and skimpy management controls."*

More than a thousand people had already been laid off by Wall Street firms in the previous months. Kidder Peabody president Max C. Chapman, Jr., told Swartz, "We're going to have to run our firms like regular businesses, instead of with the bull market at our backs."

But investors, instead of worrying when the storm would hit Main Street, sat back to enjoy the spectacle of brash young traders brought low. After all, one had to laugh at the twenty-five-year-old bond trader, let go by Salomon Brothers, who whined to The New York Times, *"I can't face being poor again."*

The week that ended Friday, October 16, had been the worst for the market since France was invaded by Germany in 1940. The DJIA dropped more than 9 percent, on record volume. It ended at 2246, far below the 2746 it had hit in August. Over the weekend, people grew more pessimistic about the coming Monday. Some decline seemed inevitable.

Eyewitness Steve Coll is a Pulitzer Prize-winning journalist and author.

Thirty minutes before the opening bell rang out over the cavernous floor of the New York Stock Exchange last Monday morning—a day likely to be remembered as "Black Monday," 1987—a group of the most influential men in U.S. finance assembled in the sixth floor office of the stock exchange's chairman, John J. Phelan, Jr.

On chairs hastily arranged around Phelan's desk sat the chief executives of the country's largest investment banks and brokerages: William A. Schreyer, chairman of Merrill Lynch & Co.; John H. Gutfreund, chairman of Salomon Brothers Inc.; Peter T. Buchanan, chief executive of First Boston Corp.; S. Parker Gilbert, chairman of Morgan, Stanley & Co., and about ten others.

Phelan had summoned them by telephone shortly after dawn. He knew that a crisis was at hand, and he wanted support and advice from the exchange's richest and most powerful members. Between them, the men who arrived in his office controlled hundreds of billions of dollars in assets.

Like a tidal wave, panic in the world's financial markets was sweeping inexorably toward Wall Street that Monday morning. When the meeting in Phelan's office began, the London stock market was concluding its worst day ever; prices were down about 10 percent amid massive selling. The Tokyo market had closed just hours before, and it too had suffered a record-setting collapse.

"We knew it could be a bad day," First Boston's Buchanan recalled. "But I don't think anybody (at the meeting) anticipated what actually happened."

Phelan outlined his plans and sounded out the assembled chief executives. The exchange chairman said that unless the members felt differently, he was going to try to keep the stock market open all day long, no matter how severe the crisis became.

Phelan remembered telling them, "Here's what we're going to do—anybody got any other ideas?"

"There was a very clear consensus—I think it was unanimous—that the markets should remain open as probably the first priority," Buchanan said. "I recall that several of us offered to help out with the specialists (firms that facilitate stock trading on the exchange floor) if we were asked."

Concerns also were voiced about the impact on the stock market that day of computerized trading programs, especially those that generate large, simultaneous trades of stocks in New York and stock futures in Chicago. Phelan said that he, too, was concerned that computer trades might exacerbate a market collapse, but he did not propose that morning—as he would later—that member firms suspend computer-assisted trading at the New York exchange.

The meeting in Phelan's office—the only such gathering of the week—ended shortly before the stock market opened at 9:30 a.m.

Then the worst one-day plunge in U.S. history—508 points on the Dow Jones industrial average—began. The chief executives returned to their respective Wall Street headquarters, there to endure one of the most trying days in their careers.

It began Monday in the Chicago futures pits, where pandemonium reigns even on a routine day.

Minutes before trading in S&P 500 stock index futures began at the Chicago Mercantile Exchange at 8:30 a.m. Central time, hundreds of traders jammed together to hear what is known as the "opening call," a declaration of the expected opening prices of the futures contracts that are traded through shouting, wild hand signals, and eye contact in the pit.

S&P futures contracts, which began trading on the Chicago Merc just five years ago, are one of a number of new financial products that have changed the way U.S. markets function.

The contracts bought and sold in the pit allow investors to speculate on the overall movement of the stock market in New York, as measured by the Standard & Poor index of 500 leading corporations.

Investors can buy an index futures contract—an obligation to buy or sell the index package at a given price at a given future time—in hopes that the stock market will move up. They also can sell futures contracts "short," speculating that index prices will fall in the weeks or months ahead.

The opening call in the pit that morning stunned the crowd of traders, several said later, even though they knew that panic selling of stocks in London and Tokyo—and on Wall Street the previous week, when the Dow had twice suffered record plunges—would create a heavy downdraft in the futures markets that morning.

Few were prepared for the free fall that occurred in the first minutes after the pit's opening. The S&P index price plummeted 18 points—more in five minutes than in all of Friday, which had seen the worst drop ever.

"Everybody just had sell orders," said one trader. "We had huge, huge orders that we haven't ever had before."

"Brokers were saying, 'Give me a bid—anywhere.' It was an absolutely scary, horrible feeling," said Jerry Friedman, an independent trader.

While there is sharp disagreement about the role played by computerized trading later on Monday, experts in both Chicago and New York agree that "program trades" were a primary factor in that initial collapse in the Chicago futures market, which signaled a later free fall on the New York Stock Exchange.

The experts disagree, however, about whether the first wave of computer trading in Chicago supported or undermined the overall performance of the country's financial markets on Monday.

The first wave of massive selling in the S&P futures pit, investors and exchange officials agree, was led by large institutional investors seeking so-called portfolio insurance.

Managers of many large pension and other funds responsible for tens of billions of dollars in stock holdings attempt to use the futures pit to protect themselves against precisely the sort of disaster that occurred Monday.

The managers own millions of shares of stock and are necessarily worried about what would happen to their assets if the market collapsed. One way to hedge their risk is to sell S&P futures short; if the market dives, they can then offset stock losses with profits gained by the futures contracts. Precise formulas, sometimes computerized, have been devised by fund managers to determine how many futures contracts need to be sold short in order to protect a fund's stock holdings against a crash.

The problem in the pit Monday morning, experts agree, was that too many institutional investors were trying to obtain their insurance too late. Everyone was selling S&P contracts at once, and in unprecedented amounts. The pit was overwhelmed by the volume, and prices went into a tailspin.

"These people were using us to write insurance in the midst of an earthquake," said William Brodsky, president of the Chicago Merc.

That morning, collapsing futures prices became an instant measure of where stock prices were headed. And since futures prices are monitored on computers by investors who trade stocks on Wall Street, it became clear within minutes that panic selling was about to occur in New York.

The collapse of futures prices in Chicago accelerated the disaster in New York, but the pressure to sell stocks on Wall Street was at first pent up like steam in a kettle.

With investors panicked by the free fall in futures, specialists in

New York were swamped by sell orders and were forced to delay the opening of trading in many individual stocks.

That delay both increased the selling pressure and threw the moment-by-moment relationship between futures prices in Chicago and stock prices in New York drastically out of whack. Futures prices fell, but stock prices couldn't keep up because of the trading delays.

Available evidence about the early stock selling in New York does suggest that in the morning it was large institutions—pension funds, corporations and other professional investors—that led the panic, not individual investors.

Statistics generated by New York Stock Exchange computers show that single-block trades involving 200,000 or more shares—that is, trades so large that they were likely made by institutional investors—occurred mainly in the morning. Seventy-two such block trades occurred between 9:30 and 11:30 a.m., with the largest number—23—taking place between 10:30 and 11 a.m., when trading in many of the blue chip stocks finally opened after early delays. In contrast, only 22 such trades occurred between 1 p.m. and 3:30 p.m.

Similarly, single-block trades involving more than $10 million in stock market value were heavily concentrated in the morning. Sixty such trades occurred between the New York opening and 11:30 a.m., while only 36 occurred during the rest of the day, according to exchange statistics.

Those numbers are generally supported by the observations of traders, investors and exchange executives. They said that while the futures free fall in Chicago triggered a wave of morning selling by institutions in New York, panic selling by individual investors took over in the afternoon.

According to collated reports of telephone operators at Fidelity Investments, the large Boston-based mutual fund company that serves 2.5 million individual investors, fears of small investors across the country escalated sharply Monday afternoon after the early selling waves in Chicago and New York had sent prices skidding downward.

"Nervous concern became high anxiety, and the exchanges (from stock funds) into money market funds shot up," said Rab Bertelsen, a Fidelity vice president.

"Every once in a while, they (government officials) would ask what we thought was the cause of this," Phelan said. "I just thought it was a confluence of different kinds of things," he said, including inflation fears, rising interest rates, computer trading and the fact that the stock market had risen without a significant correction for five years.

Investors were not calmed by President Reagan's apparent lack of interest. "This is purely a stock market thing and there are no indicators out there of recession or hard times at all," he said. After a bounce in the next two days, stocks dipped again. Specialist firms, obliged to buy stocks themselves when no other buyers could be found, faced bankruptcy.

Prior to the market opening on October 20, the Fed released this announcement: "The Federal Reserve System, consistent with its responsibilities as the nation's central bank, affirmed today its readiness to serve as a source of liquidity to support the financial and economic system." As Fed governor Robert T. Parry later recalled, "Performing the lender-of-last-resort activity transferred the systemic risk from the market to the banks and ultimately to the Fed, which is the only financial institution with pockets deep enough to bear this risk. This allowed market intermediaries [such as the specialists] to perform their usual functions and helped keep the market open."

Though DJIA would not again reach its pre-crash highs until July 1989, a depression was avoided. The Federal Reserve lowered lending rates to increase the money supply and stimulate the economy, rather than tightening credit as it had done after the 1929 crash.

The Pit, 1986–1987

Laura Pedersen

Countless experts told us the crash of 1987 was caused by program trading—vast computer systems working at nanosecond speed to place bets on the market's direction. As thrilling as it sounds, we all learned wrong. Computers may have accelerated trading, and multiplied the effects of a single decision, but orders eventually traveled to a world that was all too human.

Laura Pedersen, who wrote about trading options on the American Stock Exchange in her book Play Money, *recalled that the real character of the trading pit was revealed when it was being redesigned.*

Like a Broadway theater, there was the "stage"—in our case, a high platform on which the specialists stood, looking across a chasm at the hordes of traders who were stationed atop a series of graduated tiers. In between, in the orchestra section, was a long passageway, ostensibly reserved for the waves of brokers who, during trading hours, moved in and out of the pit like spawning salmon. At least that was the way it was supposed to work, on paper. It never did. Chaos is not the sort of thing that lends itself to space allocation.

One thing that went wrong almost from the start was that the carpenters were designing this thing from blueprints instead of from observation. Had they bothered to see us in action, understood human greed, they'd have seen instantly that what mattered more than unobstructed vision—sight lines between traders and specialists—was (a) the proximity between the two groups and (b) the need to be in voice contact with the specialists, to catch the hand signals, eye movements, and so forth. The problem was that the higher the traders and specialists were placed, the greater the distance. The communications gap became a chasm in which a lot of hand-to-hand combat took place. To keep the brokers from being overrun by the surge of frenzied traders, it became necessary to install a long metal railing, similar to the one found in every zoo around the polar bear cages. Actually, the analogy isn't that far-fetched. Before the railing was built, the poor brokers found themselves quite literally bulldozed up the other side of the pit by a swarm of angry traders, pinning us specialists against the makeshift wall behind us, and leaving us no choice but to use our feet to violently shove these bodies back down. There were days it looked like that famous castle-siege scene in any one of half a dozen Hollywood epics. Thanks to all those discarded ketchup packets, we even had the "bloodstains," to show our battle worthiness.

Efforts at noise abatement proved equally futile. The walls of the enclosure were wrapped in thick industrial carpeting to muffle the ungodly combination of noises that emerged from there. On top of the roaring of three hundred or so maniacal traders, there was the noise of the beeping monitors, the overhead public-address system, and thirty phones incessantly ringing off the hook. All at once.

Even before the opening bell, well in advance of trading, the players would jockey for position in the pit so as to be the first to be recognized by the specialists, standing slightly above them on the podium overlooking the floor of the pit.

The best way for X to get a front-row position was to finagle Y out of the pit. This was often accomplished by the simple expedient of arranging for Y to be paged out front—usually by X's clerk standing two feet away, using a wall phone. The minute Y left, X would slip into the vacated spot and stay there, not budging an inch. By the time an infuriated Y returned to the pit, he would find it impossible to worm his way back in.

Given that sort of competitive environment, mistakes were bound to occur that could test the best of friendships.

One particularly active day, my clerk jotted down that I had bought "fifteen options contracts at the price of thirteen and a half," while the opposing trader yelled back that he'd sold me "fifty contracts at thirteen and a half."

The difference between saying fifteen and hearing fifty led to a $47,250 misunderstanding that had to come out of one of our pockets the following day. What made it particularly awkward was that the aggrieved trader was a rather good-looking guy I'd had a date with the evening before, one of those rare occasions when my restricted life-style allowed me a night out. Because the transaction reporter standing next to me during the trade also swore to having heard me say "fifteen," my opponent had a tough time proving the error to be mine.

Either of us could have sought a ruling by a floor referee or gone to formal arbitration, which would have put a crimp in our budding romance. Moreover, arbitration is not a viable alternative for settling such trading arguments, because it can take hours and cost both traders precious floor time, often a sacrifice of more money than the amount being disputed.

So, instead, we grudgingly agreed to split the loss. The pit had been too loud for anyone to hear correctly. My adversary left with his copy of the rejected trade notice, but not before calling me a "first-class bitch." At least he still thought of me as first class. But not enough to resume dating me. In fact, he told me afterward that whenever he looked at me, all he could think of was losing $23,625.

The Fall of the House of Hutton, 1987

Brett Duval Fromson

"When E. F. Hutton talks, people listen." That memorable slogan of the 1970s suggested intelligence and integrity. It helped grow the firm's revenues from $85 million in 1970 to $1.1 billion in 1980—a decade when many brokerages were struggling. Hutton ranked second only to powerhouse Merrill Lynch. "We used to look down our noses at the PaineWebbers, the Dean Witters, and the Shearsons as they went through their traumas in the 1970s," a Hutton executive told Brett Duval Fromson, an editor at Fortune *when he wrote this account. "We were sure that nothing like that could happen to us."*

The company didn't survive through the next decade. "Hutton had been a great brokerage," Fromson said. "It was murdered by the stupidity, selfishness, and greed of its top executives."

Even at sixty-three, E. Robert Fomon can't sit down. For five hours he paces his living room, trying to explain the demise of E. F. Hutton, the brokerage house he ran for sixteen years. A haze of cigarette smoke covers the English antiques and sporting paintings that decorate his Fifth Avenue apartment. "Did I let the firm down?" he asks. "Did I let the employees down? No, I don't think so." To hear Fomon talk, there are no good explanations for Hutton's collapse and subsequent sale to Shearson Lehman Brothers, no large lessons to be learned.

Fomon just doesn't know a good story when he hears one. The Hutton saga is a managerial morality tale that has everything but a hero: an actress, a baseball commissioner, several villains, pretty girls, not to mention mismanagement, selfishness, arrogance, and greed. Call it "The Fall of the House of Hutton."

Was Hutton's collapse inevitable? Had the eighty-four-year-old franchise outlived its usefulness? As a laid-off former Hutton employee—one of five thousand—asks: "Did we have to be laid naked at the feet of Shearson?" The answer to each question is "No."

Hutton's problem, says a former management director, is that it "made every mistake in the book, and no one was ever punished." The blunders ranged from the ridiculously extravagant (investing $100 million in a glitzy new headquarters when the firm was losing money) to the downright illegal (check kiting). But the seminal error was allowing Robert Fomon to wield absolute power for so long. He hired and promoted whomever he wanted, including close friends. He personally reviewed the salaries and bonuses of more than one thousand employees. Like a feudal lord, he banished organization, budgets, and planning from his domain. "His whole life was holding court, making all the large and small decisions," says a former Hutton managing director and Fomon confidant. "When Friday night at six o'clock rolled around, a tear would come down his cheek because he was wondering what the hell he was going to do till Monday. Outside of work, he was the loneliest man who ever lived."

As Hutton grew, however, it became far too complex to be run so autocratically. After a broken leg and two small strokes between 1983 and 1985, Fomon, says a former Hutton officer, "lost control of the firm and no one ever regained it."

Hutton's senior officers contributed to the chaos because so many lacked managerial skills. In the firm's entrepreneurial culture, executives usually came up through the ranks of brokers or dealmakers; they did not regard managing as macho. Bad decisions by the officers tended to be ratified by the board of directors. Until 1986, eighteen of the twenty-three members, on average, were insiders. The outside directors included actress Dina Merrill, E. F. Hutton's daughter, and Edward Cazier, Jr., one of Fomon's personal lawyers, whose firm, Hahn Cazier & Smaltz, received large fees from Hutton.

The firm's vaunted but poorly organized retail brokerage, which produced about 75 percent of Hutton's revenues, had problems too. Executives focused so much on increasing revenues that they lost sight of costs. Hutton did not know which brokers made money and which ones did not. Retail brokers retained large clients whose orders could have been executed more cheaply by lower-commissioned institutional brokers. Two executives cite an example of run-amok management: Hutton was expensing party girls from escort services as temporary clerical and secretarial help. From 1981 on, profits slipped steadily at the retail brokerage. Still, Hutton's legendary perquisites continued. Though the firm lost $90 million in 1986, according to a former top executives, it spent $30 million to send its best-producing brokers and their wives on all-expense-paid trips.

Between 1980 and 1982, Hutton was not just squandering its own money; it was also using funds from a $4 million check-kiting scheme. Hutton managers intentionally overdrew the firm's checking accounts for a day or two to earn additional interest income. The firm pleaded guilty to two thousand counts of mail and wire fraud in 1985 and never recovered from the scandal. Not even Robert Rittereiser, a top-notch manager brought in as president from Merrill Lynch, could save Hutton. He says that when he agreed to join Hutton, "I had no idea that the firm was in such bad shape."

He began to get the picture the first day. Fomon told him that a client of Hutton's most productive broker, Houston's Don Sanders, had bounced a check for $48 million but had been allowed to resume trading in another account he had with the firm. "I told Fomon that if it were up to me, I'd close the account today," says Ritt. "And I wondered why he hadn't." But the decision had already been made to let Sanders's client keep trading. Rittereiser was powerless to do anything more than shake his head. Rittereiser spent his first six months soothing state regulators who wanted to close Hutton down and bankers who wanted to pull the firm's credit lines.

The relationship between Fomon and Rittereiser began to deteriorate in late 1986. Fomon, perhaps realizing that he was losing control of his firm, actively tried to sell it. Several companies, including Chrysler, seemed interested but backed off when they realized the extent of Hutton's problems. Fomon frequently complained about Rittereiser behind his back. "I wanted to sell the firm because I could see that he was a consensus guy, not a leader," says Fomon.

A blowup between the two was inevitable.

The board had to decide who was going to run its company: Fomon or Rittereiser. Clearly the two could not work together any longer. At the initiative of [board member Peter] Ueberroth, the board directed Fomon and Rittereiser to decide who was in charge. But the members left little doubt that they preferred Rittereiser. The next day, Fomon bought Ritt lunch at an Upper East Side hotel and in a tense meeting said, "You want to be CEO? Okay, I'll do it."

Although Fomon was as good as his angry word, he remained chairman for six months while he negotiated an $11 million golden handshake. At his final appearance before the board, Fomon took one more swipe at Rittereiser by nominating Ueberroth as chairman. According to Hutton officers, Fomon hoped Ueberroth would take the job and sack Rittereiser. When Ueberroth refused, Fomon said, "I'm going to put Hutton in play," and left the room.

Fomon made his move after the crash of October 19, 1987, trying—unsuccessfully—to secure an offer from Sandy Weill. Instead the board arranged a quick sale to Shearson American Express. (Shearson had offered $50 per share a year earlier, but because the crash had knocked Hutton's stock from $35 to $15 it paid only $29 per share.) One of the board's final acts was to vote itself multimillion-dollar retirement benefits. Meanwhile, the deal they had structured left most Hutton managers and employees with no benefits at all.

The ending was no surprise, concluded Fromson: "Although the directors' special treatment of themselves seems unfair, it is in keeping with the long tradition of me-first-manship at Hutton. Robert Fomon was the exemplar of that spirit. 'People around here believed that if they could get away with something, they should do it,' says a former Fomon associate. At Hutton, selfishness was a way of doing business. The company lived—and died—by it."

Barbarians at the Gate, 1988

John Helyar and Bryan Burrough

If takeovers became a spectator sport in the 1980s, this one was the Super Bowl—halftime show and all. Meanwhile, from the press box, pundits denounced it as the worst sort of greed.

Top management at RJR, who had a habit of granting themselves innumerable perks, began the action by announcing a leveraged buyout (LBO) of the company—meaning they would borrow money to buy all the outstanding shares and take the company private. Seven executives would then own as much as 18 percent of the company, simply for having been around at a time when buyout financing was available. The burden of the leverage, estimated at about $20 billion, making it the largest deal ever, would be carried by employees. Many would lose their jobs in the cutbacks necessary to repay the loans.

In Barbarians at the Gate, *their brilliant best-seller that later became a television movie,* Wall Street Journal *reporters John Helyar and Bryan Burrough illustrated the excesses of RJR and its grandiose chief executive, Ross Johnson.*

"Oh hell, we'll never do a buyout," Johnson said. "Just think of all the people that would be affected; we can't do that. Do we want to have to fire thousands of people? Can we live with that?" Besides, he added, "we have the best jobs in America."

It was no lie. RJR executives lived like kings. The top thirty-one executives were paid a total of $14.2 million, or an average of $458,000. Some of them became legends at the Waverly for dispensing $100 tips to the shoeshine girl. Johnson's two maids were on the company payroll, and Johnson's lieutenants single-handedly perked up the upper end of Atlanta's housing market.

No expense was spared in decorating the new headquarters, highlighted by the top-floor digs of the top executives. The reception area's backdrop was an eighteenth-century $100,000 lacquered Chinese screen, complemented by a $16,000 pair of powder blue

Chinese vases from a slightly later dynasty. Visitors could settle into a set of French Empire mahogany chairs ($30,000) and ogle the two matching *bibliothèque* cabinets ($30,000) from the same period. In each was an English porcelain dessert service in a tobacco-leaf pattern ($20,000). The visitor might be ushered in to see Bob Carbonell and pad across his camel-colored $50,000 Persian rug. Or, if the visitor was lucky enough to see Ross Johnson, they could jointly admire the $30,000 worth of blue-and-white eighteenth-century porcelain china scattered throughout his office.

If the visitor was really lucky, he was an antique dealer in town to take more orders. RJR was the toast of dealers in London, Paris, and New York. Laurie Johnson personally supervised many purchases on European jaunts with her decorator. Despite the $50 million cost of moving the headquarters, multimillion-dollar decorating projects were also underway at the old tobacco headquarters and the new Washington office. "It was the only company I ever worked for without a budget," gasped one grateful vendor.

It was, literally, the sweet life. A candy cart came around twice a day, dropping off bowls of bonbons at each floor's reception areas. Not Baby Ruths but fine French confections. The minimum perks for even lowly middle managers was one club membership and one company car, worth up to $28,000. (For serious luxury cars, executives had to kick in some of their own money.) The maximum, as nearly as anyone could tell, was Johnson's two-dozen club memberships and John Martin's $75,000 Mercedes.

Sweet as the surroundings were, the new headquarters developed a clear caste system. About a third of the 400 people working there had moved from New Jersey. Many were Standard Brands veterans. Another third were Reynolds people from Winston-Salem. The remaining third, mostly secretaries and support staff, were new hires from Atlanta. The Reynolds veterans felt they shouldered much of the menial work. Some began calling themselves "the mushroom farmers" because they worked in the dark and just kept shoveling manure. An inescapable air of the transitory pervaded the new headquarters. Instead of the grand old tobacco building in Winston-Salem, or even the Glass Menagerie across the street from a cigarette factory, Johnson had moved RJR Nabisco into a spec office building in a mall-hotel-office park complex that overlooked a highway cloverleaf. Some of Johnson's lieutenants—Ed Robinson and Andy Hines, the controller—hadn't even bothered to sell their houses up north. Ward Miller, the corporate secretary, hadn't even moved to Atlanta. Everything about RJR Nabisco said, "We're just passing through."

But it was at nearby Charlie Brown Airport, where corporate Atlanta housed its jets, that the air of new money and restlessness found its ultimate expression. There Johnson ordered a new hangar built to house RJR Nabisco's growing fleet of corporate aircraft. Reynolds had a half-dozen jets, and Nabisco a couple of Falcon 50s and a Lear, tiny planes an executive like Johnson wouldn't be caught dead in. After the arrival of two new Gulfstreams, Johnson ordered a pair of top-of-the-line G4s, at a cool $21 million apiece. For the hangar, Johnson gave aviation head Linda Galvin an unlimited budget and implicit instructions to exceed it.

When it was finished, RJR Nabisco had the Taj Mahal of corporate hangars, dwarfing that of Coca-Cola's next door. The cost hadn't gone into the hangar itself, but into an adjacent three-story building of tinted glass, surrounded by $250,000 in landscaping, complete with a Japanese garden. Inside a visitor walked into a stunning three-story atrium. The floors were Italian marble, the walls and doors lined in inlaid mahogany. More than $600,000 in new furniture was spread throughout, topped off by $100,000 in objets d'art, including an antique Chinese ceremonial robe spread in a glass case and a magnificent Chinese platter and urn. In one corner of the ornate bathroom stood a stuffed chair, as if one might grow fatigued walking from one end to the other. Among the building's other features: a walk-in wine cooler; a "visiting pilots' room," with television and stereo; and a "flight-planning room," packed with state-of-the-art computers to track executives' whereabouts and their future transportation wishes. All this was necessary to keep track of RJR Nabisco's thirty-six corporate pilots and ten planes, widely known as the RJR Air Force.

The aviation staff presented the plans for all this to Johnson with some trepidation. He had said state-of-the-art, but this cost $12 million. He had wanted everything a corporate-jet hangar could possibly have, but this came out to 20,000 square feet. Johnson looked over the drawings, heard out the architects, and made his recommendation: add another 7,000 square feet.

The RJR Air Force was a defining symbol for Johnson. It was all about restlessness and restiveness. It was also about dispensing favors. Frank Gifford got rides home from "Monday Night Football" games. Gifford and his talk-show host bride, Kathie Lee, were whisked away to their honeymoon on an RJR Nabisco jet. (Johnson was best man at the wedding.) When Roone Arledge needed a lift from Los Angeles to San Francisco, an RJR jet was dispatched from Atlanta. Johnson's old buddy Martin Emmett, long gone from the company, racked up more miles on Johnson's jets one year than nearly anyone still employed.

The jets were also a symbol of the increasingly fuzzy line between what constituted proper use of a corporate asset and what constituted abuse. Some thought the case of Johnson's German shepherd, Rocco, fell in the latter category. At the Dinah Shore that year, Rocco bit a security guard, setting off a flurry of concern in the Johnson household.

Would he be seized by the authorities and quarantined, or worse? Rocco, it was decided, had to go on the lam. He was smuggled onto a corporate jet and secretly flown out of Palm Springs to Winston-Salem, one jump ahead of the law. Escorted by a senior vice president named Dennis Durden, Rocco was listed on the passenger manifold as "G. Shepherd." It wasn't the only Rocco adventure: The company would later pay an insurance claim for a bite inflicted on the Johnsons' gardener.

The RJR Air Force was Johnson's ticket to the high life. Each weekend the planes disgorged Don Meredith from Santa Fe, or Bobby Orr from Boston, or the Mulroneys from Canada. The jocks of Team Nabisco were frequent flyers on Air Johnson. [He] took excellent care of them, paying more for occasional public appearances than for an average senior vice president: Meredith got $500,000 a year, Gifford $413,000 (plus a New York office and apartment), golfer Ben Crenshaw $400,000, and golfer Fuzzy Zoeller $300,000. The king was Jack Nicklaus, who commanded $1 million a year.

Johnson claimed his jocks yielded big benefits in wooing supermarket people, but the line between corporate and personal services was a blurry one at RJR Nabisco. LPGA pro Judy Dickenson gave Laurie Johnson golf lessons. Gifford emceed benefits for Johnson's favorite charities like the New York Boys Club. A pair of retired New York Giant fullbacks, Alex Webster and Tucker Frederickson, maintained offices at the Team Nabisco office in Jupiter, Florida; Frederickson ran an investment counseling business from his.

For all the money Johnson doled out for Team Nabisco, some of the athletes weren't easily managed. Nicklaus was notoriously difficult. For one thing, he didn't like playing golf with Johnson's best customers, which was his highest and best use. And he considered himself above the task of working the room solo at some Nabisco function. Although he was making more money than anyone at RJR Nabisco except Johnson and Horrigan, the "Golden Bear" growled at doing more than a half-dozen appearances a year. After several run-ins with subordinates, an arrangement was struck where only Johnson and Horrigan could personally tap Nicklaus's services.

Then there was the O. J. Simpson problem. Simpson, the football star and sometime sports announcer, was being paid $250,000 a year, but was a perennial no-show at Team Nabisco events. So was Don Mattingly of the New York Yankees, who also pulled down a quarter million. Johnson didn't care. Subordinates took care of those and most other problems. He was having a grand time. *"A few million dollars,"* he always said, *"are lost in the sands of time."*

Time has a way of changing minds, too; and in time Johnson changed his mind about a buyout. But when his $75-per-share bid was announced, the company's directors, embarrassed by reports of excesses they had also enjoyed, recoiled from their benefactor. They accepted a rival bid (arguably lower, depending on the value of securities) from Kohlberg, Kravis, Roberts. The final price: $109 per share, a total of $25 billion.

The Pru-Bache Scandal, 1983–1991

Kurt Eichenwald

In October 1990, a sixty-one-year-old widow, Eloise Burg, picketed the Manhattan offices of Prudential-Bache. Her sign read:

"PRUDENTIAL-BACHE HAS FINANCIALLY AND
IMMORALLY RAPED ME. INVESTORS: BEWARE!"

Burg claimed Pru-Bache had cost her hundreds of thousands of dollars by lying to her about unsuitable investments. She took her protests to the streets after being awarded just $45,000 in arbitration. Jackson Taylor, a thirty-year-old Columbia University student who claimed Pru-Bache had also conned him, joined Burg. They were the first public outcry against what is by far the largest swindle in the history of Wall Street.

"One at a time," wrote New York Times *reporter Kurt Eichenwald, in his best-seller* Serpent on the Rock, *"until they numbered in the hundreds, then the thousands, then the hundreds of thousands, people in every state and around the world awoke to realize that they had been victims of the most destructive fraud ever perpetrated on investors. . . . It was not engineered by the shady penny-stock promoters or crooked savings and loan operators who exist in the underbelly of the financial world. Rather, the scheme emerged full-blown from the New York headquarters of one of the brokerage industry's brightest lights, an investment firm with a name that conveyed the essence of reliability and trust. . . . More than $8 billion worth of risky partnerships packaged by Prudential collapsed after they had been falsely sold as safe and secure. Even after the partnerships lost most of their value, the investors had no idea what had happened. Every month, on millions of account statements, Prudential-Bache lied about the true worth of the portfolios, showing them as never having lost a penny in value. And so the damage spread unchecked for more than a decade. . . ."*

As Eichenwald describes, the deal was dirty from the start:

Three executives from Graham Resources walked into a cocktail party at a hotel near Fort Lauderdale, Florida. They were scheduled to meet a group of thirty Prudential-Bache brokers and managers who were attending a sales conference in the late summer of 1983. It was Graham Resources' first opportunity to size up the types of people who would be selling the new Energy Income Fund.

The Graham executives—Rich Gilman, Paul Grattarola, and Rusty Renaudin—fanned out in the massive marble room. They walked among the Prudential-Bache brokers and managers, who were busily munching on shrimp hors d'oeuvres and downing free drinks. Waiters in white gloves walked through the crowd, silently whisking away the empty plates and glasses that the brokers scattered haphazardly about the room.

James Parker, the Direct Investment Group's chief marketer for Florida, introduced the Graham executives to as many brokers as he could. After about half an hour, the crowd moved to a conference room. There, the Graham executives were scheduled to make a presentation describing the new energy income partnership.

Before leaving Louisiana, the three executives had plotted how to handle this group from Prudential-Bache. This, they decided, would be the best opportunity to get some intelligence on the firm's brokers and managers. Graham had done business with Merrill Lynch in the past and knew the high level of training that those brokers received. Renaudin and Grattarola, both regional marketers for Graham, were former Merrill Lynch stockbrokers and felt they understood the salesman's mentality.

The best pitch, the group had decided, was to treat the Prudential-Bache brokers as if they were from Merrill Lynch. That meant making a sophisticated marketing presentation about the way the Energy Income Fund worked and how it might perform. This would not be like hocking shoes; instead, Graham would provide an educational lecture that would help the brokers understand the product and see where it might fit with their clients' investing needs. If the presentation went over the heads of the crowd, then Graham, in coordination with Prudential's marketing team, could dumb it down a little the next time.

The task of making the presentation at the Florida meeting was given to Gilman. As all the brokers and managers found their places, Gilman sat down at the head table, reviewing his notes. Finally, he was introduced and stood up before the assembled group.

"I'm here today to introduce you to an exciting new product that will provide your clients with a unique way to participate in the oil and gas industry," Gilman began. "It is called the Prudential-Bache Energy Income Fund."

As planned, Gilman launched into a sophisticated description of how the partnerships worked. While the presentation was technical, it was not financially complex. He described how the partnerships would use investor money to buy oil in the ground, then pump it and sell it. The cash from sales—minus expenses—would be returned to the investors in distributions. Included in each distribution was the original cash used to buy oil plus the profit from its sale. It was like investing in a car for $1,000, souping it up, and selling it for $1,500—the money received included $500 in profit and $1,000 in original investment.

Finally, Gilman explained that determining the value of the oil in the ground was somewhat complex. While a reserve was purchased all at once, it would be pumped out over decades, with the price of oil always changing. He described how values are assigned to the reserves. He used the parlance of the industry, mentioning the "present value" of the reserves and the "internal rate of return" of the partnership.

Gilman paused and looked up. A sea of blank, uncomprehending eyes looked at him. The brokers and managers had absolutely no idea what he was talking about. Nor did anyone look like they much cared.

A hand went up, and Gilman pointed toward the man. "Do you have a question?" he said.

"Yeah," the Prudential-Bache broker said. "What are you guys going to pay in commissions?"

As complex as the Energy Income Fund was to understand, the first thing that the brokers cared about was how much money was in it for them.

For the next few minutes, Gilman fielded question after question about the commission structure of the partnerships, from how much would be paid overall to how much would end up in the brokers' pockets.

Grattarola sat back in disgust. Great, he thought. We've got a bunch of guys here interested in just three things: commissions, commissions, and commissions.

Eventually, the brokers started asking some questions about the oil business. But the queries were either pointless or so idiotic that Gilman seemed to have trouble keeping a straight face.

"Is oil going to $100 a barrel?" The Graham executives did not know. "Well, how long do you think it would take for it to go that high?" Again, they said they did not know if it ever would.

Near the end, they called on a broker who was eagerly waving his hand.

"Yes," the broker said. "Is it true that the oil is in huge underground lakes?" Grattarola took that question. After pausing for a minute to catch his breath, he answered. No, it was not true.

The meeting drew to a close, and a number of branch managers walked to the front of the room. Several of them looked extremely mad. One short, overweight manager pushed himself into the Graham executives' faces.

"What the hell were you people talking about?" the manager demanded angrily. "Present values? Internal rates of return? We don't want to hear any of this fancy stuff. You just talk about yield. How much money would somebody who put $10,000 in an oil partnership get each year?"

The Graham executives could not believe what they were hearing. Yield was the return on investment—for most retail clients, it usually referred to the amount of fixed interest they were paid on a bond. Even in the sloppy parlance of Wall Street, telling investors that the partnership's cash distributions were a yield would not only be misleading, it would be fraudulent. Perhaps part of the money—the difference between the costs of purchasing and selling the oil—might be referred to loosely as "yield." But as Gilman had just explained, the distributions also included a return of the original capital that was used to buy the oil in the first place. Describing the distributions as "yield" would be like telling bank customers that all cash withdrawals from their own accounts were interest payments. It was simply false.

"Calling this 'yield' does not tell the whole story," Gilman answered. "It would be very misleading."

"Well, then it's too damn complicated," the manager replied. "If you guys can't break this down and make it simple, then nobody at this firm is going to sell it. Let me tell you, if your sales pitch is longer than three minutes, then I don't want you talking to my brokers. They've got better things to do."

After a few more tense minutes, the meeting broke up. The three Graham executives hustled out of the room. They were supposed to drive a rental car to the airport, where they were scheduled to fly to another meeting of Prudential-Bache brokers. But they decided to take a limousine. They needed the driving time to start preparing a much slower, less sophisticated presentation. They hired a car and piled into the back.

"Well," Gilman said. "What do you think?"

"I think we're in deep shit, guys," Grattarola said. "These are the dumbest bastards I've ever run into. We've got managers who don't understand, and are a bunch of hustlers. We've got brokers who are stupid, and not well trained."

Renaudin agreed. "These guys don't know their ass from a hole in the ground," he said.

The three discussed whether it was possible that the ignorance they were seeing was just in Florida, or if it was throughout the firm.

"I'll tell you, we don't need sales material for this bunch," Grattarola said. "We're going to need educational material. We've got to keep it real simple for these guys, and go back to the very, very basic stuff."

Some questions were raised about whether educational material alone would help the brokers sell the partnerships. But Grattarola was insistent.

"These guys don't understand investments," he said. "They don't understand the terminology of the Street. And they sure as hell don't understand oil and gas. We could end up with some serious compliance problems."

All of them knew what Grattarola was saying. These brokers could easily fall out of compliance with the securities laws requiring them to accurately describe investments to their clients. How could they be accurate if they didn't understand what they were selling?

Getting the brokers educated was the top priority. Otherwise, they might start breaking the law.

"Today, I want to tell you about an investment opportunity with potential high cash flow, a superior structure, a unique sharing arrangement, and low risk."

By the late summer of 1983, hundreds of Prudential-Bache brokers across the country heard those words in the opening seconds of the first marketing video for the Energy Income Fund. The video, put together by the Direct Investment Group, began with a shot of Ron Gwozdz, the department's first product manager for the energy partnerships. As he recited the opening line, he walked to an office door and grabbed a hard hat. He threw open the door, and the scene dissolved to an oil field setting. For the next few minutes, Gwozdz talked about the experience of Prudential Insurance and Graham Resources in the oil business. He introduced John Graham, who discussed how low oil prices made the timing for the investment perfect.

"Ron, I've never seen a better time to buy products in the ground at distressed prices," Graham said.

Graham dismissed the idea that there might be a glut of oil and natural gas. "That's somewhat misleading," he said. "This should not be the case."

When Grattarola saw the video, he thought it was a disaster. It didn't explain the partnerships—if anything, it oversimplified them. It made them seem safer than they actually were. It didn't discuss the risks. It didn't raise any of the important compliance issues. It offered none of the education that was so critically needed. But few people in the senior ranks of Graham or the Direct Investment Group seemed to care. The video was simple. It would get the partnerships sold.

Eloise Burg, the widow who picketed Pru-Bache headquarters, told reporters "I'm working to get them out of business." After several months the firm made restitution to her. But by then the story was out. Most shocking was the involvement of Prudential, "the essence of reliability and trust," as Eichenwald put it. The rock-solid company had bought the Bache brokerage as part of its quest for the Holy Grail of Wall Street, the "financial supermarket."

Burg and Taylor paid a price for being first, but they also gained an advantage. Prudential-Bache fought hard against a legal settlement for investors who followed her lead. Even after a judgment was awarded in a class-action suit, the company's lawyers tried to trick investors into giving up their claims by deliberately miswording forms. Only a small portion of the stolen capital was returned.

Prudential is still in business.

Capitalist Tool, 1990

Christopher Buckley

Here was Malcolm Forbes aboard his yacht, the *Highlander,* a few years ago going up the Amazon River, watching a skeet shooting contest taking place on his afterdeck between the ex-king of Greece and the ex-king of Bulgaria.

"Aren't you going to take a turn?" I asked.

He was endowed, along with a lot else, with these great eyebrows that made the caricaturist's job easy. They arched, he winked, declined: "The last thing I shot was Germans."

I liked him before I ever met him, when I read in an interview in which the reporter asked him to what he attributed the secret of his success. He answered, diligence, hard work and my father leaving me a ton of money.

I come to praise Malcolm (for whom I recently went to work as an editor), not to dump on Mr. Trump and his ilk, but you never had to apologize for liking him. Whatever he was, he was no malefactor of great wealth. (What is the opposite of miser? Spendthrift isn't quite the right word. Is there a word for it?) He was of the money-is-like-manure school. You know, pile-it-up-in-one-place-and-it-stinks, spread-it-around-and-it-does-some-good.

In the aftermath of the—ahhem—much remarked upon 70th birthday bash in Morocco last summer, one writer reported a scene around a table where a half dozen of the richest people in America engaged in a little philosophical shop talk on the subject: Who among us is happiest? The answer was unanimous: Malcolm.

He was the last happy millionaire—or billionaire, for that matter—an antidote to the Henry Potters (the "meanest man in town" in Frank Capra's movie "It's a Wonderful Life"), the Gruesome Rich with their pay telephones in the foyer and their brutalized offspring who spend the balance of their ruinous lives litigating against their siblings, making the only case left for the doctrines of Karl Marx. In struggling to find some good in his premature death this weekend I can only think of this: that it adds an inoculating coda, a grace note to a decade that will not be remembered for the grandeur of its displays of wealth. His obituaries, dated 1990, may convince some people years from now that perhaps they all weren't Milkens or Kravises or Boeskys.

What made him happy—despite all the money, I mean? I think one clue lies in his maternal genes.

Malcolm's father was a self-made Scotsman who for all his dapperness and jauntiness was a Scót who stretched his dimes. His wife was a Catholic girl, who didn't. I heard this story: that one day he looked up from the latest bill from Tiffany and exploded at her: "Woman, how can you spend so much money!"

"Bertie," she replied calmly, "I like spending money."

On the last day of our trip from Manaus to Iquitos, I went out on deck to watch the sun melt into the jungle and stumbled onto him. He was sitting on a fold-out chair next to his helicopter, reading a biography. White hair aside, he looked like a boy who has left the grown-ups to go read a story by himself in the corner.

Here is another reason he was happy: he never quite grew up. He was the Eternal Boy, surrounded by his toys: his Harley-Davidsons, his hot-air balloons, his boats, his castles, his . . . things. For a man who liked his comforts, he thrilled in discomfort. In his life he crashed his motorcycle and plunged into icy Chesapeake waters after ballooning across the continent. A friend of his told me a story about flying to Europe with him aboard his plane. There was a foursome, playing bridge. She looked out the window and saw that the engine was on fire. She said, "Malcolm, the engine is on fire." Malcolm looked out the window. The pilot had already started to turn back to Gander. "Your bid," he said. How karmically right that he should have died at home, in bed, after returning from a bridge tournament in London.

And yet . . . this happened 10 years too soon. He was 70, going on 60. I saw him last Wednesday. The energy field around him was crackling. He was robust, the cigar was lit, he wanted to see the samples from the prospective art directors. For a man with an empire, he cared down to the last detail. Finally he saw one he liked. The face creased into a grin. "Now this," he said, pointing to one of the boards. "Now this is good." After a moment, he added: "What do you think?" I think he did this out of courtesy.

Then suddenly the meeting ended, as meetings with busy men tend to, without your realizing it. Swifty Lazar was on the phone. This is my last image of Malcolm: leaning forward—I don't think he did much sitting back in chairs in 70 years—growling, "Err-ving!"

Who will speak for capitalism now? Václav Havel and Mikhail Gorbachev. But who will make it fun?

"The Cartel," 1991

David Wessel

Salomon's decades-long dominance of the Treasury market was the foundation of the firm's pride. But as the Bible warns, "Pride goeth before destruction, and a haughty spirit before a fall."

Not content with merely making the market in Treasuries, Salomon tried to corner it. At the auction of two-year notes on May 22, 1991, Salomon trader Paul Mozer, using unsuspecting clients as fronts, bought far more than the legal limit. Of the $12.26 billion sold, Salomon bought almost 90 percent.

The scandal revealed Salomon had abused its position as one of the 39 "primary dealers" entitled to buy notes directly from the Treasury. The system, which made sense at one point, created an orderly market that the Treasury could trust. It needed to know, for instance, that the firms bidding on the notes could actually make payment. After Salomon's corner, the market was anything but orderly. Anyone who needed those notes — smaller firms, for instance, who were prevented from buying the notes directly, but had promised delivery of them — had to pay Salomon's price. Some estimates put the losses among those smaller firms at $100 million. Many laid off traders.

The scandal made some investors think about the multitrillion-dollar Treasury market for the first time. As Wall Street Journal *reporter David Wessel explained, experts in Washington hadn't thought about the system for a long time either.*

Back in 1981, when interest rates were sky-high, U.S. Treasury Undersecretary Beryl Sprinkel came up with a way to save taxpayers billions. Convinced that interest rates would fall, he proposed suspending the sale of bonds that lock the government into paying stratospheric rates for 30 years.

But Mr. Sprinkel ran into two implacable foes: in New York, bond dealers and investors who advise the Treasury, and in his own building, Wall Street's allies in the Treasury bureaucracy. At a closed-door meeting at the New York Federal Reserve Bank, all but one of the bond dealers lined up against Mr. Sprinkel. Fearful, among other things, of seeing their finely tuned market disrupted, they told the Treasury secretary that the proposal was "uncertain, unknown and untested."

It turned out that Mr. Sprinkel was right. Interest rates did come down.

But as Treasury secretaries usually do on such matters, then-Secretary Donald Regan took Wall Street's advice. And for years, taxpayers will be paying 14.56% interest on those bonds, at a total additional cost of $1.5 billion—enough, for example, to completely immunize five million children. Moreover, there were a dozen other bond issues at similar double-digit rates.

Privately, Secretary Regan railed about "the cartel"—a select band of "primary dealers" in Treasury securities to which the Treasury Department has long granted something very close to a veto over changes in its borrowing practices. But in the end, he deferred to it.

Along with the New York Fed, the Treasury has long tolerated restrictive practices and ossified technology that allow the 39 primary dealers—the middlemen between the Treasury and investors—to keep others from obtaining valuable information about the world's biggest financial market.

Now, the silver lining of the Salomon Brothers Inc. scandal may be that it is revealing just how much of an insiders' game the Salomon-dominated system had become. Salomon has admitted that it repeatedly violated Treasury-auction bidding rules. Some at the Treasury, realizing that the department is perceived as a patsy, are beginning to think about changing the way it does business with Wall Street.

"The primary-dealer system has worked very well for us," says Jerome H. Powell, assistant Treasury secretary for domestic finance, "but we are taking a careful look at it. There are aspects of it that raise real concerns." Such as? "The perception and the reality that the primary dealers have benefited from it because of an unfair advantage."

Until the Salomon scandal, top officials rarely raised such explosive questions. Instead, the Treasury's aim was to avoid uncertainty and rattling the market, which often boiled down to the primary dealers. Without them, the argument went, the Treasury might someday find itself without buyers for the government's debt. In an era of global markets, this apprehension is probably outdated. But the fear—along with the practice of filling important jobs at Treasury from the ranks of the primary dealers—accounts for the cartel's remarkable success in beating down almost every effort to change the rules of its game.

At the core of the bond dealers' club is an inner elite, a little-known group blandly called the Treasury Borrowing Advisory Committee. This self-selected group of primary dealers and other bond-market players has made sure that, in return for getting Wall Street's bids, Treasury did the bidding of Wall Street.

Ostensibly, the advisory committee recommends how much the Treasury should borrow in one-year notes, how much in 10-year securities, and so on. In fact, it's essentially an old-boy network. "I have been uneasy, to be honest, about that particular mechanism for some time," Gerald Corrigan, president of the New York Fed, recently told a congressional committee. He never said so, publicly at least, before the Salomon scandal.

For years, committee members have come to Washington four times a year, always on a Tuesday, to get, among other things, a valuable one-day advance peek at the Treasury's estimated quarterly borrowing needs. In a throwback to the days when gentlemen simply didn't cheat, the members are told not to call their offices until the Treasury's public announcement the next day—and there's no evidence anyone ever broke the rule. But the Treasury, trying to dispel the perception that it's too close to the dealers, says that before the committee meets again, next month, the borrowing estimate will be released publicly.

That's one small adjustment in an otherwise unchanging ritual. After the briefing at the Treasury, the members sit down for a chat with the entire Federal Reserve Board and then head for Washington's stately Madison Hotel for lunch. After coming up with recommendations that are presented to top Treasury officials the next morning, they meet for dinner, usually with Treasury and Fed officials. The committee is so hidebound that for years the menu never changed—salmon at lunch, lamb chops at dinner.

"Apologies don't mean [expletive]," Salomon chairman John Gutfreund said with characteristic charm after the story broke. "What happened, happened."

The government wasn't mollified by that explanation. It opened Treasury auctions to all broker-dealers. It later examined the sale of other government debt, such as federal home mortgages and student loans. Eventually it found enough false records and rigged bids of the sort Salomon had used to force nearly a hundred firms to sign "cease and desist" agreements and pay $5 million in fines. The firms included major players such as Citicorp, PaineWebber, and Bear Stearns.

Salomon was the lone holdout.

The scandal led to difficult times at Salomon, and to the resignation of John Gutfreund and other top executives. In 1997, Salomon was bought and absorbed by Sandy Weill's Travelers Group.

PART ELEVEN

Bull Without End, Amen

"If the curve you're grading on is 'What's attainable by mortals,' he certainly deserves an A."

Federal Reserve governor Lawrence Lindsey on
Fed chairman Alan Greenspan

Timeline

1991 — Soviet Union dissolved, December 8

1994 — Mexico devalues peso

1994 — Huge derivatives losses announced by Gibson Greetings, P&G, and Orange County, CA

1995 — DJIA closes above 4000, February 23

1995 — DJIA closes above 5000, November 21

1995 — Many thousands of mergers and acquisitions, including Chemical and Chase Manhattan banks merge

1995 — AT&T splits into 3 companies

1995 — Mexican bailout finalized

1995 — "Rogue trader" in Singapore sinks Barings Bank

1996 — DJIA closes above 6000, October 14

1996 — Dow 6400: Greenspan warns of "irrational exuberance"

1996 — Real-time NYSE quotes on CNBC and CNN-FN

1997 — DJIA closes above 7000, February 13

1997 — Thailand triggers Asian currency crisis

1997 — DJIA closes above 8000, July 16

1997 — DJIA drops 554, triggers "circuit breakers," October 27; rebounds 337 the next day, on 1+ billion volume

1998 — Long-Term Capital Management uses Nobel Prize-winning options-pricing theory, goes bust

1998 — DJIA closes above 9000, April 6

1998 — Russia announces it won't pay debts, August 17

1999 — DJIA closes above 10,000, March 29

THE SCENE IN THE 1990S

Everybody's Invited

Peter Lynch

*A*ccording to the proverb, success has many parents but failure is an orphan. Many people—a lot of them, not surprisingly, with addresses inside the Washington, D.C., beltway—have taken or been given credit for the long bull market of the 1980s and 1990s. Yet one person rarely mentioned may have done the most to increase the personal wealth of the average American investor. Theodore Benna of Pennsylvania was an employee benefits consultant in 1979 when he found an interesting loophole in a retirement income law. That loophole in clause 401(k)—sound familiar?—could be interpreted to allow companies to make payments directly into an individual employee's retirement plan. Moreover, that plan could follow the employee from employer to employer, producing a lifetime of contributions even if the employee didn't spend an entire career with one company.

Benna convinced his bosses to use their own company as a test case. In 1980, the IRS approved the plan. Millions of Americans who never thought they would invest in the markets became direct owners of mutual funds.

Eyewitness Peter Lynch, the longtime manager of Fidelity's Magellan Fund, retired in 1990 after building his fund into the largest in the world. Along the way, he had become a celebrity, simultaneously producing outstanding returns while comforting investors that his success was the result of common sense instead of inside knowledge. (Is that Gap store at the mall always crowded? Consider buying the stock.) But he looked back on his last decade in the business with one regret.

Who could have had a greater advantage than yours truly, sitting in an office at Fidelity during the boom in financial services and in the mutual funds?

I'd been coming to work here for nearly two decades. I know half the officers in the major financial-service companies, I follow the daily ups and downs, and I could notice important trends months before the analysts on Wall Street. You couldn't have been more strategically placed to cash in on the bonanza of the early 1980s.

The people who print prospectuses must have seen it—they could hardly keep up with all the new shareholders in the mutual funds. The sales force must have seen it as they crisscrossed the country in their Winnebagos and returned with billions in new assets. The maintenance services must have seen the expansion in the offices at Federated, Franklin, Dreyfus, and Fidelity. The companies that sold mutual funds prospered as never before in their history. The mad rush was on.

Fidelity isn't a public company, so you couldn't invest in the rush here. But what about Dreyfus? Want to see a chart that doesn't stop? The stock sold for 40 cents a share in 1977, then nearly $40 a share in 1986, a 100-bagger in nine years, and much of that during a lousy stock market. Franklin was a 138-bagger, and Federated was up 50-fold before it was bought out by Aetna. I was right on top of all of them. I knew the Dreyfus story, the Franklin story, and the Federated story from beginning to end. Everything was right, earnings were up, the momentum was obvious.

How much did I make from all this? Zippo. I didn't buy a single share of any of the financial-services companies: not Dreyfus, not Federated, not Franklin. I missed the whole deal and didn't realize it until it was too late.

By 2000, an estimated 34 million Americans had 401(k) plans, and the assets in them totalled about $1.7 trillion. Not only did those funds give individuals the benefit of the high returns in the equities markets, they also pushed up the markets in a self-fulfilling prophecy. When monthly "in-flows" from employers are used to buy stocks, prices are supported. So what will happen when the demographic bulge of baby boomers cash out of their 401(k) plans? No one knows.

The Cult of Greenspan, 1996

Rob Norton

More than a decade of success at a job so complicated that few people even agree on the questions, much less the answers, has earned Federal Reserve Board chairman Alan Greenspan the reputation of a magician.

He arrived with—or just before—a bang. "If I were Greenspan I'd worry about the next surprise, whatever that might be," economist Murray Weidenbaum warned Time magazine's Lee Smith in July 1987, when Greenspan took the post. "How he handles it will be how he makes his mark as chairman." The surprise arrived just three months later, on October 19, when Black Monday hit.

Many investors remember that day as a crash. Years later, Greenspan called it a "big one-day decline." At least in retrospect he was unruffled, explaining, "There's no guarantee that even if you get a [crash like] 1929, you'll end up with a [depression like] 1932." After Black Monday, Greenspan and the Fed moved quickly to make the currency market more liquid, supporting financial institutions that were strained by the sell-off. A "1932" was avoided. Greenspan had made his mark. Economics, once called the "dismal science," had produced a celebrity.

Smith's story foreshadowed other crises also: "What if all those Third World countries repudiate their debts? Will the international financial system collapse? . . . And, hold it! Is that inflation stirring again?" Over the next ten years, as Mexico, Russia, and Asia faced loan defaults that threatened American banks and world markets, Greenspan stepped in, as "lender of last resort," to keep markets liquid.

"So who is this guy?" asked Fortune magazine writer and unabashed Greenspan fan Rob Norton in 1996, examining the first decade of the chairman's tenure.

Thank God for Alan Greenspan. Arguably as important as who wins [the presidential election] in November—maybe even more important—is the fact that Greenspan will still be running the Federal Reserve—the closest thing the U.S. economy has to an economic pacemaker.

"He's the best chairman the Fed has ever had," says Allan Meltzer, a professor at Carnegie-Mellon University and longtime critic of Fed policy. Meltzer isn't just shooting the breeze—he's in the midst of writing a history of the Federal Reserve System. Says Lawrence Lindsey, one of Greenspan's fellow Fed governors: "If the curve you're grading on is 'What's attainable by mortals,' he certainly deserves an A."

Greenspan's highest marks are for the so-called soft landing that the economy is in the process of accomplishing right now, slowing from the hot and potentially inflationary growth of 1994. "What he did was very unusual," says Meltzer. "He acted against inflation before it got started—the first time the Fed has done that in at least 30 years." Here's an inside observation, from Rick Mishkin, chief economist at the New York Federal Reserve Bank: "In hindsight, it was as good as we could have hoped. We just nailed it." Says Alan Blinder, who recently departed as vice chairman of the Fed: "This is perhaps the most successful episode of monetary policy in the history of the Fed." Because of that policy success, there are no worries about triggering inflation; the Fed now has room to take out some "monetary policy insurance"—as Greenspan told Congress in February—by cutting interest rates as we face a period of slowing economic growth.

Not everyone loves Greenspan, of course, and he doesn't walk on water. He presided over one of America's worst recessions as chairman of Gerald Ford's Council of Economic Advisers. Lots of people—including business people—remember that well and think he was and is too worried about inflation and not enough about growth. There are even some who positively hate him, and concoct dark conspiracy theories about how he's subverting the will of the people to benefit Wall Street.

So who is this guy? And why should we bet that he can continue to keep the economy on track? If you think you know, wait a second. Sure, you know his public persona: the professorial bureaucrat who speaks before Congress about boring subjects in intentionally ambiguous cadences. But the real man is more interesting. His is a story of intellect and street smarts—of how he learned to examine the clockwork of the U.S. economy and how he built a hugely successful business by explaining its workings to executives. How he turned himself into the ultimate Washington operator and how he became chairman—as if by destiny—of the Federal Reserve just when it most needed him. There's even a lighter side somewhere behind his opaque mask: He's a wry observer of the political folkways of Washington, and though he has a monastic streak—sometimes spending entire weekends lost in the data, preparing for congressional testimony—he's also a bit of a bon vivant, making the Washington party scene and playing tennis at mountain resorts with his longtime companion, NBC news correspondent Andrea Mitchell.

. . . Greenspan began visiting Washington in the late Sixties, first as an adviser to then presidential candidate Richard Nixon. He served in the Ford Administration during the tumultuous middle 1970s. Along the way, he developed the perfect Washington personality: rock solid in his own beliefs and impervious to the ritual abuse that comes with the territory. He became a master at suffering fools—patiently if not gladly—and he learned when not to take things too seriously.

A story about Greenspan in the Ford years goes like this: Once he was waiting to testify before a Senate committee chaired by the late Hubert Humphrey. Greenspan had back trouble at the time, and Humphrey knew it. As another administration official's testimony dragged on, Humphrey sent Greenspan a note saying, "Alan, I can see you're having trouble with your back. Why don't you leave, and we'll say you were called by the President." Greenspan replied by note that he was okay. Later, as the questioning of the other official droned on, Humphrey motioned Greenspan to the dais and whispered, "Go. We've got enough testimony. I don't want you to be in pain." Again, Greenspan declined.

Finally it was time for Greenspan's testimony, and the red light came on, signifying Humphrey's turn to ask questions. "Dr. Greenspan," he intoned balefully, "are you ashamed, as you should be, about how destructive your policies have been to this country?" Greenspan gritted his teeth and answered without smiling.

Such training was invaluable for a future Fed chairman. Think of the ranks of nitwit Congresspeople who take shots at the Fed chairman today during his appearances on Capitol Hill, sometimes as often as once a week and for several hours at a time.

Today Greenspan's power as the undisputed leader of the Federal Reserve System is downright awesome—but he had to earn it.

The Fed is a strange governmental creature. It's made up of the 12 regional Federal Reserve banks, each with a president, board of directors, officers, and research staff, plus the Washington-based board of governors, with the largest phalanxes of research economists. The Fed is secretive by nature, suspicious of outsiders, and possessed of an esprit de corps that borders on fanaticism. When Greenspan was appointed chairman in 1987 by Ronald Reagan, he was greeted with some suspicion. "You get a new chairman who hasn't had a career at the Fed, and there's a period of intense observation," says one Fed official. "Greenspan was different; he was a political guy, a bit of a celebrity." And remember, he succeeded Fed insider Paul Volcker, the towering, glowering legend who had slain the demon dragon of the 1970s: double-digit inflation.

Two things helped right away. First was his manner. Greenspan is libertarian in person as well as in theory—a believer in individual liberty and rights. He treats everyone from hotel waiters to heads of state with respect, and there's not a hint about him of the snobbery that's typical of academic economists. The other things that helped were his mastery of the theory and details of the economy, and his obvious love of data. That impresses people at the Fed, and it can't be faked.

Greenspan's first big test was the stock market crash of 1987. It came just two months after he showed up at the Fed. His cool and decisive reaction to the crash—guaranteeing enough liquidity to preclude the cycle of asset deflation and monetary contraction that drove the economy down after the 1929 crash—has been widely praised. Inside the Fed, though, his ability to see that the stock market problem was transitory and his willingness to reverse policy and raise interest rates in mid-1988 were equally important. It sent the signal that the Fed was determined to keep its foot on the throat of inflation and was willing to take risks to do it. A case can be made that this attitude helped produce the 1990 recession—or at least prevented Greenspan from fighting it more aggressively once it began.

Greenspan bonded, early on, with the Fed's research staff. Fed economists at the time were studying a way of predicting inflation called P (don't ask). Greenspan supported the project and got involved personally. When the research paper was published, buried in a list of acknowledgments, in alphabetical order, was the name Alan Greenspan. It was a classy, egalitarian touch, and Fed economists beam even today when they tell the story.

Leading by example and winning over the staff is especially important at the Fed because of its idiosyncratic management structure. The chairman's power derives almost exclusively from his position as presiding officer over two committees. One is the Board of Governors—made up of himself and the six other presidential appointees who serve in Washington (it is mostly concerned with regulatory and administrative matters). The other, which holds the real statutory power over monetary policy, is the Federal Open Market Committee (FOMC), made up of the seven governors and the presidents of five of the 12 regional Federal Reserve banks (they take turns voting).

Outside the committees, the chairman has little pure executive power. There's a story about the short, unhappy reign of G. William Miller—a former CEO of Textron who was appointed Fed chairman by Jimmy Carter in 1978—that makes the point. A nonsmoker, Miller was bothered by the fumes emanating from his left—the seat of then New York Fed president Paul Volcker (his tastes ran to cigars that were short, but not too big around)—and from the right, where governor Henry C. Wallich, a distinguished monetary economist, smoked a large and malodorous pipe. Miller had little THANK YOU FOR NOT SMOKING signs placed at each committee member's seat. They were ignored, and barely visible through the haze. "I can remember looking over and not being able to see Miller for the smoke," recalls Al Broaddus, now president of the Richmond Fed, then a staffer—with a laugh. The signs eventually disappeared, as did Miller. Volcker succeeded him as chairman and was still smoking when he left the Fed in 1987.

Running the Fed, then, depends crucially on the chairman's ability to run a meeting. Greenspan, by all accounts, is very good at it. Newly released transcripts of FOMC meetings (they are published with a five-year lag) show him at work, letting all members have their say, softening the edges of disputes, and suggesting areas of compromise when there is disagreement. "He shows a lot of respect for other people," says former vice chairman [David] Mullins, "and he has the confidence to defer to their expertise." Greenspan, they say, has only been on the losing side of one vote during his entire time at the Fed, and that was a bank regulatory matter so arcane that no one seems to remember what it was about. "By the time I arrived on the scene, in the middle of 1994, this was Alan Greenspan's Fed from top to the bottom," recalls Alan Blinder. "It was like the Fed was an orchestra being played by an expert conductor."

Main Street's Heroes: Schwab, Bogle, and Buffett

Carol Vinzant and Roger Lowenstein

CHARLES SCHWAB AND JOHN BOGLE

The technology and customer service innovations of discount broker Charles Schwab & Co. have been widely followed. John Bogle's Vanguard, historically important because it was the first to offer an index fund to consumers, also stands out for its low management fees. Both firms have become the darlings of investors tired of doing business on Wall Street's terms. Fortune *writer Carol Vinzant sketched their significance.*

Between the '40s and the mid-'70s, the ranks of investors grew from two million to 25 million. When the SEC put an end to fixed commissions in 1975, the final popularizing mechanism fell into place. While full-service brokers actually raised commissions for small investors, discount brokers such as Charles Schwab stepped in and lowered rates by as much as 75%. Schwab, who had previously tried his luck at a walk-in law firm and a drive-through zoo (neither worked out), set up convenient branch offices nationwide. He offered no advice but did introduce then-radical innovations like 24-hour phone service, touch-tone and eventually online trading, and fund supermarkets. Now valued at $42 billion, Schwab's company revolutionized retail investing and served as a model for firms like Fidelity, Merrill Lynch, and countless others, a market whose collective impact is almost incalculable when ripple effects are taken into account.

For all the easy access to the market that Schwab and his followers were providing, many small investors still felt safer in mutual funds, which let experts make the hard decisions. Problem is, even experts don't beat indexes over the long haul. John Bogle was one of the first to recognize that fact; after being fired by an actively managed fund in 1974, he started Vanguard. Among its initial offerings was the mutual fund industry's first index fund. Vanguard proved that low management expenses give both index funds and actively managed funds a critical edge over the competition. "I've always been a fairly thrifty kind of Scot, even at high levels," Bogle says.

One reason Vanguard's expenses are so low is that the company is mutually owned—shareholders of Vanguard's funds own the company itself. But if Vanguard's success has made Bogle rich, he doesn't have anywhere near the $15 billion to $20 billion that the company would be worth if it were structured like a conventional fund company. "It's not the essence of my personal capitalism to grab everything you can get," says Bogle. He recalls that a speaker at a fund conference once called him a communist and Marxist: "So I went up to him with a big smile and said I appreciated the compliments. In the office I'm known as a fascist."

Many customers for Bogle, Schwab, and their kind were investors emboldened by new investment theories of the 1960s and 1970s, which claimed a randomly selected portfolio could perform as well as stocks touted by a broker. At the time, this was Wall Street heresy. One was supposed to rely on professionals to learn which companies would show good results. But publications by University of Chicago economists Eugene Fama and Paul Samuelson, and some amusing dart-throwing demonstrations—including one in a congressional committee—supported a do-it-yourself mentality. Malcolm Forbes and two editors of his magazine tossed a dartboard portfolio of twenty-eight stocks that rose 370 percent from 1967 to 1977, more than ten times the gain in the DJIA. (Alas, other random portfolios did not fare as well.)

WARREN BUFFETT

Warren Buffett symbolizes the promise that anyone can get rich in the stock market. You don't need inside information, just common sense. You can live in Omaha rather than New York. You don't need to trade every day—you'll hold shares for decades. And it's safe, because everything you buy is undervalued. If only it were that easy.

Roger Lowenstein is the author of Buffett, *from which this account comes.*

In the annals of investing, Warren Buffett stands alone. Starting from scratch, simply by picking stocks and companies for investment, Buffett amassed one of the epochal fortunes of the twentieth century. Over a period of four decades—more than enough to iron out the effects of fortuitous rolls of the dice—Buffett outperformed the stock market, by a stunning margin and without taking undue risks or suffering a single losing year. This is a feat that market savants, Main Street brokers, and academic scholars had long proclaimed to be impossible. By virtue of this steady, superior compounding, Buffett acquired a magical-seeming net worth of $15 billion, and counting.

Buffett did this in markets bullish and bearish and through economies fat and lean, from the Eisenhower years to Bill Clinton, from the 1950s to the 1980s, from saddle shoes and Vietnam to junk bonds and the information age. Over the broad sweep of postwar America, as the major stock averages advanced by 11 percent or so a year, Buffett racked up a compounded annual gain of 29.2 percent.

The uniqueness of this achievement is more significant in that it was the fruit of old-fashioned, long-term investing. Wall Street's modern financiers got rich by exploiting their control of the public's money: their essential trick was to take in—and sell out—the public at opportune moments. Buffett shunned this game, as well as the more venal excesses for which Wall Street is deservedly famous. In effect, he rediscovered the art of pure capitalism—a coldblooded sport, but a fair one.

The public shareholders who invested with Buffett also got rich, and in exactly the same proportion to their capital that Buffett did. The numbers themselves are almost inconceivable. If one had invested $10,000 when Buffett began his career, working out of his study in Omaha in 1956, and had stuck with him throughout, one would have had an investment at the end of 1995 worth $125 million.

And yet, the numbers alone do not account for the aura that Buffett cast on Wall Street. Once a year, disciples and money men would flock to Omaha like pilgrims on a hajj, to hear Buffett deconstruct the intricacies of investing, business, and finance. His annual meetings became a piece of Americana, like an Elvis concert or a religious revival. Financial groupies arrived in Omaha clutching Buffett's writings like a Bible and reciting his aphorisms like excerpts from the Sermon on the Mount.

His grasp of simple verities gave rise to a drama that would recur throughout his life. Long before those pilgrimages to Omaha, long before Buffett had a record, he would stand in a corner at college parties, baby-faced and bright-eyed, holding forth on the universe as a dozen or two of his older, drunken fraternity brothers crowded around. A few years later, when these friends had metamorphosed into young associates starting out on Wall Street, the ritual was the same. Buffett, the youngest of the group, would plop himself in a big, broad club chair and expound on finance while the others sat at his feet.

On Wall Street, his homespun manner made him a cult figure. Where finance was so forbiddingly complex, Buffett could explain it like a general-store clerk discussing the weather. He never forgot that underneath each stock and bond, no matter how arcane, there lay a tangible, ordinary business. Beneath the jargon of Wall Street, he seemed to unearth a street from small-town America.

It is a curious irony that as more Americans acquired an interest in investing, Wall Street became more complex, more abstruse, more arcane, and more forbidding than ever: When Buffett was born, in the midst of the Depression, the few Americans who did have capital felt personally equipped to manage it. This they did by salting it away in blue chips and triple-A bonds. The Depression cast a long shadow, but the postwar prosperity eclipsed it. Today, tens of millions have at least a small grubstake, but very few feel comfortable with handling it, and fewer still have the old habit of prudence. At best, they anxiously scan the financial pages, as though each day's twitch in the data on housing or inflation might bring the long-awaited "answer." At worst, they switch in and out of mutual funds with an impatience that would have shocked their grandparents.

In such a complex age, what was stunning about Buffett was his applicability. Most of what Buffett did was imitable by the average person (this is why the multitudes flocked to Omaha). Buffett's genius was largely a genius of character—of patience, discipline, and rationality. These were common enough virtues, but they were rare in the heat of financial passions, and indispensable to anyone who would test his mettle in the stock market. In this sense, Buffett's character and career unfolded as a sort of public tutorial on investing and on American business. Buffett was aware of his role from the very beginning, and he nurtured a curious habit of chronicling his escapades even as he lived them.

As an investor, Buffett eschewed the use of leverage, futures, dynamic hedging, modern portfolio analysis, and all of the esoteric strategies developed by academics. Unlike the modern portfolio manager, whose mind-set is that of a trader, Buffett risked his capital on the long-term growth of a few select businesses. In this, he resembled the magnates of a previous age, such as J. P. Morgan, Sr.

But the secretive Morgan was a Wall Street archetype; Buffett, a plainspoken Midwesterner, was its antithesis. He was famous for quipping that it was the bankers "who should have been wearing the ski masks," or that, as he said to a friend who had been offered a job in finance, "You won't encounter much traffic taking the high road in Wall Street." He once wrote that he would no more take an investment banker's opinion on whether to do a deal than he would ask a barber whether he needed a haircut. This commonsensical crackerbarrel wit made him an archetype of something larger, and far more basic, to the country's past. It answered to a deeply American need for authentic heroes.

This has always been America's secular myth: the uncorrupted commoner from the Midwest or West who stands up to the venal Easterners, be they politicians, bankers, big businessmen, or other. It is a ransom to the country's origins, a remembrance that the first authentic and pure Americans were destroyed. Let Europe have its princes; the American ideal has always been a self-made man from the midcountry—a Lincoln, a Twain, a Will Rogers. In an age without heroes, this, too, is what Buffett's disciples were seeking in Omaha.

As Jack Newfield wrote of Robert Kennedy, Buffett was not a hero, only a hope; not a myth, only a man. Despite his broad wit, he was strangely stunted. When he went to Paris, his only reaction was that he had no interest in sight-seeing and that the food was better in Omaha. His talent sprang from his unrivaled independence of mind and ability to focus on his work and shut out the world, yet those same qualities exacted a toll. Once, when Buffett was visiting the publisher Katharine Graham on Martha's Vineyard, a friend remarked on the beauty of the sunset. Buffett replied that he hadn't focused on it, as though it were necessary for him to exert a deliberate act of concentration to "focus" on a sunset. Even at his California beachfront vacation home, Buffett would work every day for weeks and not go near the water.

Like other prodigies, he paid a price. Having been raised in a home with more than its share of demons, he lived within an emotional fortress. The few people who shared his office had no knowledge of the inner man, even after decades. Even his children could scarcely recall a time when he broke through his surface calm and showed some feeling.

Though part of him is a showman or preacher, he is essentially a private person. Peter Lynch, the mutual-fund wizard, visited Buffett in the 1980s and was struck by the tranquillity in his inner sanctum. His archives, neatly alphabetized in metal filing cabinets, looked as files had in another era. He had no armies of traders, no rows of electronic screens, as Lynch did. Buffett had no price charts, no computer—only a newspaper clipping from 1929 and an antique ticker under a glass dome. The two of them paced the floor, recounting their storied histories, what they had bought, what they had sold. Where Lynch had kicked out his losers every few weeks, Buffett had owned mostly the same few stocks for years and years. Lynch felt a pang, as though he had traveled back in time.

Buffett's one concession to modernity is a private jet. Otherwise, he derives little pleasure from spending his fabulous wealth. He has no art collection or snazzy car, and he has never lost his taste for hamburgers. He lives in a commonplace house on a tree-lined block, on the same street where he works. His consuming passion—and pleasure—is his work, or, as he calls it, his canvas. It is there that he revealed the secrets of his trade, and left a self-portrait.

The Intel Generation, 1997

Amy Virshup

Never fall in love with a stock, experts say. Yet investors remain hopeless romantics.

For most investors, Intel isn't about chip geometries. And it's not even about a stock certificate or the steadily rising figures on their account statements. It's more like, well, a religion. One in which evanescent shares are transmogrified into very solid objects: For John Lee it was a "dream house"—a 4,800-square-foot, four-bedroom home with a bar and a wooded lot. For Jon Maakestad and Bev Turbin, it's a cabin in the Wisconsin woods. For Fred Runkel it's the down payment on a home—if and when he cashes in. And the Intelites are more than willing to evangelize: Peruse [the newsgroup] misc.invest.stocks on the Internet or the Intel bulletin boards on America Online (there are two) and you'll find such blandishments as "Buy Intel for today, tomorrow and forever" and "You will talk about this stock to your kids and grandkids" and even "INTC reminds me of a situation similar to Edison in 1900." Dare to raise doubts about the stock, and be prepared for digital scorn—if not outright vilification: "YOU ARE A WHINER!!!!!!" one Intelite recently berated someone who'd posted a message complaining about alleged manipulation of the stock. "WHA!!! WHA!!! ... [go] put your money in bank CDs and be [happy] with 5 percent a year, you crybaby!!!!!" The faith even has its own sins—of omission (not buying in the first place) and commission (selling too soon), and a patron saint: Andy Grove.

Dave Fox, a 33-year-old sales auditor from Mountain View, Calif., is an Intel believer: When Fox started investing, he split his stocks between short-term holds and a handful of "long-term, forget-about-it kinds of plays," including US West, Motorola and Intel, which he bought in May 1995 for $112.25 a share. (It subsequently split.) Then, about a year ago, Fox needed cash for the down payment on a condo. Out went the short-term plays, followed by Motorola (and US West a bit later). But not Intel. "I never considered selling Intel," he says. Nor, when the stock ran up to almost $165 in early February, did he consider taking some profit and diversifying his holdings. "I couldn't," says Fox. "I just couldn't."

What does he plan to do with his profits, should he ever take any? "I'm thinking maybe college tuition for my child," says Fox. "Which . . ." He pauses. "I don't even have a girlfriend right now," he admits. "But at some point I'd like to meet someone, get married, have children—the money could be there for my child's education." Then he thinks again. "If I have the means to pay for my child's tuition without selling my Intel stock, I would probably find a way."

Bev Turbin and Jon Maakestad never expected a stock to play such a key role in their lives. Until last year most of their savings were tied up in real estate, including rental properties they'd owned and managed for almost seven years. The couple—he runs his own advertising firm in Minneapolis, she's a former CPA who now stays home with their two children—lived modestly. "Jon is very conservative," says Turbin. "He puts money in a savings account and it never comes out." But back in 1994 Maakestad was looking for an investment for his retirement account. A neighbor in his office building worked for semiconductor maker SGS-Thomson and one day, while they were standing in the hallway, Maakestad asked him about tech stocks. "I said, 'You're a smart technology guy, what stocks would you buy?' And he said 'Intel.' " So Maakestad picked up 300 shares. Over the next two years, as the stock climbed to $119, split and then stayed in the $60 range, Maakestad kept adding to his stake, until he held 1,800 shares.

Then in May 1996 the couple, both 41, sold one of their buildings. For two months they debated what to do with their profit. Every night at the dinner table they'd talk about it, mulling over the pros and cons of various options—clearly, leaving it in their money market account wouldn't bring them the return they wanted, but they didn't want to take too much risk. "The biggest thing we were afraid of was putting it in a stock and having the stock go down," says Maakestad. Finally, he turned to Bev and said, "Why don't we just buy more Intel?" (It never seemed to occur to them that Intel could go down as well as up—despite plenty of evidence to the contrary. Over the years, Intel has shown itself more than capable of plummeting 10 or 20 points in a matter of days.)

Maakestad doesn't want to hear about the inherent risk in his eggs-in-one-basket strategy. "I've listened to all these people who say, 'Well, you should have your portfolio diversified,' so I said, 'Okay, I'll buy some Fidelity Southeast Asia and Pacific Basin,' and I sat there and watched them go down, then they'd go up a little and they'd go down, they'd go down more, and I thought, why diversify?" Bev, meanwhile, thought Intel's P/E looked solid and figured the stock was as good a place as any to park their money short term—she thought it might go from $76 to $80 over the next month. So the couple bought an additional 1,000 shares at $76.

A few days later the Maakestads went north to Eagle River, Wis., for their annual summer vacation. And Intel went south, dropping to $69. Mercifully, the cabin they'd rented didn't have a phone, so they didn't find out what had happened to their nest egg for a few days. On Thursday it started to rain, so Maakestad drove into town to pick up some groceries, then checked in with his broker. How did Turbin take the news? Well, she says diplomatically, "It did put a damper on the vacation." In fact, they packed up the family car and drove home a day early.

Between August 1996 and February 1997, of course, Intel's trajectory moved relentlessly upward. But if you think watching your money double in eight months would be a relatively stress-free experience, think again. "I don't like the fact that when you own so much of one stock it can affect your emotions as much as this one can," sighs Jon. "[Over] the last nine months there were a lot of really high days where every day it'd go up three or four dollars. And when you own a lot of shares, that adds up. But there's always that uneasy feeling that somebody could take that away." The stock has become a presence in the family's life: Turbin and Maakestad talk about it at the dinner table and on weekends. (When Intel's had a pretty good week, it's more likely they'll go out to eat, she adds.) Even their five-year-old son's gotten into the act: He recently asked his mother to explain what "156 and a quarter" meant.

Meanwhile, Turbin, whose previous investing had been limited to making a once-a-year purchase for her SEP-IRA, has turned into a market hound. After their vacation she began checking the price daily, then tuned her television set to CNBC—permanently. In October she sold some Norwest stock she'd held "forever" and put that into Intel, too (giving the couple 3,800 shares and warrants— for a total of 60 percent of their portfolio). Emboldened by their success, she even began day-trading from home—using their Intel stock to trade on margin. Now she goes nowhere without her cell phone so she can check her stocks every hour. On a recent morning she called her broker from the parking lot of the St. Paul zoo, where she'd accompanied her son's kindergarten class, to put a stop order on some Western Digital. "Where are you?" he asked, puzzled by all the screaming in the background.

The Maakestads are the first to admit that Intel has been very, very good to them. The first week in May, they closed on a cabin in Wisconsin made possible by their stock. (They've joked about getting an "Intel Inside" plaque to hang over the fireplace.) Turbin and the kids are moving up there for the summer, though they won't exactly be getting away from it all: She's signing up for a stock-charting service, getting a second phone line installed and bringing along her fax machine and cell phone. "It's a risk we took, and it paid off," says Maakestad, who finally sold 1,300 shares in May, just after Digital and Cyrix announced their suits against Intel. (Turbin also sold 500 warrants.) "And you can say that it was a dangerous thing to do and we're not diversified enough, but we were right. No matter what you say, we were right!"

"In retrospect," says [Howard Ward of the Gabelli Fund], "selling the stock has always been a mistake in anything other than the short term."

Still, [investor Fred] Runkel has tried to prepare himself for the idea that someday—however distant the date—he might not be an Intel stockholder. But it's been hard. And he's been down this road before: About the same time he bought Intel, he picked up some shares of Wal-Mart. For the first few years he watched as the share price kept going up. Every now and then, [their broker, PaineWebber's Tim] Watters would call and suggest that it was time to take some profits. "He said, 'Don't fall in love with the stock.'" But Runkel just couldn't bring himself to sell. Even after Wal-Mart stopped going up. For three years he sat on the stock as it went nowhere, all the time losing out on other opportunities in the market. Finally, last year, he got himself to sell.

"It's almost like I learned my lesson with Wal-Mart," says Runkel, speaking of his new resolve to be an unsentimental investor. "But as Intel keeps going higher and higher, I [think], 'Oh my goodness, what am I going to do when I have to sell Intel?' It's kind of like I know the rationale and I know in my mind, don't get married to this stock. But as long as I feel the company has the growth potential and isn't really overvalued . . ." Runkel trails off.

The day we spoke, Intel had dropped 15 points in the previous week's trading, after falling from a high of $164 in February to trade in the $140 range. "I think if Intel drops another 20 points, I wouldn't say I'm getting out," says Runkel. "I would say 'This is a buying opportunity, because this is a great company.'"

The Little Guy
October 28, 1997

Art Buchwald

Almost ten years to the day after the crash of October 1987, the markets experienced another sharp sell-off. The DJIA had dropped 554 points, from 7715 to 7161—not the worst percentage drop, but the largest point drop ever. For the first time, the decline triggered "circuit breakers"—rules instituted after the 1987 crash to halt trading when the market falls too far, too fast. At 2:35 P.M., after the DJIA dropped 350 points, trading was halted for thirty minutes; trading resumed on schedule at 3:05, but less than half an hour later the DJIA had lost another 200 points, which ended trading for the day. (The prescribed one-hour pause was longer than the remaining half hour of scheduled trading.)

"It was never realistic to think [the circuit breakers] would stop a big slide," Stephen Buser, a professor at MIT's Sloan School of Management, told Steven Wilmsen of the Boston Globe. *Andrew Weiss, an economics professor at Boston University, agreed: "Markets are ruled in the long run by fundamentals, and there's nothing you can do to change that. The forces are too big. You can think of the weekend as a long circuit breaker, and historically that hasn't worked."*

But the sell-off didn't last. Within a week, the DJIA had gained back nearly all its losses. Columnist Art Buchwald credited a human circuit breaker.

It is now common knowledge that the little guy saved the stock market from its worst crash in history.

All the big guys at the Bull and Bear Grill were talking about it the other evening. There were partners from Goldman Sachs and Morgan Stanley, investors for the large pension funds, players in billion-dollar mutual funds, and traders who lived and died by junk bonds.

Into this motley crowd entered a man in cowboy boots, blue jeans, and a worn T-shirt.

"Who is it?" whispered a banker in an Armani suit.

The man sitting next to him at the bar said, "I can't believe it. It's the little guy, the one who saved us all from going belly-up."

The word spread like wildfire through the bar. Suddenly a cheer went up from the crowd, and they hoisted the little guy up onto their shoulders and carried him around the room.

"Have a Chivas Regal," yelled a broker from Merrill Lynch.

"I'd rather have a beer," the little guy answered.

A man from Smith Barney said, "You didn't panic. Tell us your secret."

The little guy said, "Why panic? All I saw on Monday was a much-needed correction. We little people expect glitches in the market, and you have to be a fool to unload just because Bill Gates had a bad day."

The crowd strained to hear every word he said.

He blew the foam off his beer. "You big guys panicked because you kept looking at the numbers. The little guys knew that if they waited until Tuesday they could pick up stocks at going-out-of-business prices. Once you big guys knew the little guys were buying, you regained your courage and jumped back into the game."

A man wearing a double-breasted Calvin Klein suit said, "It's true. We had no idea what you people would do. It's hard for the big guys on Wall Street to read the mind of the little investor. Thank God he has ice in his veins."

The little guy finished his beer and said, "Thanks, but I have to be going."

"Where are you going?"

"I have to buy a lottery ticket. I feel that after Tuesday I can't lose and, besides, there's no difference between the lottery and the stock market."

While You Were Trading, 1992–1998

Judith Helen Rawnsley, Joseph Jett, Frank Partnoy,
Gretchen Morgenson, and Dr. Anirudh Dhebar

No investor is an island unto himself. The 1990s were more than a collection of growth stocks, IPOs, and effortless gains in index funds. A few things happened while you were trading.

After the collapse of the Soviet Union in 1989, American banks loaned—and lost—hundreds of billions of dollars in the former Eastern Bloc. The collapse of the Thai currency helped trigger a crisis in Asia that threatened the U.S. economy. Mexico needed another bailout. The Euro, the new currency of the European Economic Community, threatened the American dollar's hegemony in international transactions. Congress and the President battled over balancing the budget, at one point leading to a government shutdown.

Those incidents, lo so many Nasdaq points ago, didn't halt the bull market. Nonetheless, some of them brought down companies and even countries, and ruined innumerable individuals. They also demonstrated that Wall Street's connections to world markets are increasingly complex.

In the accounts that follow, eyewitnesses describe four public mishaps and crises: the collapse of Barings Bank due to a "rogue trader"; the Kidder Peabody bond scandal, in which another trader was blamed by a company eager to conceal the larger story; the surprise losses in derivatives that hit many companies in 1994; and the sudden failure of Long-Term Capital Management, the hedge fund whose founders included two Nobel Prize winners.

I. THE COLLAPSE OF BARINGS

The news first broke in London, home of the 233-year-old Barings Bank. On February 26, 1995, The Times of London put this bulletin on the wire:

Barings, the City's oldest merchant bank, is today hours away from collapse and is desperately trying to arrange a rescue takeover to avert a financial disaster that could badly damage the City. The Bank of England is helping Barings find a buyer or buyers for the business in a move to raise sufficient cash to cover the loss of $600m (pounds 375m) by two dealers in its Singapore securities office trading derivatives on the Tokyo stock market.

Barings has until midnight tonight, when the Tokyo market opens, to find a buyer prepared to shoulder the derivatives losses, or to raise enough cash through piecemeal disposals to cover the deficit.

More than just an old bank, Barings was one of the most important institutions in international finance. It had once been named alongside Britain, France, Austria, Russia, and Prussia as the "sixth great power of the world." Among other notable achievements, most tied to the old British Empire, Barings helped finance the Louisiana Purchase.

The trades that threatened it, however, were part of a relatively new business. After "the Big Bang"—Britain's 1986 deregulation of the finance industries—Barings recognized the need to become more aggressive. But, as a British analyst told John Darnton of The New York Times, *"The merchant banks have been terrifically caught out by their move into securities and trading. They've paid too much to get into it. It's an extremely competitive and risky business. It's new for them and it involves an entirely different culture."*

The day after the first warnings were made public, Barings effectively vanished. Blame was placed on a young British trader in Singapore, Nick Leeson, who had himself disappeared. As The New York Times *reported:*

About noon today, four plainclothes officers with two locksmiths in tow entered Mr. Leeson's fifth-floor apartment in a luxury building in the stylish and leafy Orchard neighborhood here.

The investigators spent about 40 minutes inside the apartment and declined to speak to reporters when they emerged.

Two neatly covered mountain bikes and two racks of drying laundry were evident on a back balcony of Mr. Leeson's apartment.

Mr. Leeson, 28, who worked for the Barings office in Singapore since 1992, disappeared with his wife, Lisa, 23.

Mr. Leeson was reported to have fled Singapore with his wife on Thursday, driving his Porsche across the causeway into neighboring Malaysia, where he checked into the luxurious Regent Hotel in Kuala Lumpur, the capital. The manager of the Regent Hotel confirmed that Mr. Leeson had registered on Thursday evening, but had left on Friday.

The Malaysian police also confirmed that Mr. Leeson had entered the country, and that he was being sought for questioning. Reuters has reported that Mr. Leeson owned several pieces of property in Malaysia as well as a large yacht.

Despite rumors that Mr. Leeson had been caught trying to cross the border from Malaysia into Thailand, there was no announcement of an arrest by tonight.

Police spokesmen in Thailand said they were following up on other rumors that Mr. Leeson had set sail in his yacht from Malaysia for waters near the resort island of Phuket in southern Thailand. Still more rumors in Southeast Asian financial circles had him in a Malaysian hospital, or sailing off the eastern coast of Malaysia.

. . . An official of the Philippine National Police confirmed that the authorities in Singapore had asked police agencies in all neighboring Southeast Asian countries to be on the lookout for Mr. Leeson.

While Leeson was on the run, the press dubbed him a "rogue trader," and tried to uncover how the disaster had occurred. Judith Helen Rawnsley, previously a financial journalist and a researcher at Barings' Japan office, knew Leeson.

I remember Nick as a friendly, down-to-earth, almost meek guy, whose loudness when drunk merely seemed to over-compensate for his shyness on other occasions. On visits to the Tokyo office, he was cheerful and helpful. In the evenings he was always ready to go out for drinks and to nightclubs with his colleagues.

The metamorphosis of Nick Leeson's character was not specific to either himself or the environment created at Barings. It was symptomatic of a certain type of trading culture: one of individualism, competition and insecurity, in which greed and fear are paramount characteristics. Such an environment negates traditional management and risk controls, namely the cultivation of teamwork rather than individual competitiveness, the sharing of information and the nurturing of self-confidence. Arrogance is not self-confidence. The latter helps you to admit when you are wrong and be open with colleagues and bosses. Arrogant traders suffer from an illusion of invulnerability, which is encouraged by less confident colleagues deferring to them, and managers being unwilling or unable to challenge them.

"He wasn't exactly turning into a jerk, but he was feeling a hell of a lot more confident than when he was just a futures and options clerk because he was getting a lot of accolades from everyone. Management, the clients loved him," says Mike Killian. "It was go, Nick, go, Nick, go, go, go! His head was spinning. He was the Michael Jordan of the trading floor." He became, both in his own eyes and in the eyes of those around him, the king of the trading floor. In 1994 he changed the password for his electronic mail to Superman.

Around town Leeson increasingly epitomized the worst excesses of an expat trader abroad; although revered by fellow traders, he clashed with the local population and, like many a highly strung dealer, went on loud and crass drinking sprees with his colleagues and behaved badly. He felt that he was riding the wave, he was the master and could get away with anything.

It soon became apparent that Leeson's fraud had begun as soon as he arrived in Singapore in 1992. As a trader told Rawnsley, "He lied about everything; none of his profits were real." By 1995, instead of having produced immense profits, he was hiding losses of £827 million—about $1.3 billion. Rawnsley explained how he did it:

Leeson's experience in London and Jakarta had given him an intimate understanding of the settlements process. This knowledge, in conjunction with his command of the back office, enabled him to easily pull the wool over the eyes of his superiors, internal and even external auditors. He was in a position where no one could challenge him without seriously questioning his fundamental integrity, a confrontation which he successfully gambled would never occur. The account records that were printed daily for all internal and client trades were retained in the settlement archives and the second copies sent to clients. For the misused Account 88888 [which he had established to book his fraudulent trades], Leeson left standing instructions with his settlement staff to shred the bottom copy and give him the top copy, so the only record of his trades in the whole company was in his hands. "The girls in the back office were naive really," comments a member of the settlements department in Hong Kong. "Everyone really rated Nick and did what he said. Even if they had known something was wrong they would have been too scared to say it. That's office politics."

Leeson primarily traded options in the Nikkei 225 index—roughly the Japanese equivalent of the S&P 500.

From the beginning of 1994, Leeson wrote so-called straddles, a bet that the index would trade only in a narrow range. The straddle is one of the most aggressive techniques for shorting volatility and exposes the option writer to considerable risk where markets move in a sudden and unexpected fashion. It appears, however, that Leeson made no attempt to hedge his portfolio, as the profit and loss swings correlate closely to moves in the index over this period.

Leeson had not reckoned with the forces of nature. The trouble began in the early hours of 17 January [1995] when the great Hanshin earthquake rocked Japan's industrial heartland around Kobe and Osaka, reaching a mammoth 7.2 on the Richter scale. The damage was immense. Over 5,000 lives were lost. As the bill for the damage scaled colossal heights, sentiment changed drastically over the weekend. On Monday, 23 January, the bottom got knocked out of the stock market when the Nikkei 225 dropped by over 1,000 points from 19,241 on the day of the quake to 17,785.

Lesson had bet the index would stay within 19,000 and 21,000.

Suddenly Leeson went berserk, but none of his trading counterparts were aware of the madness that had overcome him. His buying spree in Nikkei futures for Account 88888 following the Kobe earthquake was unprecedented by any standards. Within four weeks, his position on SIMEX had reached 55,399 contracts that expired in March and a further 5,640 in the June contract.

By that stage Leeson was under mounting pressure. It was becoming increasingly difficult for him to conceal the scale of the losses and the flows of money required from London to cover margin calls. Yet he continued to act calmly, his sang-froid carrying into both his work and social life.

Finally, two executives from the London office, frustrated by Leeson's repeated excuses, flew to Singapore to question him:

[On February 23, Leeson] sat down with [Barings Group Treasurer] Tony Hawes and [Senior Settlements Clerk] Tony Railton to discuss the matter of the missing money, but walked out in the middle of the meeting, never to return.

The next day, Friday, 24 February, a handwritten letter from Leeson was faxed to [Barings' regional managers James] Bax and [Simon] Jones in Singapore from the Regent Hotel in Kuala Lumpur, where he had just checked in. It begins: "My sincere apologies for the predicament that I have left you in. It was neither my intention or aim for this to happen but the pressures, both business and personal, have become too much to bear and after receiving medical advice, have affected my health to the extent that a breakdown is imminent." The letter said he was tendering his resignation immediately, and promised to make contact early in the following week "to discuss the best course of action," a promise that was never kept. The fax is signed "Apologies, Nick."

Leeson was captured in Frankfurt, Germany. He had hoped to avoid Singapore's unforgiving criminal justice system, but was extradited. Tried and convicted, he served about half of his six-year sentence before being released. In his memoir of the affair, Rogue Trader, *his regret about committing fraud was tempered by his condemnation of his superiors for allowing him to do so—an unusual defense.*

The Dutch bank ING bought what was left of Barings, for £1.

In June 2000 Leeson appeared in a Swedish television commercial for an online brokerage that wanted to present a conservative image. "We thought to ourselves, 'Who could warn people that this is a dangerous game?' " said an executive from the advertising agency that conceived the commercial. As with his other earnings, he split his appearance fee equally with Barings' creditors, to whom he owes £100 million.

For some time, Leeson's spot on the SIMEX floor was marked off with duct tape. None of the superstitious traders dared step within the box.

II. KIDDER'S PHANTOM TRADES

Not long after naming him "Man of the Year" for 1993, Joseph Jett's bosses at Kidder Peabody called him a criminal. They said he alone was to blame for falsifying $350 million in profits—that he was a loner scheming to increase his bonus, an outsider who couldn't have been successful without fraud.

Then they really got dirty. Jett was portrayed as a stereotypical angry black man—a martial arts buff with a hyperactive libido but not enough intelligence to know his deception would be obvious. Sadly, some of the press listened.

The true story, revealed by Jett in his book, Black and White on Wall Street, *was much more interesting. It began with an early-morning announcement by GE that made reporters rush to Jett's apartment building in New York:*

My apartment buzzer started ringing: shouting came over the intercom: "Mr. Jett! We know you're up there! Come down and talk to us! It's for your own good!"

Jett spent hours watching the television news reports and trying to decide how best to word a statement. He then braced himself to run the gauntlet outside the lobby.

Taking a deep breath, I pulled the door open. A blaze of lights erupted, blinding me. I could feel a crowd surge forward and I blinked, trying to make out shapes of people in front of the lights. For a second or two I couldn't see anything but the glare. My vision cleared in time to see the group begin to relax, break up and retreat. Directly in front of me the face and hair of a young blond woman emerged from a silhouette as the lights dimmed. She was thrusting a large microphone toward my face. Suddenly it fell limp in her hand, the metal stem dangling for a second from its cord as she looked at me blankly, slightly exasperated. Then she, too, turned away. All the lights were off, no one was looking at me anymore, and I heard the now familiar voice resume shouting. Behind me, the guy was wedged behind the lobby doors, pressing again on the buzzer: "Mr. Jett, Mr. Jett! We know you're in there! Come down and talk to us!"

I pushed through what was left of the milling crowd and started walking toward the corner, shaking with the rage rising in my chest. Reality had shifted under my feet again, only this time the jolt was all too familiar. I wanted to turn around and bellow: "I am Mr. Jett!" Instead I kept walking. The crowd of reporters let me go. They were looking for Joseph Jett, Harvard graduate and multimillionaire Wall Street bond trader. They weren't looking for a black man.

The reporters missed a great story:

It was simple. Greed, for money and for power, had driven the managers at Kidder into a scheme to wrest the company away from GE, but the plan was built on a foundation of juggled books, forward trades and doctored balance sheets that simply gave way under its own weight. It was akin to a classic pyramid scheme in which ever-growing deposits are required to support the original investment. In Kidder's case, the deposits took the form of increasingly complicated ruses for creating the impression that the ailing Kidder was instead healthy and viable. Pyramid schemes are illegal, but we broke no laws. Instead, we "window dressed" Kidder's books, a common enough practice at banks and other financial institutions. But we lost our common sense, and the ability to see reality gave way to hubris, competition and internecine warfare among angry, bitter enemies. When the pyramid finally collapsed, we were all left standing in the rubble with hands dirty from grappling to prop it up.

Kidder was in terrible shape when I joined the company. Only the Mortgage department made any money. Ed Cerullo ruled that area, and he was an intensely competitive manager who didn't broach any interference from his superiors. They were powerless against him because [GE's CEO] Jack Welch and GE were unhappy with sickly Kidder and unwilling to invest any more money in the floundering company. Kidder needed Cerullo because he alone made money. Cerullo wasn't as charitable. He [believed] Kidder should be led by a man like him, Cerullo. In the right hands, it had tremendous potential. But those hands had to belong to a man at the top of his game, someone who could run a billion-dollar empire as if it were a triathlon. [Kidder CEO Michael] Carpenter had tried but failed to find a suitor to buy the ailing company. Cerullo desperately sought another parent, a company to buy the Fixed Income department away from GE and free him to run it as he saw fit. But who would buy us? Kidder could attract a buyer only if it earned huge profits. We had to invest. So we spent more than GE allowed, and then had to trick GE into believing that we operated within their guidelines.

The trick was a change in accounting practices that allowed the removal of all forward settling trades from our balance sheet. With that tweak of the books, mortgage assets disappeared from Kidder's reported balance sheet. Sixteen billion in assets vanished. GE never knew we were over budget by $30 billion. Our lenders never knew we were over-leveraged and in violation of our loan terms. We juggled our books, and the benefit was twofold. We hid the true balance from GE, while at the same time we showed potential investors the huge profit earned with the illicit $30 billion.

Unfortunately, as Jett said, "The pyramid disintegrated. For months each lie had required another, each juggle of the books mandated further juggling, each churn of bond trades made it necessary to flip other bonds or Strips. For months we'd been flailing away, desperately trying to prop up sections of the pyramid only to see the cracks and decay start elsewhere. Finally, the pyramid collapsed. . . . GE had to explain to its shareholders how it had been so amateurish and so ignorant in its dealings with Kidder, and it had to explain what—or who—had caused this debacle."

A few months later, a report by Gary G. Lynch, formerly chief of enforcement for the Securities and Exchange Commission, cleared everyone above Jett of wrongdoing. Nonetheless, as The New York Times noted, in the first three months of 1994 Jett had reported phony trades of $1.7 trillion—a rate that would have made his annual trading volume twice the value of all privately owned Treasury securities. (Jett's daily $30 billion was one-tenth of GE's assets.) Apparently GE failed to do the math. The explanation offered was that Jett's managers had not watched his trading as closely as they might have. That seems odd, considering they had extensive records of Jett's actions, especially his contact with white female employees.

In 1996, the case came to a muddled conclusion. A National Association of Securities Dealers inquiry cleared Jett, while an SEC investigation found "intent to commit fraud." A crucial piece of evidence was never considered. GE had removed from its computers the software Jett had supposedly used to commit his "secret" scheme. However, Jett was able to present taped telephone conversation in which a superior was instructing him regarding the trades.

Throughout the case, GE froze Jett's personal accounts, which held millions of dollars in past earnings and bonuses. At the time the verdict was announced, he was nearly homeless, working as a mover and part-time construction worker. As part of the verdict, his millions were returned.

Ed Cerullo escaped serious harm. Though fired, his penalty was merely a fine of $50,000 and suspension for one year.

Michael Carpenter was also fired.

Within months of the scandal first breaking, GE cleaned up Kidder's balance sheet—blaming Jett rather than mismanagement or bad trading—and sold the company to PaineWebber.

III. DERIVATIVES

On April 12, 1994, Gibson Greetings, Inc., shocked investors by announcing that it had lost $20 million trading "derivatives." The same day,

Procter & Gamble announced a derivatives loss of $100 million. Neither company could define a derivative in simple terms. (As suggested by its name, it is a financial instrument that "derives" its value from the value of another financial instrument.)

Other firms soon admitted similar losses. Billions of dollars had been lost by baffled corporate treasurers. Many companies sued the investment banks that had sold them the products.

Then Orange County, California, presumed to be one of the richest in the nation, announced it was bankrupt because of bad derivatives trades made by its comptroller, Robert Citron.

Clients had reason to be angry. "No one seemed to care about whether clients actually understood what they were buying, even when the trades had hidden risks," said Frank Partnoy, a derivatives salesperson at Morgan Stanley in the early 1990s. "The [derivatives product] group simply continued to pile trade on top of trade. Year by year, client by client, trade by trade, the venerable House of Morgan was building a precarious house of cards."

Early on I learned about one derivatives trade that I think exemplifies the group's business. This particular trade, and its acronym, were among the group's most infamous early inventions, although it still is popular among certain investors. The trade is called PERLS.

PERLS stands for Principal Exchange Rate Linked Security, so named because the trade's principal repayment is linked to various foreign exchange rates, such as British pounds or German marks. PERLS look like bonds and smell like bonds. In fact, they are bonds—an extremely odd type of bond, however, because they behave like leveraged bets on foreign exchange rates.

With PERLS, investors who were not permitted to bet on foreign currencies could place such bets anyway. Because PERLS looked like bonds, they masked the nature of the investor's underlying bet. For example, one popular PERLS, instead of repaying the principal amount of $100, paid the $100 principal amount multiplied by the change in the value of the U.S. dollar, plus twice the change in the value of the British pound, minus twice the change in the value of the Swiss franc. The principal repayment was linked to these three different currencies, hence the name Principal Exchange Rate Linked Security.

If the currencies miraculously aligned precisely—and the probability of that was about the same as that of the nine planets in our solar system forming a straight line—you would receive exactly $100. But more likely you would receive some other amount, depending on how the currencies changed. If you understood what you were buying, you hoped to receive a lot more than $100, although you knew you could receive a lot less. If the foreign currency rates went the wrong way—if the dollar and pound zigged while the franc zagged—you could lose every penny.

PERLS were especially attractive to devious managers at insurance companies, many of whom wanted to place foreign currency bets without the knowledge of the regulators or their bosses. PERLS were designed to allow such cheater managers to gamble in the volatile foreign exchange futures and options markets.

But there were other types of PERLS buyers who lacked the training and experience to understand them at all. They looked at a term sheet for PERLS, and all they saw was a bond. The complex formulas eluded them; their eyes glazed over. The fact that the bonds' principal payments were linked to changes in foreign currency rates was simply incomprehensible. These are the buyers I call widows and orphans. These are the buyers salesmen love.

. . . I have heard many stories about salesmen selling PERLS to widows and orphans, but this one, which I heard just after I arrived at Morgan Stanley, is my favorite:

A few months after one successful salesman sold a stodgy insurance company an $85 million string of PERLS it obviously did not understand, a senior treasury officer from the company called the salesman to find out how much the PERLS the company had bought were worth. The officer had assumed they still would be worth $100—or perhaps $99.99 or $100.01—and was incredulous to learn that the bonds already had plummeted to a fraction of their original value. The conversation the salesman relayed to me went like this:

"But how did we lose so much money on this bond already? It's only been a few weeks. And it's a government agency bond, for God's sake. My boss is going to kill me."

"Well, you know, the various currencies reflected in the principal redemption formulas have depreciated significantly against the U.S. dollar since you bought this security several weeks ago. Also, time decay and volatility changes in the foreign exchange markets have decreased the value of the options embedded in the PERLS."

"What? Tell me again—in plain English this time. What does all that mean?"

"It means you made a big foreign exchange bet, and you lost."

At this point the company officer was flustered. "Foreign exchange bet? What the hell are you talking about? We didn't bet anything, and we shouldn't have lost anything. We didn't make any foreign exchange bet. We're an insurance company, for God's sake. We aren't even allowed to buy foreign exchange."

"Well, when you buy PERLS, you take the foreign exchange risk. That's why you were getting an above-market coupon on the bond. I told you that. I warned you. You just don't remember. I tried to explain this formula to you. Come on, why did you think you'd be getting such a high coupon if you weren't taking any risk?"

The officer was dumbfounded. "Oh, my God. You mean to tell me we were taking the foreign exchange risk? I thought you were taking the foreign exchange risk."

This salesman had earned a giant commission on this PERLS trade, and he laughed uncontrollably at his story. I laughed, too. When he finished his story, he asked me if I knew what it was called when a salesman did what he had done to one of his clients. I said I didn't know. He told me it was called "ripping his face off."

"Ripping his face off?" I asked, wondering if I had heard him correctly.

"Yes," he replied. He then explained, in graphic, warlike detail how you grabbed the client under the neck, pinched a fold of skin, and yanked hard, tearing as much flesh as you could. I never will forget how this salesman looked me in the eye and, with a serious sense of pride, almost a tear, summed up this particular PERLS trade.

"Frank," he said, "I ripped his face off."

Why did Morgan Stanley and other banks push derivatives? The commission on a normal bond might be one-half of 1 percent. On PERLS, Morgan Stanley received a commission of more than 4 percent. In Partnoy's two years with Morgan Stanley he and his seventy colleagues in the derivatives sales department produced about $1 billion in commissions.

IV. LONG-TERM CAPITAL

In 1973, three economists devised an equation that eventually won two of them the Nobel Prize. (One of the men had died; the Nobel is not awarded posthumously.) Their formula calculates an appropriate price for options, futures, and other financial products. It "created an entire new industry," a finance expert told New York Times *reporter Gretchen Morgenson.*

John Meriwether, who was both publicity-shy (he had bought the rights to most photographs of himself) and famous (he had played a leading role in the incident that gave the title to Michael Lewis's best-seller, Liar's Poker), *had traded successfully for many years with variations on the equation. Forced from Salomon Brothers after a scandal, he formed a hedge fund called Long-Term Capital Management. Among his partners were the two Nobel Prize winners, Myron Scholes and Robert Merton. After raising billions of dollars, Meriwether and his team, with advice phoned in by the Nobel laureates, began to trade. Using leverage, they held investments worth 30 to 100 times their working capital, which ranged from $2 billion to $5 billion. They performed well at first, but by 1998 had begun to show large losses. Gretchen Morgenson of* The New York Times *explains what went wrong, and what happened next.*

Long-Term Capital used sophisticated computer models to track and predict prices in the bond market. It got into trouble when those models failed.

Bond prices, particularly prices of bonds that are related, generally move in the same direction, but not always at the same rate. For example, one bond's price may temporarily rise faster than another's. Usually these price discrepancies eventually correct themselves. And usually the discrepancy in the relative price movements of two related bonds does not vary outside a certain range.

Long-Term Capital specialized in finding these price discrepancies and predicting which way prices would move. The fund got into trouble when it detected price discrepancies between U.S. Treasury securities and other bonds, including high-yield corporate bonds, mortgage-backed securities and European government bonds. Long-Term Capital decided to short U.S. Treasuries, a bet that their prices would go down, and go long on the other types of bonds, betting that their prices would go up.

Unfortunately for Long-Term, emerging markets stalled. In June, the fund lost 15 percent of its value. Then on August 14, Russia announced its decision to default on its debt. Markets around the world fell sharply.

The plunges in many stock markets caused investors to pour money into the U.S. Treasury market, a haven when there is economic turmoil, driving up the prices of Treasury securities. The falling yields on U.S. Treasuries, which move in the opposite direction to their prices, led to a decline in the interest rates for mortgages, pushing down the prices of some mortgage-backed securities. The flight to U.S. Treasuries also took its toll on the European and high-yield bond markets, where prices declined. With all of their bets going in the wrong direction, Long-Term Capital was squeezed.

In August the fund lost 44 percent of its value, bringing its year-to-date losses to 52 percent. "A series of events occurred that were outside the norm," NYU finance professor Martin Gruber told Morgenson. "These catastrophes happen. The fault isn't with the models."

The Federal Reserve quickly organized more than a dozen banks and brokerages to bail out Long-Term Capital with $3.5 billion. Finance professionals were "agog," Morgenson reported. "Cries of crony capitalism, Wall Street style, are growing louder. And with some justification." At the time, the United States was pressing Japan and other countries to let weak financial institutions fail. Supporters of the bailout countered that the collapse of Long-Term Capital would hurt small investors. "But the retail investor is only part of the story," explained Morgenson, "and hardly the heart of it. The bailout was in the bankers' self-interest, too. Most of the firms that executed Mr. Meriwether's trades piggybacked on them, putting on the same positions. So a mass liquidation of Mr. Meriwether's portfolio would have slashed the value of their holdings. Furthermore, some of the rescuers — Merrill Lynch and UBS A.G., for example — had stakes in the fund."

Not surprisingly, many of the most dangerous mishaps arose from the new technology that came to dominate the world markets, accelerating decisions and amplifying their effect.

Following the collapse of Barings, Dr. Anirudh Dhebar, who has taught at the Harvard Business School and MIT's Sloan School of Management, offered some cautionary observations:

I would like to lay some of the blame on the computer terminal on [trader] Nicholas Leeson's desk.

The ease, economy and speed with which computers and increasingly sophisticated software allow us to cut and paste, calculate, format, graph and act are making a mockery of a creative and nourishing act: the thinking process.

I call it the "F9-key syndrome." F9 is the "CALC," or "calculate," key in most spreadsheet software and is used to recompute the spreadsheet after a change. Editing spreadsheets is relatively easy and inexpensive. Don't like an answer? Change some entries, press F9 and you have a new one. Don't like that either? Repeat the process.

Unchecked, CALC itself—and not the decision for which the analysis is intended—becomes the game as the analyst gets sucked into a black hole of re-re-re-recalculations. It is soon unclear what is driving the exercise: mindful analysis or mindless CALC?

I speak from several years of observation. In my teaching, I have business school students—M.B.A. and executive-education participants alike—work on spreadsheets. I constantly caution the students: DO NOT rush to the computer, open the spreadsheet, monkey around with the numbers and graphs until 2 a.m. and then think. Think FIRST, and you may be done in a fraction of the time. Do the students listen? No. Unfailingly, computers' superfast calculators, graphing aids and fancy formatting features snare the mind and destroy the discipline.

. . . Often, the computer keyboard and its mouse are the trigger points for decisions themselves: press a key or click a button and you can outwit a rival in a video game, change the setting of factory equipment, buy options on billions of dollars of securities, launch a satellite or incite violence and broadcast bigotry with surprising ease.

Are we, as individuals and as a society, ready for this? Can we rapidly process all the information we get, so soon after the events that caused it, and act on it so swiftly? I urge the reader to reflect. Immediate answers are neither wanted nor desirable.

Federal Reserve chairman Alan Greenspan offered a similar thought: "The one thing the Barings episode illustrates," he said, "is the productivity for making losses has gone up very significantly in the last twenty-five years. You couldn't write the execution slips fast enough twenty-five years ago to lose as much money as was lost by one individual, aided by terrific technology."

PART TWELVE

Net Gains

"I'm unbelievably excited about Netscape the company, and I'm absolutely terrified about Netscape the stock. The enthusiasm for the deal is so totally out of proportion that it's hard to imagine it will trade at a reasonable valuation."

Roger McNamee, Integral Capital Partners, 1995

Timeline

1991 — World Wide Web created by Tim Berners-Lee

1993 — President Clinton gets an e-mail address: president@whitehouse.gov

1995 — Online networks Compuserve and America Online offer web access

1995 — Netscape IPO

1996 — Microsoft's Internet Explorer browser battles Netscape Navigator; antitrust suit to follow

1997 — Number of WWW sites tops 1 million; will rise to 4+ million by January 1999, 10 million by January 2000, and 20+ million by January 2001

1998 — Purdue University researchers discover that adding ".com," ".net," or "Internet" to company name causes short-term stock rise of 125 percent compared to similar companies

1998 — NASD and Amex emerge

1999 — Euro currency introduced

1999 — Almost 100 IPOs double share price in first day

1999 — IPO of VA Linux Systems rises 700 percent first day

1999 — DJIA closes above 11,000, July 16

1999 — Nasdaq composite closes year above 4000

1999 — 66 mutual funds return 100 percent or more; 11 top 200 percent

2000 — Nasdaq composite hits 5000 in March, just weeks after passing 4000

2000 — Abby Joseph Cohen warns of overvalued tech stocks, March 28

2000 — Nasdaq down 35 percent in April

2000 — Microsoft loses antitrust suit; begins appeal

2000 — Nasdaq attempts to connect with European exchanges

2000 — Decimalization introduced

2000 — Feds catch mobsters working the market

2001 — Nasdaq falls to nearly 1600, down 70 percent in a year; many Internet companies close doors

THE SCENE IN THE 1990S

Virtual Friends

David Owen

In 1995, author David Owen confessed a secret in the pages of The New Yorker.

I've become a compulsive viewer of CNBC, the cable television network that covers business all day long.

CNBC has a lot to offer the homebound worker, including thoughtful predictions about the direction of interest rates, and stock prices that glide continually along the bottom of the screen, even during commercials. What I love about it, though, is not its content but its companionship. I have come to view the members of the CNBC staff as my home-office co-workers.

Turning on my TV the first thing in the morning is like coming in to work early and putting my feet up on my desk. Running CNBC in the background makes my home office seem not like a solitary prison cell or torture chamber but like a beehive of cheerful, important activity. No matter how unmotivated I feel about doing my own job, the people on the screen seem enthusiastic and engaged, even if all they're doing is discussing a sudden small decrease in the number of yen to the Deutsche mark. If I lose interest in some project of my own, I lean back and watch CNBC until I feel like making money again. If I really have to buckle down, I press the mute button on my remote control—the electronic equivalent of closing my office door—but I never turn off the TV.

Virtual co-workers are better than flesh-and-blood co-workers in several respects: they are paid to be entertaining,

326 • Eyewitness to Wall Street

they are always in the same mood, and they don't duck into the bathroom when they see you coming down the hall. Most of the people at CNBC seem to me to be about my age (which means, I suppose, that they are five or ten years younger), and some of the guys don't wear jackets. There's quite a bit of kidding around, even with the C.E.O.s of big companies. I can nurse my powerful crushes on Sue Herera and Maria Bartiromo without endangering my marriage or risking accusations of sexual harassment. (I'm pretty sure Sue Herera has a thing for me, too, although it's difficult to read the body language of someone whose body usually ends at her armpits.) The only guys in the office I don't really like are Dan Dorfman and a guy who smiles too much and always nods when he talks.

CNBC is not the perfect virtual office. There's no health plan, most of the men wear makeup, and I don't know who our boss is. I wouldn't presume to tinker very much, though. I might add an after-hours segment set in a bar. It would be like "Cheers," but the people having drinks would be Joe Kernen, David Faber, Ron Insana, and all my other best buddies from the regular show. I might also add a whole separate channel about the receptionists and mailroom guys, who invariably know the best dirt. In a decade or two, perhaps, CNBC will be available in a holographic format that will make the show appear to take place not on my television screen, but in my actual office, at desks right next to mine.

I'm probably making it seem that all I do is work. Believe me, I don't. Today was a good example. At three o'clock this afternoon, a full hour before the closing bell on Wall Street, I said goodbye to the guys at the office and went over to ESPN for a round of golf.

Netscape Fever
August 9, 1995

Molly Baker and Joan E. Rigdon

*The Internet stock boom of recent years began with the initial public of-
fering of Netscape, the maker of World Wide Web software. Just prior to
the IPO, Molly Baker and Joan E. Rigdon of the* Wall Street Journal
*had encountered full-fledged mania: "I've never seen another offering
where getting a one-on-one session was like getting a one-on-one with
God," commented an analyst who was lucky enough to get an hour of attention from Netscape management. Another said, "I'm unbelievably excited about Netscape the company, and I'm absolutely terrified about
Netscape the stock. The enthusiasm for the deal is so totally out of proportion that it's hard to imagine it will trade at a reasonable valuation."*

*No one looking for a big story was disappointed the day the stock
debuted.*

It took General Dynamics Corp. 43 years to become a corporation worth today's $2.7 billion in the stock market. It took Netscape
Communications Corp. about a minute.

That's the value investors were putting on Netscape yesterday after the software company's first public shares started changing
hands among technology-crazed investors. Never mind that the
firm had only $16.6 million of revenue in the first half of this year
and has never earned a profit. Or that its main product is one that's
given away free on the Internet.

Having been priced at $28 a share Tuesday—a figure that had al-
ready been doubled from what was planned a few weeks ago—
Netscape opened trading an hour and a half late yesterday at a
breathtaking $71 a share. That times the 38.1 million shares in exis-
tence yielded the stunning "market cap."

The problem, of course, was that not all of those 38 million shares
were buyable. Only five million were. It just shows what the law of
supply and demand can do when it gets really, really out of whack.

Robert Strawbridge got an inkling of that nutty supply-demand imbalance even before yesterday. Two weeks after starting his job as a summer intern at Hambrecht & Quist Inc., one of Netscape's underwriters, Mr. Strawbridge was put in charge of emptying the San Francisco firm's voice mailbox. Every hour of every working day for the past six weeks he has listened to 75 or so pleas from around the world seeking the Holy Grail—a share of Netscape at the offering.

Or Netscope.

Or Netcap.

Whatever.

"People were desperate," Mr. Strawbridge marvels. "The calls would come in from people saying, 'I've never opened an account before, but this one I have to own. Can someone please, please, call me back?'"

Tough luck. At best, most got a prospectus in the mail.

It all called to mind some other one-day manias for initial public offerings that just about everybody had to have. A piece of Genentech in 1980, for instance—opening its first day of trading at $35 and closing at $71.25. Home Shopping Network going from $18 to $42.625 its first day in 1986. Most recently, Boston Chicken (now known as Boston Market) priced its IPO at $20 in November 1993 and saw the stock open at $45 the next day.

One player yesterday, having finished up a couple of fast phone calls to his brokers, had the grace to put the Netscape saga in this historical perspective. Harold Davis, a retired veterinarian in Zionsville, Ind., bought 3,000 shares at $71 and sold them 10 minutes later for $73.625. "It was a Boston Chicken moment," he exults.

Dr. Davis, like so many other would-be owners of the latest red-hot technology start-up, was flabbergasted when Netscape's shares opened at 2½ times the offering price yesterday. But like so many of those investors, he wasn't deterred.

Also like them, he wasn't all that familiar with what his $213,000 was buying. "I don't really know anything about the company," Dr. Davis says.

. . . A little shaky on these details, Dr. Davis figured that "I didn't want to own it when I went to bed." Hence the sale of his whole position minutes later.

It was a good move. Before the day was over, the stock had cooled to a close of a mere $58.25. That left the little Mountain View, Calif., company with a market cap of a more reasonable $2.2 billion on the Nasdaq Stock Market. Trading volume: 13.8 million shares—or 2¾ times the number outstanding.

In late 1998, America Online bought Netscape for $4.2 billion.

Internet Stock Scams, 1998

Katrina Brooker

In the 1920s, shady stock promoters found gullible customers by telegram. In the next decades, boiler room operators did the same by making unsolicited telephone calls. It did not take long for crooks to realize the Internet offers a new way to sell an old idea.

For Matthew Bowin, a petty con man who currently resides in the Santa Cruz County Jail, prosecutors say that suckering investors into a phony stock scam was easy: He did it on the Internet. All it took was a slick ad that slowly flashed across a popular online investor site: "The next Microsoft is offering its stock to the public . . . over the Internet! . . . click here for more information."

With that simple pitch, during the spring of last year Bowin lured nearly 100,000 investors to a Website touting his high-tech startup, Interactive Products & Services. The site included extensive technical information about the firm's revolutionary Internet devices, named NetCaller and PC Remote; a claim that the company had a partnership set up with Microsoft; and instructions on how to invest in the promising startup.

Trouble was, nearly everything about Interactive Products & Services was phony, according to court documents. Its cutting-edge product didn't work. Its partnership with Microsoft didn't exist. Its claim that the company had filed its IPO with the SEC was false. The engineers and consultants listed as "key employees" developing the NetCaller say they had nothing to do with the company. As for its CEO, well, it seems the 36-year-old Bowin's day job was running an escort service (he's currently charged with pimping and pandering).

But so legitimate looking was Bowin's pitch that Elvin East, an entrepreneur from Georgia who was thinking about conducting his own Internet IPO, called Bowin for advice. Nearly 3,000 investors from around the world E-mailed him for information, Bowin says, and 150 actually sent in checks. One investor from Hong Kong wired $10,000. Another, a California attorney, invested $1,500. In three months Bowin pulled in $190,000. Not bad for a guy with such a colorful rap sheet.

Fortunately, Bowin is not a good crook—he was arrested last April and is now on trial, charged with theft. As for investors? "I guess I'll keep looking for the next Microsoft," says a wistful Steven Fujita, a 31-year-old bankruptcy clerk in Los Angeles who entrusted Bowin with $500.

Welcome to the seedy underbelly of online investing: the World Wide Web of securities fraud. The Internet has become a breeding ground for stock scamsters. Where else, after all, can crooks find as many millions of potential victims so quickly, cheaply, and anonymously?

In the old days, conning investors was hard work. Since most stock fraud involves micro-cap stocks—or other securities no one has ever heard of—scamsters who work the traditional way, hunched over telephones in boiler rooms, have to make hundreds of cold calls; to succeed they need to have the personality of a pit bull. On the Internet, however, a single E-mail or Website can reach millions of potential investors instantly, effortlessly. Besides, using the Internet is cheap. Bowin, for one, never spent a dime on his scheme. Using a computer manual as his guide, he set up his Website on his own. He then got his ad displayed for free by promising to pay for it after his IPO went through.

There is nothing particularly new or clever about the types of scams on the Internet. Indeed, most rely on devices perfected by boiler-room artists decades—even centuries—ago. But if the Internet hasn't introduced new types of stock scams, it has definitely made the business of fraud far more efficient. Now, instead of having to go out and find their victims, cyberscamsters can sit back and let investors come to them.

Surfing on the Slippery Skin of a Bubble, 1999

Po Bronson

In the 1960s, it was impressive enough to be a stockbroker. In the 1980s, one had to be an "investment banker." In the 1990s, nothing less than "venture capitalist" would do.

Eyewitness Po Bronson, who brilliantly sends up Silicon Valley in his novels Bombardiers *and* The First $20 Million Is Always the Hardest, *is also just as entertaining when reporting on real people.*

For a homeless shelter's annual charity auction not long ago, Steve Jurvetson, a venture capitalist, donated a breakfast with himself at Buck's Restaurant. Buck's is a bustling diner in Woodside, Calif., a single-intersection hamlet nestled into an oak grove at the base of the San Mateo County foothills. The booths at Buck's are upholstered in ocher Naugahyde and the menus have the feel of political-action newsletters and the owners are mighty proud of their coffeecake. Buck's also happens to be the place where Netscape and many other high-tech companies were hatched.

"Breakfast at Buck's" was sold off by way of the Internet site eBay at the end of February; 78 bids after the auction started, a budding Manhattan entrepreneur named Mark Hernandez offered to pay $4,400 for the privilege of flying out to Silicon Valley two weeks later to present his business idea. That might sound like a lot of money to have breakfast with someone, but Jurvetson is a venture capitalist with a reputation—young, enthusiastic, open-minded. He can be found at Buck's most mornings. He bounds in like a kangaroo, exuberant, flashing a joyous smile, his youthful face tanned from his noon-hour games of ultimate Frisbee. He is generally more dapper than his colleagues, wearing a charcoal Czechoslovakian handmade suit over a cobalt shirt with faint royal blue pinstripes. His tie picks up these colors perfectly; the black wing tips on his large feet shine. In the plastic window of his wallet is the bridal portrait of his wife of eight years, Karla, who is a psychiatrist at Stanford.

He has a prototypical résumé for a Silicon Valley V.C.: earned B.S. and M.S. degrees from Stanford, designed microchips at Hewlett-Packard, learned management consulting at Bain & Company, returned to Stanford for his M.B.A. and then beat out 250 other applicants for a position at Draper Fisher, the venture firm. Prototypical résumé, except for the date column: as an undergrad, he tricked the registration computer—which blocked signing up for more than 20 units—by penciling in just two units of credit on what were five-unit classes. In this way, he was able to take eight classes at once and finish in two and a half years with an A plus average. Think that's fast? The conventional wisdom in Silicon Valley is that it takes three years to learn the craft. Steve Jurvetson made partner in six months. He was 28.

Venture capitalists' favorite unit of measurement is the factor X. They live life on multiplication scale, and anything less than X is inconsequential. When they invest, they ignore 12 percent or 15 percent or 18 percent returns. They start to take notice when they see potential for 10X returns. In this lingo, Jurvetson blasted through college at nearly 2X the normal rate, and made partner at 6X speed.

Now he's accelerating—straight into what could be a precarious stretch of road. Only 32, Jurvetson is in for the summer of his life, with no fewer than 11 of the Internet-related companies he has backed (Wit Capital, Goto.com, Tumbleweed and Netzero among them) at various points along the road to an initial public offering. The brand name he has built for himself with investments in a couple of other successful Internet start-ups—his firm's specialty and the hottest destination for venture capital—will be put to the test.

That's because the market's taste for Internet stocks appears to have soured: bellwethers are way off their peaks and new issues are coming out of the box more cautiously. Dave Marquart, a Silicon Valley veteran who was the only venture investor in Microsoft and the co-lead investor of Sun Microsystems, warns: "To be a bona fide venture capitalist, you have to go through a complete cycle. Those who've entered the business since the mid-90's have never seen a down cycle. Everything has been to the right and up—very up."

To understand why Jurvetson is a folk hero for so many of those looking to convert their dreams and visions into Net wealth, consider what happened in February 1996. Sabeer Bhatia was an immigrant from India with zero experience running a company, zero experience in consumer products and zero experience in software. (He had been a hardware engineer at Apple.) He was Jurvetson's age less two years, or J − 2.

Bhatia had already been turned down by 21 other venture capital firms. He had produced no prototype, not even a graphic printed on a piece of paper. What he did have was what Jurvetson called "hallucinogenic optimism" and one intriguing idea, which he sketched out on a conference room white board. Jurvetson invested $300,000 to buy 15 percent of the project. Less than two years later, the company that emerged from that meeting, Hotmail, was sold to Microsoft for $400 million. Jurvetson became an instant legend, the guy every young entrepreneur wants to meet, even if it means paying 250X the cost of breakfast at Buck's.

Increasingly, successful venture capital firms are sheltering themselves from the hail of unsolicited business plans by invoking the Inverse Rule of Referrals: all good ideas come by referral, so if it didn't come by referral it must not be a good idea. Here's how a typical venture firm might catalogue the incoming slough: administrative staff scans the first paragraph of the cover letter for a referral by a "trusted third party," which is entered in a database. Partners scan the database; they'll look at the plan only if they trust the referral. "It makes being a venture capitalist 90 percent simpler," Jurvetson comments.

Draper, Fisher, Jurvetson has cultivated a reputation for ignoring that rule. The firm is located in Seaport, a sailing harbor in Redwood City—psychologically far from V.C. ground zero, Sand Hill Road (but close enough to zip there in 10 minutes for a meeting). The problem with referral networks, as D.F.J. sees it, is that as the venture capitalists age, so does their referral network, cutting them off from the original thinkers. They say they read every one of the 5,000 plans sent to them each year. Theirs was the first venture capital firm to run an advertisement.

D.F.J. is a "seed" firm, meaning it gets in on the first round of financing for nascent businesses. "Getting companies started is the hardest part," says Tim Draper, the firm's founder, "and it's the most rewarding—both financially and personally." To Jurvetson, it's even more rewarding than being an entrepreneur. "I get bits and pieces of several success stories, sort of a highlight reel," he says.

Jurvetson has succeeded so far by making himself accessible to the kind of young people who he figures come up with unusual ideas—as opposed to what the industry calls "Me, Too" product. One recent month's "Me, Too" was on-line gift registries. He saw 30 business plans on that concept. The month before, it was Web-calendar companies. He saw three Web-calendar plans out of Sun Microsystems' employees alone. Having lunch in San Francisco one day, he bumped into an old friend who said he had left Netscape to found his dream start-up; without much tact, Jurvetson jokingly blurted out, "I hope it's not another Web-calendar company!" His friend's face fell. They always think they're the only ones with the idea.

"Truly original thinkers tend not to be entrepreneurs who've spent 10 years at Cisco and can be trusted to know what they're doing," Jurvetson explains. "They tend to be 26 years old and highflying. They often have a very childlike mind, with some naiveté. We're impressed by people who don't know what can't be done."

Mark Hernandez, the winner of the Breakfast at Buck's auction, is J − 3 years old. He shows up at Buck's wearing a navy blazer, khakis, tortoise-shell Clark Kent glasses and his Stanford class ring. He resigned from his position as director of Merrill Lynch's Latin American derivatives desk four days ago to pursue a new life, though it's not clear just yet what that life will entail. Their conversation swells and fades, never coming to a head with the Pitch. Hernandez has a lot to choose from. Since winning the auction, he has been besieged by other Manhattan entrepreneurs offering finder's fees for connecting them with Jurvetson. On top of that, he has invested his own money into four start-ups, and he obligingly runs down the list, getting strategic feedback.

Not until the plates are cleared does he get around to his dream project: he's going to raise $5 million from cash-rich friends on Wall Street and pair it with a special $15 million loan into a highly leveraged kitty called Transformation Capital. It's a seed fund!

He'll be looking for 20 start-ups to invest in.

Mark Hernandez doesn't want to be the Steve Jobs of the next century. He wants to be the Steve Jurvetson of lower Manhattan.

"Ever since I read that Hotmail story," he says, "I wanted to get in touch with you."

Do You Believe?: How Yahoo!
Became a Blue Chip, June 1999

Joseph Nocera

In 1995, software maker Netscape went public and achieved a first-day market capitalization of $2.7 billion. Four years later, veteran business writer Joseph Nocera tried to understand the psychological shifts that had occurred in the world of Internet stocks by the time Yahoo!—with a P/E ratio of more than 1,000—was decreed a "blue chip."

Under the old, pre-Internet rules, a company with Yahoo's revenues and projected growth rate might be able to justify a market cap of, oh, $3 billion. Instead, Yahoo's market cap stands at $34 billion. Its P/E ratio in mid-May was around 1,062. This is uncharted territory: for the day traders who have helped run up the stock so far and so fast; for the short-sellers who've gotten killed again and again on Yahoo; for the retail investors deciding whether to take the plunge; even for the pros at Fidelity Investments, who by the end of last year held close to 1.8 million Yahoo shares. Half of those were owned by Fidelity Magellan, the nation's largest mutual fund, which brings us to the most astonishing fact of all: Despite its unfathomable market cap, Yahoo is now viewed as a stock "safe" enough to be held by mutual funds that manage retirement money for tens of millions of Americans. Analysts routinely categorize it, along with AOL, Amazon.com, and eBay, as an Internet "blue chip." Fund managers buy Yahoo for "defensive" purposes.

There are plenty of people who still think that Netmania will turn out to be a bubble—and they may well be right. But for now, the more illuminating question is the more prosaic one. How did we get here? How did it come to pass that a company with $16 million in quarterly earnings could have $34 billion market cap—and that no one dares suggest that its stock is overpriced? That story, the story of Yahoo the stock, is the story of the relationship between investors and Internet stocks. It's about how we all learned to abandon our valuation bias.

"These valuations are such a distraction," Michael Moritz is say-ing, affecting his most world-weary tone. The 44-year-old venture capitalist is slouched in his small office, his face propped against one arm; he appears to be struggling to stay awake in the face of such dreary questioning. "Clearly," he continues, "this has mesmerized all sorts of people." He sighs. "But I don't think it's that healthy for Sil-icon Valley—or for those trying to build a company."

Just months [before the April 1996 IPO], the Japanese company Softbank had sunk $100 million into Yahoo, becoming its largest shareholder. So the company didn't need money—the classic "old economy" reason for going public. Yahoo Chairman and CEO Timothy Koogle didn't even want to do an IPO that April. "I really wanted a few more quarters. I wanted to be sure we could deliver our numbers consistently and ahead of (Wall Street's) expectations," he says.

In the end, though, the Yahoo CEO felt he had no choice. Two competitors, Lycos and Excite, had announced plans for IPOs, and Koogle felt Yahoo couldn't be left behind. If Yahoo waited to go public, it might be perceived as a laggard, and forfeit what Wall Street calls the "first-mover premium." "We couldn't afford to be boxed in," he says.

Lycos and Excite went public just weeks before Yahoo, and nei-ther shot the lights out. Yahoo, on the other hand, priced its offer-ing at $13 a share (these are pre-split prices), saw the stock jump to $43, and closed the day at $33—up 154%, giving it a first-day mar-ket cap of over $800 million. Yahoo's stock had outperformed the others; by the tortured logic of the Internet, that made Yahoo the leader in portals.

There is one other crucial fact about Yahoo's IPO—and indeed all Internet IPOs—that helps explain some of the giddy rise in Net stock prices. The "float" was tiny. When Yahoo went public, it had around 26 million shares outstanding. But only 10% were made available to the public. The rest remained in the hands of the founders and other insiders, such as Sequoia and Softbank. With a float that small, Yahoo was virtually guaranteed a successful IPO, since demand for its shares would far outstrip supply. As Michael Parekh, the Internet analyst at Goldman Sachs, puts it, "Float mat-ters." Truth to tell, in the early days of a Net stock's life, little mat-ters more.

In the beginning especially, Yahoo's stock wasn't moving as a result of a superior business model. Yahoo's stock was moving because of its small float. With less than three million shares in circulation, it wasn't that hard to make [the price] move. "I want to be in a stock with a two-million-share float," says a New York day trader named Lee Ang. "All you need is the littlest hype, and it will run up."

For day traders, "valuation is meaningless." Anyone who thought otherwise got his head handed to him. Short-sellers, believing the stock was overvalued, would make periodic runs at it. But these were suicide missions. With the float so small, it was relatively easy for people on the long side to snap up most of the available shares and "squeeze the shorts"—forcing them to capitulate and buy stock to cover their positions, which drove the price even higher. Hedge-fund managers who had started out shorting Yahoo often switched to the other side and began buying it up instead.

This wasn't the only form of capitulation to the power of this stock. There was also a kind of intellectual capitulation, perhaps best exemplified by a man named Bob Walberg. Walberg is an analyst who writes for an Internet site, Briefing.com. But Walberg did not instantly warm to Internet stocks. Having spent 15 years working at regional brokerages, Walberg thought of himself as an analyst who took "a conservative, value-oriented approach." He was horrified by Internet valuations. And he said so.

"Once you reach the conclusion that it is the supply-demand equation that is moving these stocks, and not valuation, you have to make a choice," Walberg says. "You can ignore what is driving the stocks and opt out of the game. Or you can ignore valuation and stay in the game. We decided we didn't want to opt out. Besides, you have to recognize that investors are trying to pick winners—and Internet stocks have been the big winners."

The analysts who covered Yahoo could still love the stock because, like Bob Walberg, they had all gotten their minds into that different place—the place where you acquiesce to the logic of Internet valuations. All relied on relative valuation measures—thus keeping the comparisons within the Internet universe. That was the key, really: Once you viewed Net stocks in relative terms, it all seemed to make sense. Some analysts liked revenue per customer measures, while others pointed to the growing number of visitors to the Web-sites. One analyst smushed these together and came up with a "value per customer" metric. ("We then take the steady-state per-customer operating income and apply a dividend discount model to come up with a value per customer," he helpfully explained.) Analysts who liked to crunch numbers favored "discounted cash flow" models as a way of defending the valuations. They made cash-flow estimates five or six years into the future, then worked backward to the present. The problem is that since we know so little about where the Net is headed, predicting cash flow so far into the future is largely meaningless. While it looked like old-fashioned valuation analysis, it wasn't. Rather, it was a kind of disguised justification: an implied acknowledgment by the analysts that investing in this new technology was a bet—just as Graham and Dodd had said back in 1934.

In the end, that's the lesson the stock has imprinted on those who follow it: If you get hung up on valuation, you'll get hurt.

"Do you know why people like me own this stock?" asks Roger McNamee. "We own it because we have no choice."

A general partner of Integral Capital Partners, a Silicon Valley technology fund, McNamee is one of the best-known tech investors in America. He was in on Yahoo's brief life. He appreciates the "brilliance," as he calls it, of Yahoo's business model and the abilities of Yahoo's management. He likes Tim Koogle a lot. None of that entirely explains why he's of late been loading up on Yahoo and other Internet stocks: "I buy these stocks because I live in a competitive universe, and I can't beat my benchmarks without them." What he thinks about their valuations is irrelevant. "You either participate in this mania, or you go out of business," he says. "It's a matter of self-preservation."

By the spring of 2001, Yahoo's stock had dropped to less than one-tenth of its high a year earlier, and Tim Koogle stepped aside from the CEO post. The market cap of the company was still more than $9 billion.

Riding the Mo in the Lime Green Glow, 1999

Matthew Klam

Often confused with simply buying and selling stocks online, day trading is a specific kind of speculation: the practice of buying and selling within a day to capture small moves in a stock, often ending each day entirely in cash. There have always been day traders, but with the growth of online trading, and the wide availability of real-time quotes, the term has become part of the common lexicon.

For The New York Times Magazine, *Matthew Klam looked inside a day trader's mind.*

The stock market opens and Dave Goehl immediately makes a $230 profit on 500 shares of eGroup, which he bought yesterday, by accident. Dave is buying and selling securities on the Nasdaq exchange in his shorts and a T-shirt from the convenience of his spare bedroom. "It's the neatest thing in the world," he says. Taped to the wall in front of him is a list of his daily reminders: to trade 12,000 shares a day, to avoid sticking with losers for too long, to choose each transaction carefully. Dave reminds me, constantly, that "trading is 99 percent emotional," and since trading stocks online in real time with lots of his own money is like roasting marshmallows on the *Hindenburg*, he must keep his wits about him. On the wall above his desk he reads No. 1 of his "Top 10 Habits of a Successful Trader": "Be Disciplined: Discipline! Discipline! Discipline! Discipline! Discipline!"

He wakes up at 6 most days, turns on CNBC, reads the financial newspapers, *USA Today*, online journals like "The Bull Market Report," Steve Harmon's "Internet Stock Report"; he scans the free message boards on Silicon Investor and Yahoo Finance for any mention of the stocks he's following, some timely nugget that big institutional investors—firms like Fidelity or U.S. Bancorp Piper Jaffray—got before the rest of the markets, reports on new research, hearsay of analysts' opinions, any other rumors of upgrades or downgrades that will turn out to be either dependable information or panic or borderline fraud. Thanks to the Internet, Dave has facts at his fingertips not even professionals had in such volume until recently, reports, analysis, a river of opinions on every stock, but so what? How's his gut?

"Usually, the more trades I make, the worse I do," he explains. "In one of the books I read, the guy compares a trader to a ninja—the way they hide out, they're in black and they can sit there and you can't even hear them breathe. They wait for the perfect moment and then they strike. It's like you could go a whole week and not trade at all until you find the perfect stock."

We try to piece together what we remember from comic books, that the ninja are Japanese warriors who employ lethal, razor-sharp throwing stars, nunchuk sticks, silent footwear. Dave has no formal training in the martial arts; he has no formal training as a stock trader either. He didn't mean to buy eGroup last night. He meant to short it (that is: bet that its share price would fall) but buying it is what he did, which ended up being good, because it went up, not down. Sometimes even a ninja needs luck.

Dave turns to the screen, shoulders slightly raised, with a look of fury and excitement. Now what? His body is motionless but his eyes blaze, his smile gleams. Since 9:45 he has been racing through online charts of Harbinger, Fatbrain.com, About.com, some of his favorite stocks, pausing, thinking, shifting, staring.

Above the bed is a magnetic board that lists certain publicly traded companies, separated into: "dot-com stocks," "e-tailers," "box makers" (computer manufacturers), advertising, "wireless and broadband" (telecom and cable companies), many of them new, soaring growth stocks that share the potential to explode. An I.P.O. section lists companies that are on deck or trading. There's some laundry on the floor, athletic tape on the windowsill and a set of golf clubs in the corner.

Dave is watching CheckFree, which he also bought yesterday, at just under $33 a share. "They're the infrastructure behind bill payments online," he says. "Supposedly Amex is using them and hasn't made it public yet." Dave pieced this theory together from tips on the Yahoo and Silicon Investor chat rooms, plus the cagey response of CheckFree's investor relations department. CheckFree is trading at 33⁷/₁₆, Dave stares ahead, smile pasted on his face: "If you can break through 35, you've got 40." Discipline.

On the green plastic table beside the bed are messy piles of papers: the record of Dave's 3,500 trades so far this year, an accumulation of notes on new business ideas, magazines, books on options trading. On the shelf are more books: *Liberation Management*; *Thriving on Chaos*; *Think Like a President*; *Control Your Destiny or Someone Else Will*; *What They Don't Teach You at Harvard Business School*; *Secrets of the SOES Bandit*; *The Complete Idiot's Guide to Making Money on Wall Street*. There are glow-in-the-dark stars on the ceiling.

Beside Dave's mouse pad sits *Trading for a Living*, by Dr. Alexander Elder, a psychiatrist who speaks of himself as an addict hooked on trading. Dave shows me Chapter 10, "Losers Anonymous." Elder explains that we are all losers with a tendency to sabotage ourselves. "If you win big, you get euphoric, you're less disciplined; you figure, Why not bet it all?" That, says Dave, is "the addictive part." He has written in the margins and scribbled across its pages in gassy script: "Control your feelings—if not, stop." "You must be prep'd to win."

A skinny dog walks into the room, climbs up onto the bed and falls asleep, its feet sticking up in the air. Mrs. Beasley, a 3-year-old beagle mix. Another dog, Doc, comes in behind her, 14 years old, black and gray with a wet nose. I just waterproofed my shoes, and he's smelling them.

"Elder realized that Alcoholics Anonymous was a good model for anyone who trades," Dave says to me. "Basically what he says here is that you have to wake up each day and tell yourself you're a loser."

The price of CheckFree begins to drop. Dave starts banging the keys. "Yuck. Now I'm disappointed."

Still smiling, he unloads his 1,000 shares in two lumps over 30 seconds for a gross profit of $346.

So this is the neatest thing in the world?

Over the summer, when I first met Dave, the day-trading industry was promoting itself with the moronic glee of a Publishers Clearing House Sweepstakes: a 12-year-old buys a helicopter with stock-market winnings, a dude without a job drives away in a Rolls-Royce towing a yacht. But then the message shifted. In a new ad, a goateed hipster with an annoying, satisfied puss—calculated to look cutting-edge—tells you: We're pioneers. In another, a classroom of immigrants ostensibly trying to learn some English begins rhapsodizing about an Internet broker called Ameritrade; they've mistaken it for the word America, they think their English teacher wants to talk about online trading and they all love this new country!

See, this is not about money-grubbing; it's a new democratic revolution. Day trading, like the right to own dirty magazines, the privilege of serving in our armed forces, is a fail-safe against the loss of individual freedom—which for Americans is the same thing as collective freedom—and for that matter is the only sure way to keep your soul intact. Now an investor controls his own life so he can make the final call, so no one can delude him into thinking that the buying and selling of stocks is more complicated than a couple of mouse clicks, so nothing can obstruct his inherent right to unload his losers on the next bigger dope to come along. And what could be more American than that?

Five years ago not a single person traded online. Today a quarter of all individual investors do so. In the vanguard are the full-time day traders like Dave—a revolution of guys in relaxed clothing trying to turn their computers into cash registers. I came to see this revolution. I wanted to watch day trading up close, see a grown man exhaust himself with fears of bankruptcy and dreams of ascendance, hollowed out of everything but dread, terror, release, desire. I imagined a crazy Elvis fan, finally sucking on that sweat-soaked scarf.

I sat in day-trading shops—the places that became abruptly notorious when an Atlanta trader shot one up in July—little purgatorial way stations of American greed; rooms full of men not working, giving this thing a shot. I met a tanned Iraqi gentleman in a black Lycra T-shirt with the soft, intelligent brown eyes of a movie star and watched him bleed money on all 11 stocks he'd bought that morning. I met a graphic designer who ran Fibonacci programs, Elliott waves, mathematical prediction models that never worked for him; he didn't have the heart for it. A 27-year-old guy, on a roll, up $124,000 for the day, eating Taco Bell, loving it. A Taiwanese trader who made a thousand buy and sell executions between 9:30 a.m. and 4 p.m., sometimes trading a million shares a day, his hands constantly moving like some hypnotized homunculus building a sand castle one grain at a time. His mother sat in the chair beside him, also trading, not doing as well; his 22-year-old sister sat beside Mom, still in training.

And then I found Dave. He does not belong to the comparatively small subculture of the day-trading shops, but is part of the larger, harder-to-count group that trades in high volume from home, full time, moving in and out of stocks, quickly, trying to profit on the shortest-term rising and falling. Dave is 30, with thick brown hair, muscled, athletic, his big smile buzzing bright like a bug zapper. He has been trading from this desk since October 1998, after he quit his $130,000-a-year (plus bonus) job as the national accounts manager for a booming legal staffing-headhunting organization based in Hartford.

In one important way Dave is not a typical day trader—after a difficult start, he has done well financially, and so far the research suggests that most day traders don't. Dave started trading with $80,000, some of which he parked in stocks he intends to hold for a long time, but most of which he began using for day trading. He says his total stake is now worth $300,000. This year, he says, he is up almost $200,000. But that's the gross number, so subtract $38,000 in commissions paid to Datek and the online brokerage firms he trades through. Now subtract at least another $60,000 for taxes. And subtract his expenses: $300 a month for his PC Quote, which gives him Nasdaq Level II access over the phone line; $300 for his share of rent to turn this part of the apartment into a trading room; $180 a month for newspapers, cable, newsletters, phone. Barring a drastic change in his performance, he will net $85,000 from day trading this year.

Dave spends his days in the muted, fake, unspecial world of a computer monitor. He is alone, obsessed, keeping bright-eyed, hawk-like vigil over the screen in front of him. I can't help feeling as though he has been banished to this spare room with its cheap green plastic patio furniture, an enormous bag of hockey equipment, a pile of hockey sticks along the windowsill; this is where the dogs sleep. Sometimes when they're napping on the spare bed, Dave gets up and joins them.

Against all odds, he is fervently excited. He bounces around buoyantly, undulating in his spring-loaded executive chair. Everything in Dave's scope comes across in terms of preachable love. He believes in his new obsession so strongly that I am winded from it. Every time he does a new trade he sucks all the air out of the room. "If you work hard," he tells me, "it's the ultimate."

I'm watching but, right now at least, I don't see it. Dave is a likable guy, but so far the revolution looks like a man hugging a slot machine. I'm trying to figure out what it is that makes a friendly person chuck everything to trade stock all day, alone. What would Dave be doing today if some computer genius had not invented this?

It's 10:45 A.M., and all morning a mysterious box has been appearing on top of Dave's PC Quote market maker's screen, a white square with nothing in it that Dave has to click on to remove. All this fantastic technology—small order execution system, the electronic commerce networks, the programs that draw a direct line from the capital markets to your living room by way of Web brokerages like Datek—it's all still a little screwy. It's easy to forget how new this is, but unexplainable glitches are a good reminder.

Yesterday I sat over Dave's shoulder from 9:30 to 4 trying to watch him trade. The numbers and symbols on his screen are so tiny. Today I've moved my chair up so that I'm almost sitting on his mouse pad. I see the flow of buyers and sellers moving toward a common price. An investment bank like Goldman Sachs offers up to the market a chunk of stock worth half a million dollars, and it disappears in a flicker. It doesn't look anything like the howling, seductive lure of liquid money, no invisible line from a fishhook tugging in my gut. It's lime green and bright cranberry, orange and blue, as colorful and real as any video game.

The bottom half of Dave's screen is filled with real-time tickers he has custom made, 22 of them, each with four or five stocks whose symbols whiz by. He claims he can catch individual price changes to the fraction. He offers this piece of logic as a way of explaining what stock he'll choose next: "Price, volume, a sudden move up or down; I look at the float, intermediate term high and low averages, points of resistance."

That is: he's looking at the number of shares in play, how quickly they're being traded, how the price is moving—the language of momentum traders, a language once confined not just to professionals, but to a particular subset of gunslinging money managers. Dave is a living symbol of a gigantic shift in the financial zeitgeist—the mainstreamed romance of stock picking. Peter Lynch, icon of the mutual fund industry, the man who once ran more of Main Street's money than anyone else, never talked as Dave does. Lynch is about "fundamentals"—and about trusting your retirement savings to mutual fund managers with proven track records. To the extent we care about money managers now, it's guys like Jim Cramer we admire, guys who run high-octane hedge funds and tell us we don't have to be punks on the sidelines, we can get right in the game and be winners. Why would you want to trust the next Lynch when you could be the next Cramer?

Dave tells me he watches both technical and fundamental analysis, and that's more or less true. But it's also true that he often acts when he gets a feeling—a stock "bugs" him, it "looks beat," he "loves it." Dave types VPHM in his market maker screen. "I hate ViroPharma now," he says. He watches the price move for a while, fingers twitching on the mouse. Yesterday he traded it three times for a gross profit of $50. "I should just not be trading this stock," he says.

Right now he's going to try to short it. Short selling, the full definition, allows an investor to sell a stock he has borrowed but does not own, in hopes of paying for it later, when the stock has dropped in price, thereby keeping the difference; if the stock rises he must repay the loan, plus whatever the stock has gained. Dave scrolls down to the Datek ordering screen. He types "sell," tabs to the next box and types his password, then the symbol, amount, price, seven boxes all together. But he doesn't pull the trigger yet.

Instead he looks at a one-minute chart, then a 15-minute, a 30-day, a six-month chart. Twenty seconds or more of download time pass every time he wants a new chart; all day long we're crawling between Web pages waiting for data. He flips through five other sites, checks institutional interest in the stock through the Thomson Investors Network, scans chat rooms for news, loads a sixth site, waits, checks the float, watching with the stillness in his body of someone getting ready to run across a freeway.

We're getting closer. He lifts his left hand, runs it through his hair, then again. All hair now sticking up he goes back to the market makers screen, where he can see the symbols representing the institutions that clear trades for clients large and small. Who is on the bid side (that is, trying to buy) and who is on the ask side (looking to sell)? Which side is stronger? By how much? He doesn't know the name behind every symbol, but he knows which sellers to steer clear of. He scrolls back to his Datek ordering screen, executes the order, glances at the bid side, which is suddenly gaining strength in the last five seconds. This is when he starts talking to the screen in his soft-spoken, Midwestern manner: "Get out of there, Piper Jaffray!" "Goldman Sachs is whacking everybody."

"This is weird," he says, scrolling down to see the status of his order. It hasn't been filled yet. He checks a box to cancel, withdrawing his order.

"Why did you cancel?"

"It was spooky. I don't get this stock."

This is the first of 23 cancellations just like it.

After the Revolution, June 1999

Katrina Brooker

When Morgan Stanley Dean Witter was preparing its online trading site, the most contentious issue was the name. Online trading has no class, the brokers argued. It's for the little guy. We'll devalue our business if we use the Morgan Stanley name.

The company opted instead to name the site after its Discover credit card. The brokers were relieved. That was foolish. Brokers who thought they could escape Internet trading were kidding themselves.

Katrina Brooker, reporting for Fortune, *observed the effects of Internet trading on Merrill Lynch, by far the strongest brokerage in the post-World War II era. Merrill's greatest asset had been its overwhelming army of retail brokers. Now, with individual investors moving to the Internet, those brokers looked like expensive overhead. They may have felt like it, too: on June 1, 1999, they read in the* Wall Street Journal *that their customers could now trade online, paying $29.95 for trades that would cost an average of $250 through a broker.*

The people who had sold investors on the idea of a revolution finally realized the revolutionaries were coming after them.

June 1, 1999: Merrill Lynch makes headlines around the world by announcing plans to offer $29.95 trades online. A few days later, in one of the firm's East Coast branch offices, a broker who has agreed to speak with *Fortune* on the condition of anonymity is arguing with a client on the phone.

"I can't believe this," he says. "Suddenly you've got $29.95 trades, and you're empowered." Fiddling nervously with his headset, he swivels rapidly back and forth in his chair. "Okay, fine. You want to trade on the Internet? Fine. Go right ahead. You have to do what's right for you. Just don't expect much service from me."

Now he's yelling. "Why? Because I get goose eggs!" He makes a zero sign with his thumb and forefinger. "I don't get paid, okay? So don't expect me to give you any more ideas." He pauses, listening impatiently. "I have given you ideas. Okay, maybe I haven't been as good about that as I could have. Starting today, that is going to change."

But by his look, it's clear the client's not swayed. The broker quickly changes tactics: "Look, I'm sorry. I didn't mean to piss you off. Hey, you want to go to the Mets game tomorrow? I've got tickets."

Covering his hand over the receiver, he looks over at the reporter sitting across his desk. "You wanted to know what it's been like around here lately?"

Until now, Merrill had been the old-style broker's fiercest champion. Its stance was steadfast: A broker's sound advice could beat cheap trades on the Web any day. Only a year ago, Launny Steffens, Merrill's brokerage chief, famously denounced online trading as a form of gambling. Just three months ago he reassured a roomful of brokers that the firm wouldn't allow online trading to undercut them. But now, when asked how he'd feel as a broker today facing the Internet, Steffens, a former broker, replies, "Spectacular."

And of course, the reality is that brokers can't fight the Net anymore. Too many investors are unwilling to pay a full-service broker $100 for a trade when they can do the same thing online for $10. Merrill's announcement just confirms what most brokers have known for a while: To survive, they need to figure this Internet thing out.

But where exactly do they fit in? That is not yet entirely clear. At the time of its announcement Merrill hadn't worked out how its brokers would get paid under its new system. And for most brokers, the news is only just sinking in. "I guess I'm going to have to rethink my whole business," one 30-ish Merrill broker says with a sigh.

There are some signs that a partnership between the Internet and die-hard old-style brokers could work out. Back in Merrill's branch office, the broker who has been busy all afternoon arguing with his client finally gets off the phone. His mood has turned philosophical: "The Internet?" he says with a shrug. "I may as well get to like it and figure out how to make money off it."

By the way, in October 1999, the name of Discover Brokerage Direct was changed to Morgan Stanley Dean Witter Online.

Reversals of Fortune, March 2000

James Cramer and Marianne Costantinou

Up, up and away: while the DJIA languished, and the S&P 500 rose a ho-hum 15 percent, the Nasdaq, home of tech stocks and dot.com start-ups, skyrocketed 84 percent in 1999, closing the year above 4000. Ten weeks later, it was up another 25 percent, closing at 5132 on March 10.

It almost didn't matter what a company built, or sold, or offered, as long as it was technology. In a hurricane, even turkeys fly.

As well, an astonishing 66 mutual funds had returns of 100 percent or more for 1999. Eleven of those topped 200 percent. By comparison, only six funds hit triple digits in 1998 and five in 1993. What kind of funds? Tech funds, of course. Twenty-seven of them were all tech, all the time. For the group as a whole, 60 percent of assets were invested in technology.

We were at the dawn of a "new era," the bulls said. The Internet had boosted productivity without increasing prices, allowing wealth to grow without inflation. Or perhaps the fast-growing "new economy" stocks were being offset by the "old economy" laggards, keeping inflation low. Somehow the bulls forgot that the promise of a "new era" was one of Wall Street's oldest myths; and that as investors left "old economy" companies for "new economy" stocks, the market was getting narrower.

Even some bulls admitted prices were crazy. But the professionals couldn't leave the market. With tech stocks doubling in a week or a month, taking a short breather could mean a fund manager's performance would fall behind the competition. As James Cramer, hedge fund manager and founder of TheStreet.com was still saying even a few months later, "the penalty of missing the rally has never been greater." And as long as the professionals were in, the individuals weren't going anywhere. "Don't try to time the market," they had heard often from television pundits. No one said there is such a thing as enough.

Then, on March 28, with the Nasdaq still near 5000, a few words of caution were offered by Abby Joseph Cohen, the highly respected economist at Goldman Sachs, whose accurate bullish predictions about tech stocks and the market in general had made her the Street's favorite guru du jour.

"For the first time in a decade," she announced, "our model portfolio is no longer recommending an overweighted position in technology. Many of the technology shares were given the respect they deserve over the last eighteen months, and are no longer undervalued."

"No longer overvalued" was instantly recognized as a euphemism for "too darned high." Three weeks later, on April 14, the Nasdaq had crashed to 3321—35 percent off its crest of a month earlier.

JAMES CRAMER
APRIL 2000

For weeks, I had been telling anybody and everybody to take something off the table, that this market didn't feel right, too much margin, too much craziness, too many players, too many sellers. And we had practiced what I preached at Cramer Berkowitz, our $360 million hedge fund, steadily reducing our exposure to a market that seemed to be racing through Nasdaq millennium marks as if they were meaningless base camps on the way to a light lunch atop Everest. Ho-hum, Base Camp 5,000. Hmmm, nice day. Air's not even thin yet. Not a cloud in the sky.

So when Tuesday's storm struck, we thought we were ready. We had our core positions—the ones that we vow never to get rid of—and quietly began adding to them on the way down, just like the textbooks advise. We were sharp, ice water in our veins, as we made our first tranche of buys when the market was down about 100 points. But by 10:30, we could tell this was no garden-variety sell-off, where they take them down a hundred, hold 'em, then walk them back up again as the midmorning mutual-fund contributions in the day's mail get put to work.

Our screens were bathed in red. Only some hapless gold contract and a couple of down-and-out silver-mining and gypsum companies flickered green. My right terminal, earmarked only for quotes of high fliers, was pumping red like a ripped jugular. I searched for a stock that wasn't down double digits, but as most of these companies had somehow run up to the 100s, even the most mellow of declines were teenage, as we call them.

No matter. We were in automaton buy mode—my cerebral research partner, Jeff Berkowitz, and my head trader, Todd-o Harrison, all of us schooled in the panics of the past dozen years. We knew not to flinch. Let others panic. We had raised the cash. We had taken money off the table. Now it was time to put that money to work, unemotionally.

By 11 a.m., the market was dropping faster than Skylab. We got off the trading desk—meaning we went into Jeff's office, which is twice the size of mine, because, like all traders, I never go to mine unless someone's about to lose his job—and took stock. We had put a ton of money to work in the first hour and a half, and nothing was holding. We were routinely down three points on every stock we purchased by the time we got the report back. And as swashbuckling hedge-fund managers, we get our reports back instantaneously!

We approached the developing decline precisely and levelheadedly, quietly running down our 36 positions one at a time and trying to figure out if it was time to buy "another round of 5s," meaning another 5,000 of each stock. Normally, we like to buy 5,000 shares down every point or two when we are accumulating a position. But on a day like Tuesday, we "widen the scales," and leave more space between buys. No sooner had I said "Buy 5,000 Nokia at $200 and stick a $195 bid in beneath" than Todd would shout that we had bought 10,000 shares at $192. Nokia had plummeted to levels lower than I was willing to pay. In a matter of seconds.

No sooner had we finished our droning cadence from "America Online, $64, buy 5,000," to "Yahoo!, $161, buy 5,000," than we had to start back at the top of the alphabet and work our way down again because AOL was now at $62 and Yahoo! would soon be at $151. We were clocking this sell-off at 25 Nasdaq points a minute on the velocity meter, the fastest I've ever seen. In the background, on CNBC, I heard the word crash. We don't break out that term lightly. I had traded through 1987, and I know that a lot of moves down look like a crash, but this thing was only down 4 or 5 percent so far. That's no crash.

After a couple of bad salads on the trading desk (I haven't taken a lunch in eighteen years—no money's made at lunch), we retreated to Jeff's office to go over it again. An 11:30 a.m. rally had just failed. We had come into the day with an existing call option position that allowed us to "play the upside" for the Nazzdog, trader argot for the Nasdaq, and we had quietly begun to lose millions of dollars in the position. Our scaled purchases had not anticipated a 5 percent decline on top of a 5 percent decline, but the ice-water-in-the-veins mentality kept us buying.

Now the Nazzdogs were down 7 percent for the day, and our purchases continued by rote. Off the desk, we talked about how we had seen it all and we weren't going to puke this one out at the bottom, and that the market would soon have to turn, because, well, it just had to, always did. We tried to reassure ourselves. We had been the ones calling to take money off the table. We had done so. We weren't going to be scared out of what could be the greatest trade of our lives when this market turned. "We were put on earth for this moment!" I said with determination. But at noon, with the Nazzdogs in free fall, we got off the desk again. Nobody looked like a Master of the Universe at that meeting. I knew that Todd-o had been furiously Instant Messaging Jeff at his trading turret, and I could tell we were thinking big now. "Ten percent decline, wasn't that time to double down?" our trader asked. I made a few faces, and we agreed: Time to take a big chunk of that cash we had so jealously hoarded and put it to work. Because, as my wife and former seven-year trading partner, Karen Cramer, always said, "You've gotta buy them when you can, not when you have to."

And so we did. Coolly, calmly, professionally. Like the late Tom Landry at his legendary unemotional best, sending in some precision 55-yard-touchdown-pass play with a quick dipping of his hat.

Forty minutes later, we were back in the war room. The market hadn't held. Our lunches hadn't held. Our bet had fizzled faster than anyone could imagine. Nobody spoke. CNBC droned on in the background. No more crash denial. We used the word freely.

I finally blurted: "I have a problem with this Nazzdog position. It's choking me, it is right here, going here"—I drew a line from my gut to my throat—"it's just killing me. We gotta do something. We can't take these losses. It's too big. It's the giant steaming elephant turd in the room, man." Todd-o looked at the floor. Jeff knew what was coming. All our rationality hadn't made us a dime. All our cool capital commitment and tungsten-like grit hadn't called the bottom. We had not respected the bear enough. We had not given him his due.

It was time—as it was in every serious sell-off I have crawled through—to make a sacrifice to the Trading Gods. It was time to take a loss. To admit, in some small way, that we were wrong about this market. No matter our strict scales and our levels and our precision. This sucker wasn't stopping. Not here, not now, not down 12 percent. Not unless we blinked. Not unless we took action. Not unless we threw a maiden into the volcano.

Todd-o knew I was right, but he didn't want to admit it. Jeff, Wharton and Columbia Business School scholar that he is, just looked away. No matter how many times this happens, Jeff refuses to bow to superstition, but he never fights us. He knows how bottoms get formed.

"Take some Nazzdogs and sacrifice them," I said.

"But, Jim, this is it, down 12 percent, down 24 in a matter of days, this is what it looks like at the bottom," Todd-o said. "You know that." As he spoke I glanced at the TV: Nasdaq and the Dow were down 500 points each, the worst moment of the day so far. Of course I knew it. "But how are we going to get this goddamned market going the other way," I asked him, "unless we capitulate?!"

We went back to the desk, and at 1:15 p.m., tails between our legs, we made the sacrifice, selling 1,000 contracts, a sizable chunk of our buydown bet, which we had begun at $19 the day before. Take a look at where we sold those nasty Nazzdogs. Take a look at the time: 1:23. Take a look at the price we got: $6. Oh my, six bucks, six little nothing bucks (multiplied by 100,000, of course). They reflected the maximum moment of decline in the Nasdaq, the maximum low for Intel and Sun and Microsoft and Cisco during this whole downturn. The bottom. The turn.

The moment we got the report, they lifted. Take a look at the price two minutes later: $7. Ten minutes later: $8. An hour later: almost double, as Nasdaq rose inexorably from down 3600, where we had sold the calls on the index, to 4100, the largest one-day move up off the bottom ever. That's an amazing comeback, triggered by our sacrifice to the Trading Gods.

Yes, the market bottomed when we made that sale. I can't come up with any other explanation. There certainly wasn't one on my screens or on TV or in the papers the next day. Nothing done by Greenspan or Summers or Clinton or Rubin or Buffett or Abby Joseph Cohen.

Markets bottom only when the gods of humility are appeased with offerings of arrogant strategies by steely-eyed traders designed to withstand the stress and strain of the worst markets. They bottom when guys like me can't take it anymore.

And that's why we rallied Tuesday. Fortunately, this time, we only had to throw the maiden in. One day, maybe it will have to be the whole tribe.

In the misfortune of Cramer and others like him, Marianne Costantinou, an editor at the San Francisco Examiner, *saw opportunity.*

APRIL 9, 2000

I'm one of Them now.

You know who I mean. If you live in the Bay Area, there's no escaping them, those smug twerps who have cashed in on the crazy stock market, made a killing, and are running around town driving up housing prices so much that no normal person can even afford to rent a monthly garage space, much less buy a house.

I didn't want to be a twerp but I wanted the luxury of smug. Everyone, I felt, was getting rich except me and my family. I wanted a piece of that high-tech, dot-com easy money.

This week, Nasdaq plunged and I decided to take the dive, too. I became an online stock trader.

And if I can be a little smug, I didn't do so badly for somebody who didn't have a clue what she was doing.

My timing, for once, was perfect. After a three-day scavenger hunt looking for tech stocks at bottomed-out prices, I made a 13.45 percent profit by the close of the market Friday, even after the $29.95 commission I paid for each of my 20 transactions.

And I would have made even more if I hadn't run out of money before discovering a few other nuggets just screaming to be bought. Alas, others heard the cries, snatching them from my outstretched greedy fingers literally pennies from my low-ball bids. As luck would have it, five of my wannabe tech stocks—Infospace, Vignette, Brocade, Exodus, Redback—far surpassed the achievements of my modest but stalwart keepsakes, popping up from $50 to $100 before my sorrowful eyes.

Which all leads me to three lessons I learned from my self-taught crash course:

(a) You gotta have money to make money.

(b) The three screaming meemies—Woulda, Coulda, Shoulda—will drive you crazy.

(c) You gotta get some sleep.

I don't know why they call the crazies I joined "day traders." I haven't pulled so many all-nighters since college. Who can sleep? If you're a newbie like me without some stockbroker or guru to help you, you have to spend some time researching and deciding which stocks to pick and what prices to pay.

So many choices, so little money.

I was surprised at how ill-prepared I was to jump in. I had been eyeing the stock market for months, hoarding newspaper and magazine articles talking about trends and hot stocks, seething at all these 1,000 percent run-ups on stock prices.

I was obsessed with what happened to eBay, the online auction site that I, as a compulsive shopaholic collector of all things ridiculous, knew only too well. That could have been me tripling my family's nest egg, I'd whine bitterly as eBay stock soared from $80-something, when I first started paying attention to it.

Boy, if we only had some money, I'd complain to my husband, Marty. Trouble was, creditors and expenses already had dibs on our salaries. The family nest egg was the Mickey Mouse bank on our bureau that we used for spare change. It's gotten so hard to just keep the checkbook balanced that our 12-year-old son Mark got his own savings account and won't tell us his password because we kept hitting him up.

I've obsessed about buying a house. We moved here three years ago from Philadelphia, where folks have a hard time giving away mansions for $125K. We were galled by the housing prices here, especially for tiny termite-infested bungalows. If only we had bought then. Those $300K houses in Berkeley and Oakland that we might have been able to afford with low mortgage interest are like $400K–$600K now.

My parents, Greek immigrants who still walk a mile to the supermarket that honors double coupons, could stand my self-pity no more. I had nagged my dad for a year to get rid of his respectable but snail-paced Citigroup stock that he had owned for eons and to pop aboard the Nasdaq roller coaster. Instead, he did what I should feel utterly ashamed to admit: He sent us some money—nearly the only savings my folks had left after decades working as a waiter and as a seamstress—so we could put a down payment on a house.

Being a modern-day daughter, I snatched it. I even made him FedEx it to me.

I got the check last Saturday. Alas, what was a fortune to my parents and to us and to anyone living anywhere else in the country was barely enough for a 3 percent down payment for a house here.

So, my husband and I decided that if we're going to compete with housing prices driven up by dot-com funny money, we better go after it, too.

As luck would have it, the stock market was already spiraling down, down, down last Tuesday morning when I saw that my dad's certified check had cleared my bank. My husband, having learned early on that I was a control freak dictator, just let me handle it.

He went to work.

I turned on the computer at home.

It was about 8:30 a.m. Pacific time, early for me, but 11:30 a.m. in New York, where the major stock exchanges are. I had forgotten about that in my big scheming. But not to panic. I was psyched. I was going to make a killing.

I had decided long ago that I would do all the trading online, to take advantage of those cheap commissions. I had chosen ETrade as the gateway to our fortune. I loved those goofball colors of lime green and violet blue in ETrade's logo, its sassy billboard signs, and the fact that some honcho in the company looked like he had a Greek surname.

Anyway, I'm there. I'm at the computer. I go to the ETrade home page. I click on the link to start a new account. And, ugh, first thing I learn is that I am limited to a $2,000 initial deposit. That wasn't the minimum. It was the limit.

Ugh No. 2: After filling out the application and getting my "Congratulations" note, I was told that some snafu transferring money from my bank prevented me from trading that day. I'd be getting an application in the mail that I could send back in the mail with my signature and check.

The *mail*, I screamed at their customer service reps. You're kidding, right? The stock market is going blooey, you're an online brokerage, and you're telling me I've got to wait for the mail?

Greek expletive. Greek expletive. Greek expletive.

Meanwhile, stock prices are plummeting. My dad is calling me frantically.

"Marianna, Marianna, Cisco is at 64!!!" he said, breathless.

I had CNN on in the background. I knew. I knew.

I drove to San Francisco in a rage. It was noon. The stock market was closing in an hour and I was feeling desperate. After a few more attempts with ETrade "customer service"—"Please let me wire you the money, let me drive it down to your Menlo Park office"—I called Charles Schwab.

I had nixed the idea of doing business with Schwab long ago. First, they charged more in commission for Nasdaq stocks, $29.95 vs. $19.95. And the offices there seemed too polished. It was a wingtip place, and I'm strictly Birkenstock.

But this was no time to be choosy. I called Schwab. A rep took my application over the phone. Five minutes later, I was walking over to its headquarters on Montgomery Street. I signed the application and handed over a personal check. And that was that. I was ready to make some money.

Of course, the market had closed.

Having missed out on the Cisco bargain, I decided to do some research and go after the more aggressive, riskier stocks in tech and telecommunications, the industries that had gone gangbusters last year. My husband and I really wanted to make a lot of money and we wanted to make it fast. Our hope was to double our cash so we could buy a house within a year.

We also decided that, given that we were clueless, we'd rather have a lot of different stocks in small quantities, say 10 to 100 shares of each, rather than let all our fantasies ride on one or two stocks. Besides, I later realized, I felt like I was a part of the new economy by owning a cornucopia of these Internet and tech stocks. It wasn't Them anymore. It was Us.

OK. What to buy? Ebay was too expensive. I pulled out my news clips to get some names of stocks to research. I also had a list of hot stocks from my husband's friend George, who is an avid market watcher. And I even found out about one stock, Veritas, by checking out Mayor Willie Brown's published portfolio.

I narrowed my choices by cross-referencing. Which stocks kept getting mentioned in those stories about stockbrokers' favorites? Which stocks were considered leaders in their niche?

After narrowing my choices to about 50 companies, I checked out Schwab's amazing charts and analysts' reports. I then made my own list, noting several key points for each stock: the 52-week high and low, its median price range in recent months, and the daily price range over the last few days.

I wanted to control the price I paid, rather than exposing myself to whatever price happened to be floating on the stock market floor when my order to buy went through. I was placing "limit" bids, meaning that was my top price.

Deciding on that magic price was the hard part. Depending on how much I lusted after the stock, I tried to get it for several notches below the median price I had noted on my list and within the price range of recent days' trading.

I then crossed my fingers.

Sometimes, I was too stingy, and saw the stock race away from me. But most of the time, my strategy worked. By the end of the week, I'd made a nifty profit.

If I can do it, you can, too.

Don't be intimidated. Yeah, it's all the money you have in the world and you don't know a thing. But you know enough to steal, don't you?

Read the paper, find out what stock names keep getting mentioned by all those analyst gurus. If people are talking about 'em, they must either be buying them or dumping them. Find out which. And even though they tell you that past performance is no guarantee, you got any better ideas?

Oh no, I'm giving advice. I see I'm gonna be one of those twerps.

APRIL 15, 2000

No fair.

I had climbed aboard the Stock Market Express just 10 days ago for what I had imagined would be a quick trip to the Land of Riches. But no sooner did I settle into my seat to enjoy the ride than my train got derailed. Now my caboose is all banged up. On Friday, the Dow had its worst drop ever—EVER!—plummeting a jaw-dropping 617-plus points. But my fantasies were riding on the Nasdaq, that locomotive full of high-speed tech stocks whose trips to stratospheric prices had reached dizzying heights.

Everyone was getting rich. I wanted some of that easy money, too. So when my parents gave my husband, Marty, and me their hard-earned savings so we could put a down payment on a house, we promptly invested it in the stock market.

Of course, I pop aboard and Nasdaq has its worst week ever—

EVER!—dropping 25 percent in five days, 355 points on Friday alone. As if that wasn't bad enough, I fared even worse than the market. I'm down more than 40 percent. I've lost 28.71 percent of the cash I paid for the "bargains" I bought the week before, during a deep dip in the Nasdaq.

And I also lost the 13.45 percent profit I had smugly made—at least on paper—by April 7, after just three days of scavenger-hunting. And, and, I took a 20 percent hit on four stocks I sold in disgust early Tuesday morning, irked at how quickly they had dropped at the market's first shudder. Little did I know that those four wimpy stocks were an omen. Normally I thrive on stress. But by midweek, my free-falling stocks had so unnerved me that I ended up in the hospital emergency room, convinced I was having a heart attack. I wish I was kidding.

Despite my panic, I had faith that the market would rebound—as it always does—and that my family would, one day, make gobs of money.

I had pulled all-nighters researching our stock picks, gleaning tips from friends and from the news clips I had hoarded, just waiting for some cash to plunk down and get rich quick. My parents' modest savings, too little for a down payment in this crazed real estate market, were to be our ticket.

I probably would not have been in heart attack mode if I hadn't done something that was stupid, even for me. Especially for impulsive shopaholic me. I bought stocks on margin. Until I started with this stock market business, I didn't know much about margin. I had heard of it. I knew it had to do with buying stocks on credit. And I knew it had gotten folks in trouble.

What I didn't know was how easy it was to get into big trouble real fast. My credit cards are always maxed out, testimony to the weakness I have for bargains. I can't resist them. And if there's a time limit—a "Get It Now! It'll Be Gone Tomorrow" urgency—like a sale or an auction, then I'm a goner.

. . . It was Wednesday morning, and Nasdaq was down. The prices were even cheaper than the week before.

Oh, the bargains.

I have an online account with Charles Schwab, so I sign onto my computer at home. I've got CNN in the background, keeping me posted on how Nasdaq is doing overall as I concentrate on bidding on my stock picks.

Uh-oh. It looks like a rally. My bargains are going to slip away forever.

In a mad frenzy, I keep upping my price, keeping it a shade below the last posted price, hoping to snag the stock a buck or even a quarter less per share. It's ridiculous, but there's ego riding on this, too.

Finally, I score. And it's off to another stock. And another.

I'm obsessed. I lose track of the time. I lose track of the money.

About 15 minutes later, I check my account balance. I'm $15K in the hole—money I didn't have.

I break out in a panic. OK. Not to worry. I'll just sell some of my less promising stocks.

Too late. The rally had lasted as long as my frenzy. All my stocks were down from what I paid. I couldn't sell anything without taking a hit.

And my new stocks were already heading down, too.

Again I tell myself not to worry. It'll go back up. You'll sell later.

But later never comes. The prices keep plummeting. By the end of the day, the value of my stocks had dropped about 10 percent. Far worse, my account balance showed that I could only spend another $57 on margin, which meant that if Nasdaq so much as sneezed the next day and my portfolio dropped more in value, I'd be getting the dreaded margin call.

"Hide. Don't answer the phone," my friend Anastasia advised, seeing me all knotted up.

Alas, a method I've used with other creditors would not work. The last thing I wanted was for the brokerage to start selling my stocks willy-nilly.

Money. I needed some money.

I had a few bucks in a savings account. There was the $10 a week I put away in the credit union. I eyeballed the checking account. Our car was due to be paid off next month. Now it would be a month later. It didn't matter. This was an emergency.

I raced to Schwab. It was a modest deposit, but enough to keep us out of danger. At least another day.

And then I had my heart attack.

I had a boss once who had a heart attack. He said the funny thing was, he didn't feel any pain in his chest. But his left arm got this pain and it went limp.

So when my left arm got this pain and it went limp, I was convinced.

My friend Suzanne drove me to UCSF. She told me to think happy thoughts, of my 12-year-old son Mark and what a beautiful sunny day it was. All I could think about was what a mess I made of things.

At the hospital, my blood pressure, usually low, was sky high. The nurse felt my left hand. It was cold. Off I went for an EKG test to monitor my heart. Exhausted, I fell asleep.

I woke up and felt much better. No heart attack. The doctors didn't know what it was.

But I did, only too well.

Thursday, the stock market continued to plunge. I was, curiously, less worried. Disaster had struck. I was on the *Titanic*. There was no escaping the icy waters.

By Friday morning, my husband and I were resolved. We had hit our lines of credit. We had written checks against our credit cards. We had no other choice. We would sell some stocks.

My husband wanted to sell the strongest, so we would lose the least. But I wanted to sell some of the biggest losers. I was mad at them. They had betrayed me. I wanted to be rid of them.

I put them on sale, a hair over the current asking price, praying that some blip upward would nab us a few dollars more.

I took Marty to the BART station. On my way back home, I ran into my landlord, Bijan.

He's played the stock market for years, and still thinks about the sales he made in haste.

Do not sell, he tells me. I'll regret it. Get the money somehow.

I go upstairs and do the unthinkable. I call my father.

My dad gets irked when he finds out that another supermarket is charging a quarter less for the toilet paper he just bought. It was his money I had blown. I knew he was tapped out. But before I threw away thousands of dollars by selling them at a 20 to 50 percent loss, I had to tell him.

Now it was my father's turn to have a heart attack.

He ordered me not to sell. I don't know where he got the money, but within two hours he had made the trip from his house in Queens to the Schwab office in Manhattan, and knocked the margin debt down a chunk. Short of another Great Depression, we're safe.

I promise, I said to my dad. I'll never buy on margin again.

Ten minutes later, I couldn't resist. Oracle stock was up to 68, after a low of 64, and it was climbing.

Oh no, it looks like a rally. I'll never see that price again. And before I can stop myself, I put in a bid to buy.

Even I can't believe it.

I get it for 65$^{15}/_{16}$. My bargain later goes down to 60 and closes at 62½. I'm down nearly 7 percent.

In the aftermath of the Nasdaq crash, much was made of amateurs and neophyte day traders buying on margin without understanding the risks. Surprisingly, one of the largest margin calls hit Baruch Israel Hertz, owner of the MyTrack day-trading system, who owed $45 million to four brokerage firms.

James Cramer, it should be noted, ended the year up 35 percent. He then retired from his hedge fund.

What Happened to My Money?, April 2000

David Owen

After the markets fell in the spring of 2000—when the Nasdaq dropped almost 40 percent in a few weeks—David Owen comforted grieving readers of The New Yorker.

God has taken your money to live with Him in Heaven. Heaven is a special, wonderful place, where wars and diseases and stock markets do not exist, only happiness. You have probably seen some wonderful places in your life—perhaps during a vacation, or on television, or in a movie—but Heaven is a million billion times more wonderful than even Disney World. Jesus and Mary and the angels live in Heaven, and so do your grandparents and your old pets and Abraham Lincoln. Your money will be safe and happy in Heaven forever and ever, and God will always take care of it.

Your money is still your money—it will always be your money—but it cannot come back to you, not ever. That may seem unfair to you. One day you were buying puts and shorting straddles, and the next day you woke up to find that your account had been closed forever. Perhaps you got a sick or empty feeling in your stomach when that happened; perhaps you have that sick or empty feeling still. You loved your money very, very much, and you did not want God to take it away.

Your feelings are natural and normal—they are a part of the way God made you—but God took your money in accordance with His wonderful plan, which is not for us to know or understand. You must trust God and have faith that He loves your money just as He loves you and every other part of His creation. Someday—probably a very, very long time from now, after you have lived a long and happy life in compliance with the nation's securities laws—God will take you to live with Him in Heaven, too. Then you will understand.

Even though your money is gone forever, it can still be a part of your life. As long as love and kindness and happiness dwell in your heart, your money can dwell there, too. At night, before you go to sleep, you can talk to your money in a prayer. You can think about the BMW that you and your money were going to buy, and you can remember the house on the beach that you and your money were going to build, and you can laugh about your funny old plan to send your children to private colleges. Someday, when you no longer feel as sad as you do today, you may even find that thinking about your money can give you some of the same happy feelings that spending your money used to give you.

Those feelings belong to you and they always will; no one can take them away from you. Even when you are very, very old, you will still be able to think about your money and remember how much you loved it. But you will still not be able to spend your money, or even borrow against it.

Afterword

By the spring of 2001, the losses of 2000 seemed modest. The Nasdaq was down almost 70 percent, the Dow down more than 20 percent. Companies that had rushed to add ".com" to their names removed the suffix as if it were the tattooed name of an old girlfriend. Favorites of the previous decade, like Cisco, announced poor earnings followed by layoffs of tens of thousands of workers. People even questioned the mental state of Fed Chairman Alan Greenspan, wondering if age—he turned seventy-five in March 2001—had blinded him to the slowdown they blamed on the Fed's interest rate hikes. It didn't seem to matter that he had already signaled a change in the direction of those rates. Wall Street wanted all the cuts right away. President George W. Bush claimed Wall Street's swoon made a tax cut urgent; his critics argued the cuts offered little to smaller investors who would be crucial to a recovery.

There was nothing new in any of this news. Bubbles had burst. Major corporations had succumbed to trends. Wall Street had fumed at Greenspan's deliberate pace. Politicians had spun news from the Street. The markets had gone down before, and, short of the extinction of humankind, they would go back up. Meanwhile, larger trends were creating real change in the financial industry:

—Glass-Steagall, the depression-era law that separated banks holding the deposits of individuals from investment banks that invest and speculate, was repealed in 1999. Corporate marriages that had previously been taboo—like the one between Sandy Weill's Travelers Insurance Group and John Reed's Citibank, which was arranged even before the law was actually repealed—now promise to finally create "financial supermarkets" offering all products to all customers, presumably all the time. Whether that promise will be kept is still unclear. As *Business Week* writer Pamela L. Moore commented, "When it comes to megamergers, few banks have proved that they can make one plus one add up to two."

—Increasing automation continues to threaten the existence of floor traders, even those at the NYSE. Richard A. Rosenblatt, an NYSE floor trader and a relative optimist, told *New York Times* reporter Diana B. Henriques, "For anyone to think that, five years from now, any of us will be doing business the way we do today would be dangerously naïve." But he added, "You show me a better way to trade, and I won't trade one more share on the N.Y.S.E. But nobody's shown me that yet." Laura S. Unger, an S.E.C. commissioner, identifies the central issue as liquidity: "It's mostly liquidity that determines the success or failure of any trading system," she told the National Press Club. "Without it, a trading system will end up on the trash heap of trading system history. And liquidity is a sticky thing. Once it has settled somewhere, it is hard to pry away."

—As hard as it is to displace tradition, powerful forces are trying, in what had become an international effort. The National Association of Securities Dealers, which operates the Nasdaq quotations system, is working towards partnerships with exchanges in London, Frankfurt, and Japan. "We're headed to a period where people are going to be able to trade securities anywhere in the world, anytime of day or night," says the NASD's Chairman, Frank Zarb. "You're going to see, when we stop trading Microsoft in extended hours in this country, it'll open 9:00 P.M. Pacific Time and it'll trade following the sun, as will Intel, as will the Nasdaq 100, before the middle of next year. So you're going to see the beginnings of what is called "24-hour trading" because that sounds cute, but what it really is, is the ability for companies to reflect their image where their customers are and for these companies to reflect their image where they want to raise capital. . . . We need to let Microsoft and Intel and Sun and Starbucks be shown to pools of capital outside our [U.S.] pool of capital; that means when we're closed and they are open. We have to be able to show them, these companies, to those investors."

Meanwhile, some trends are simply ridiculous. In early 2001, General Motors Corp.'s OnStar subsidiary, which operates a voice-activated wireless phone service, announced a deal with Fidelity Investments to allow drivers to make trades without even pulling to the side of the road. Lost in the rush to be thoroughly modern was a lesson from the past. The opportunity for gain—or loss—that appears during your daily commute will appear again another time or another day. History proves it.

But still we speculate, most of us learning the lessons of history only by repeating them. At least one can take comfort in this observation from Louis Rukeyser, host of PBS's "Wall $treet Week," after the "Black Monday" crash in October 1987: "It's just your money, not your life. Everyone who loved you a week ago still loves you."

Sources and Permissions

Compared to other aspects of American life, there are surprisingly few general histories of Wall Street. Fortunately, among those few are outstanding works. Charles R. Geisst's *Wall Street: A History* (Oxford, 1997) is loaded with detail. The fluid prose of John Steele Gordon distinguishes *The Great Game* (Scribner, 1999). Readers interested in the Street before the 1990s should consider the books of Robert Sobel (among them *The Big Board, Panic on Wall Street, The Great Bull Market,* and *NYSE*). Or, for a broad look at recent business history, a superb illustrated book, *The New York Times Century of Business* by Floyd Norris and Christine Bockelmann (McGraw-Hill, 2000), combines *Times* stories and photos with expert commentary.

INTRODUCTION
Wells: *The Future in America,* 1906. Bryce: *The American Commonwealth,* 1888.

PART ONE: Financing the New World
The Scene in the 1600s: New Amsterdam. *De Nieuwe en Onbekende Weereld,* Amsterdam, 1671. Quoted in *Documents Relative to the Colonial History of the State of New York,* Brodhead and O'Callaghan (eds.) 1858.

From the First IPO to the South Sea Bubble. Letter to Stuyvestant: *Documents Relative to the Colonial History of the State of New York,* Brodhead and O'Callaghan (eds.), 1858. Anonymous pamphlet: Boston, 1721; reprinted in *Colonial Currency Reprints, 1682–1751,* vol. II (Boston: The Prince Society, 1911). Defoe: *The Anatomy of Exchange Alley: or, A System of Stock-jobbing,* 1719.

Josef de la Vega: Confusiones de Confusiones, 1688. Portions descriptive of the Amsterdam Stock Exchange, selected and translated by Hermann Kellenbenz. (Boston: Baker Library, Harvard Graduate School of Business Administration, 1957).

PART TWO: The Revolution and "The Monied Men"
The Scene in the 1700s: Frugal and Industrious
Andrew Burnaby: Travels Through the Middle Settlements in North America, 1759–60 (New York: A. Wessels Company, 1904).

"Not Worth a Continental": *The Rivington Royal Gazette,* Alexander Hamilton, and the Buttonwood Brokers. Morris, Hamilton and Madison: Quoted *In The Spirit of Seventy-Six; The Story of the American Revolution As Told By Participants,* Henry Steele Commager and Richard B. Morris (eds.), (Indianapolis: Bobbs-Merrill, 1958). Duer accounts quoted in *Essays in the Earlier History of American Corporations,* Joseph Stancliffe Davis (Cambridge: Harvard University Press, 1917).

PART THREE: From the Buttonwood Tree to the Civil War
The Scene in the Early 1800s: The Great Fire and the New Exchange. *The Diary of Philip Hone,* Alan Nevis (ed.), 1927.

Girard's Bank, from *Famous Americans of Recent Times* (Boston: Ticknor & Fields, 1867).

Jackson Closes the Bank of the United States "Veto Message, Washington, July 10, 1832," Richardson (ed.) *Messages and Papers of the Presidents,* vol. II.

The Panic of 1837. *Diary in America,* 1839.

The Great Bear: Jacob Little. *Ten Years in Wall Street* (Hartford: Worthington, Dustin & Co., 1870).

The Panic of 1857, from *The Diary of George Templeton Strong,* Allan Nevins (ed.), (NY: Macmillan, 1952).

War Bonds and Greenbacks. *The Samuel P. Chase Papers,* vol. 3, John Niven (ed.), (Ohio: Kent State University Press, 1996).

The Gold Exchange. *Money and Banking Illustrated by American History* (Boston: Ginn, 1896).

PART FOUR: Wall Street in the Gilded Age

The Scene in the Gilded Age: The Idle Rich. *Society As I Have Found It* (NY: Cassell, 1890).

The Battle for Erie. *Ten Years in Wall Street* (Hartford, CT: Worthington, Dustin & Co., 1870).

Black Friday. *The New York Times:* 26 September 1869. Boutwell: *Reminiscences of Sixty Years in Public Affairs* (NY: McClure, Phillips & Co., 1902).

Carnegie's Career Begins. *Autobiography of Andrew Carnegie* (Boston: Houghton Mifflin, 1920).

The First Women Brokers. New York *Sun,* 5 February 1870.

Philadelphia's Last Gasp. George Templeton Strong [in Philadelphia's Last Gasp]: The Diary of George Templeton Strong, Allan Nevins (ed.), (NY: Macmillan, 1952).

A Bucket-Shop Education. *Reminiscences of a Stock Operator* (NY: Doran, 1923).

PART FIVE: Trust and Trustbusters

The Scene in the 1900s: Rockefeller and "The Chief Getters." *The Future in America,* 1906.

Charles Dow. *The Stock Market Barometer* (NY: Harper, 1922).

The Northern Pacific Corner. *Baruch: My Own Story* (NY: Holt, 1957).

J. P. Morgan and the Panic of 1907. *From Farm Boy to Financier* (NY: Appleton-Century Company, Incorporated, 1935).

PART SIX: Wall Street in WWI: Last Man Standing

The Scene in the 1910s: "The Corner." Baldwin, Hanson and Shepard Stone (eds.), *We Saw It Happen* (NY: Simon and Schuster, 1938).

Germany's Financiers Prepare for War. *The World's Work* [magazine], June 1918.

War News Reaches Wall Street. *The New York Times,* 1 August 1914.

Charlie Chaplin Learns to Sell Liberty Bonds. *My Autobiography* (London: Bodley Head, 1964.

"Economic Consequences of the Peace." *The Economic Consequences of the Peace* (NY: Harcourt Brace Jovanovich, 1920).

Bombing of the J. P. Morgan Bank. *The New York Times,* 16 September 1920. Borsody: private correspondence in the archives of J. P. Morgan & Co. Incorporated. Reprinted courtesy of J. P. Morgan & Co. Incorporated.

PART SEVEN: Boom and Bust

The Scene in the 1920s: Marxist Economics. *Harpo Speaks!* (NY: B. Geis Associates, 1961).

The Big Bull Market. *Only Yesterday* (NY: Harper, 1931).

CRASH! Baldwin, *We Saw It Happen,* Hanson and Shepard Stone (eds.), (NY: Simon and Schuster, 1938).

Ben Graham Calls the Bottom. *Forbes* magazine, June 1932.

Roosevelt's "Banking Holiday." Radio address to nation, 12 March 1933. Franklin D. Roosevelt Digital Library, Marist College.

"He Knows All the Tricks of the Trade." *The Money Lords* (NY: Weybright and Talley, 1972).

The Harder They Fall. Ferdinand Pecora. *Wall Street Under Oath* (NY: Simon & Schuster, 1939). *The New York Times,* "Whitney Receives 5 to 10 Year Term; Court Berates Him," 12 April 1938. Copyright © 1938 The New York Times. Reprinted by permission of *The New York Times.*

PART EIGHT: Wall Street Goes to Main Street

The Scene in the 1940s: News from the Home Front. *11 Wall.* Reprinted courtesy of the New York Stock Exchange.

Wall Street Goes to Main Street. "A Declaration of Policy." Reprinted courtesy of Merrill Lynch.

The White Shark. *The White Sharks of Wall Street* (NY: Scribner, 2000) Copyright © 2000 by Diana B. Henriques.

"Securities Bazaar." Carter Henderson. *The Wall Street Journal,* 31 October 1957.

Fidelity-a-Go-Go. *The Go-Go Years* (NY: John Wiley & Sons, 1999) Copyright © 1973, 1999 by John Brooks. Reprinted by permission of John Wiley & Sons, Inc.

PART NINE: Uneasy Street

The Scene in the 1960s: Pennies from Heaven. *Who the Hell Is Stew Albert?* (Granada Hills, CA: Red Hen Press, 2001) Copyright © 2001 by Stew Albert. Reprinted by permission of Stew Albert. Digital version: members.aol.com/stewa/abbiestock.html

Lady of the Club. *The Way It Was: An Oral History of Finance 1967–1987 by the Editors of* Institutional Investor (NY: Morrow, 1988). Copyright © 1988 by Institutional Investor, Inc. Reprinted by permission.

"Conglomerator": James Ling. *Ling* (NY: Atheneum 1972). Copyright © 1972 by Stanley H. Brown. Reprinted by permission of Stanley H. Brown.

Instinet: Personal correspondence with Jerome Pustilnik. Copyright © 2000 by Jerome M. Pustilnik.

Eyes on the Prize. *The Way It Was: An Oral History of Finance 1967–1987 by the Editors of* Institutional Investor (NY: Morrow, 1988). Copyright © 1988 by Institutional Investor, Inc. Reprinted by permission.

The Rise and Fall of Bernie Cornfeld. *The Way It Was: An Oral History of Finance 1967–1987 by the Editors of* Institutional Investor (NY: Morrow, 1988). Copyright © 1988 by Institutional Investor, Inc. Reprinted by permission.

Where Did the Go-Go Go? *Remarks to* Institutional Investor's *Fourth Annual Investor's Conference,* 18 March 1971. Reprinted by permission of David L. Babson, Jr.

Paper. *A View from the Street* (NY: New American Library, 1972). Copyright © 1972 by Donald T. Regan.

The Nifty Fifty. *Forbes,* "The Nifty Fifty Revisited" 15 December 1977. Reprinted by permission of *Forbes* magazine © 2000 Forbes 1977.

May Day. *The Way It Was: An Oral History of Finance 1967–1987 by the Editors of* Institutional Investor (NY: Morrow, 1988). Copyright © 1988 by Institutional Investor, Inc. Reprinted by permission.

The Black Box. *The Way It Was: An Oral History of Finance 1967–1987 by the Editors of* Institutional Investor (NY: Morrow, 1988). Copyright © 1988 by Institutional Investor, Inc. Reprinted by permission.

Futures. *The Way It Was: An Oral History of Finance 1967–1987 by the Editors of* Institutional Investor (NY: Morrow, 1988). Copyright © 1988 by Institutional Investor, Inc. Reprinted by permission.

T. Rowe Price. Forbes, "Thomas Row Price 1893–1983" 21 November 1983. Reprinted by permission of *Forbes* magazine © 2000 Forbes 1983.

"Silver Thursday." *The Washington Post,* "Silver Collapses," 28 March 1980; and "Hunt Brothers' Thrill Ride in Silver Takes U.S. Close to Disaster," 27 April 1980. Copyright © 1980 The Washington Post.

PART TEN: Greed Is Good?

The Scene in the 1980s: The Predators' Ball. *The Predators' Ball* (NY: Simon & Schuster, 1988) Copyright © 1988 by Connie Bruck.

Insider. *Inside Out,* Dennis B. Levine and William Hoffer (NY: Putnam's, 1991) Copyright © 1991 by Dennis B. Levine.

Den of Thieves. "Scenes From a Scandal: The Secret World of Michael Milken and Ivan Boesky," *The Wall Street Journal,* 2 October 1991, adapted from *Den of Thieves* (NY: Simon & Schuster, 1991). Copyright 1991 by James B. Stewart. Reprinted by permission.

The Confessions of Ivan Boesky. Court transcript exerpt: *Euromoney,* 1 July 1990.

Liar's Poker. *Liar's Poker* (NY: Norton, 1989), Copyright © 1989 by Michael Lewis. Reprinted by permission.

The Keating Five. Quoted in *The Big Fix,* James Ring Adams (NY: Wiley, 1990).

Black Monday. *The Washington Post,* "Crisis Chronology: The Day Wall Street Went Wild Series: The Stock Market Crisis," 25 October 1987. Copyright © 1987 The Washington Post. Reprinted by permission.

The Pit. *Play Money: My Brief but Brilliant Career on Wall Street* (NY: Crown Publishers, 1991). Copyright © 1991 by Laura Pedersen. Reprinted by permission of Laura Pedersen.

The Fall of the House of Hutton. *Fortune,* "The Slow Death of E. F. Hutton," 29 February 1988. Copyright © 1988 Time, Inc. Reprinted by permission.

Barbarians at the Gate. *Barbarians at the Gate* (NY: Harper, 1990) Copyright © 1990 by Bryan Burrough and John Helyar. Reprinted by permission of HarperCollins Publishers, Inc.

The Pru-Bache Scandal. *Serpent on the Rock* (NY: Harper, 1995) Copyright © 1995 by Kurt Eichenwald. Reprinted by permission of HarperCollins Publishers, Inc.

Capitalist Tool. "Forbes, Money and Fun," *The Washington Post,* 27 February 1990. Copyright © 1990 by Christopher Buckley. Reprinted by permission of Christopher Buckley.

"The Cartel." *The Wall Street Journal,* "The Bond Club," 26 September 1991. Copyright © 1991 Dow-Jones, Inc. Reprinted by permission of Dow-Jones, Inc.

PART ELEVEN: Bull Without End, Amen

The Scene in the 1990s: Everybody's Invited. *Beating the Street,* Peter Lynch with John Rothchild (NY: Simon & Schuster, 1993).

The Cult of Greenspan. *Fortune,* "In Greenspan We Trust," 18 March 1996. Reporter Associates Erin Davies, Lixandra Urresta, and Tricia Welsh. Copyright © 1996 Time, Inc. Reprinted by permission of Time, Inc.

Main Street's Heroes Vinzant. *Fortune,* "The Pavers of Wall St.," 5 July 1999, Copyright © 1999 Time Inc. Reprinted by permission of Time, Inc. Lowenstein: *Buffett: Making of an American Capitalist* (NY: Random House, 1995). Copyright © 1995 by Roger Lowenstein. Reprinted by permission of Random House, Inc.

The Intel Generation. *SmartMoney,* "The Intel Generation" July 1997. Copyright © 1997 SmartMoney.

The Little Guy. "Cub in a Bear Market," *Los Angeles Times* Syndicate, 6 November 1997. Copyright © 1997 by Art Buchwald. Reprinted by permission of Los Angeles Times Syndicate.

While You Were Trading. Rawnsley: *Total Risk* (NY: HarperBusiness, 1995), Copyright © 1995 Judith H. Rawnsley. Jett: *Black and White on Wall Street* (NY: Morrow, 1999), Copyright © 1999 Cambridge Matrix Publications Kit. Partnoy: *F.I.A.S.C.O.* (NY: Norton, 1997), Copyright © 1997 by Frank Partnoy. Morgenson: *The New York Times* 25 September 1998. Dhebar: *The New York Times,* "Of Thinking Caps and Computer Traps," 26 March 1995. Copyright © 1995 Anirudh Dhebar.

PART TWELVE: Net Gains

The Scene in the 1990s: Virtual Friends. "Virtual Friends" *The New Yorker,* 20 November 1995. Copyright © 1995 by David Owen. Reprinted by permission of David Owen.

Netscape Fever. *The Wall Street Journal,* "Netscape's IPO Gets an Explosive Welcome," 9 August 1995. Reprinted by permission of Dow-Jones, Inc.

Internet Stock Scams. *Fortune,* "The Scary Rise of Internet Stock Scams" 26 October 1998, Copyright © 1998 Time Inc. Reprinted by permission of Time, Inc.

Surfing on the Slippery Skin of a Bubble. *The New York Times Magazine,* 20 June 1999. Copyright © 1999 by Po Bronson. Reprinted by permission of Po Bronson.

Do You Believe?: How Yahoo! Became a Blue Chip. *Fortune,* 7 June 1999. Copyright © 1999 Time Inc. Reprinted by permission of Time, Inc.

Riding the Mo in the Lime Green Glow. *The New York Times Magazine,* 21 November 1999. Copyright © 1999 by Matthew Klam. Reprinted by permission of International Creative Management, Inc.

After the Revolution. *Fortune,* "Cold Calling in a Cold World," 5 July 1999. Copyright © 1999 Time Inc. Reprinted by permission of Time, Inc.

Reversals of Fortune. Cramer: *New York,* "The Volcano Lover," 17 April 2000, Copyright © 2000 by James J. Cramer. Reprinted by permission of James J. Cramer. Costantinou: *San Francisco Examiner,* "First-time Stock Trader: E-Agony and the Ecstasy," 9 April 2000, and "Fantasies Railroaded by Market Express," 15 April 2000, Copyright © 2000 by Marianne Costantinou. Reprinted by permission.

What Happened to My Money? *The New Yorker,* 15 May 2000. Copyright © 2000 by David Owen. Reprinted by permission of David Owen.

Afterword: Moore, *Business Week,* "Empty Aisles at the Financial Supermarkets," 8 November 1999. Copyright © 1999 McGraw-Hill, Inc.

Henriques: *The New York Times,* 29 July 1999. Copyright © 1999 by The New York Times. Reprinted by permission.

Zarb: Speech given at National Press Club Ballroom, Washington, D.C., 13 June 2000. Reprinted by permission of the NASD.

Rukeyeser: *Wall Street Week,* Maryland Public Television, 23 October 1987.

Acknowledgments

Several people made this book possible. Barbara Grossman suggested it. Stephen Rubin made a home for it at Broadway Books, the very model of the modern major publisher. My longtime editors Stanley H. Brown and Miles Kronby offered keen insight, as they always do. Steven Wheeler of the New York Stock Exchange and David W. Wright of the J. P. Morgan Bank generously opened their archives. Fearn Cutler created the design. My father read several drafts.

Most important, my mother, Nancy S. Colbert, aided greatly with both research and thoughtful discussion.

Thanks to all.

Index

David Colbert, author of the acclaimed *Eyewitness* series, began digging through libraries and pushing great writers upon his friends while still a student at Brown University, and has been doing so ever since, through a stint editing books at a large publishing house and now as an author and editor. The first volume in the series, *Eyewitness to America*, was a Main Selection of Book-of-the-Month Club and the History Book Club. Colbert is also the author of *The Magical Worlds of Harry Potter* and editor of *Eyewitness to the American West, Baseball: The National Pastime in Art and Literature*, and *World War II: A Tribute in Art and Literature*. He can be contacted at djcolbert@aol.com.